WHITEHEAD'S RADICALLY TEMPORALIST METAPHYSICS

Contemporary Whitehead Studies

Series Editors: Roland Faber, Claremont School of Theology, and Brian G. Henning, Gonzaga University

Contemporary Whitehead Studies, co-sponsored by the Whitehead Research Project, is an interdisciplinary book series that publishes manuscripts from scholars with contemporary and innovative approaches to Whitehead studies by giving special focus to projects that: explore the connections between Whitehead and contemporary Continental philosophy, especially sources, like Heidegger, or contemporary streams like poststructuralism; reconnect Whitehead to pragmatism, analytical philosophy and philosophy of language; explore creative East/West dialogues facilitated by Whitehead's work; explore the interconnections of the mathematician with the philosopher and the contemporary importance of these parts of Whitehead's work for the dialogue between sciences and humanities; reconnect Whitehead to the wider field of philosophy, the humanities, the sciences and academic research with Whitehead's pluralistic impulses in the context of a pluralistic world; address Whitehead's philosophy in the midst of contemporary problems facing humanity, such as climate change, war and peace, race, and the future development of civilization.

Recent Titles in this Series:

Whitehead's Radically Temporalist Metaphysics: Recovering the Seriousness of Time,
by George Allan

Propositions in the Making: Experiments in a Whiteheadian Laboratory,
by Roland Faber, Michael Halewood, and Andrew M. Davis

Whitehead and Continental Philosophy in the Twenty-First Century: Dislocations,
edited by Jeremy D. Fackenthal

Beyond Whitehead: Recent Advances in Process Thought,
edited by Jakub Dziadkowiec and Lukasz Lamza

Tragic Beauty in Whitehead and Japanese Aesthetics,
by Steve Odin

Creaturely Cosmologies: Why Metaphysics Matters for Animal and Planetary Liberation,
by Brianne Donaldson

Thinking with Whitehead and the American Pragmatists: Experience and Reality,
edited by Brian G. Henning, William T. Myers, and Joseph D. John

The Divine Manifold,
by Roland Faber

Foundations of Relational Realism: A Topological Approach to Quantum Mechanics and the Philosophy of Nature,
by Michael Epperson and Elias Zafiris

WHITEHEAD'S RADICALLY TEMPORALIST METAPHYSICS

Recovering the Seriousness of Time

George Allan

LEXINGTON BOOKS
Lanham • Boulder • New York • London

Published by Lexington Books
An imprint of The Rowman & Littlefield Publishing Group, Inc.
4501 Forbes Boulevard, Suite 200, Lanham, Maryland 20706
www.rowman.com

6 Tinworth Street, London SE11 5AL, United Kingdom

Copyright © 2020 by The Rowman & Littlefield Publishing Group, Inc.

All rights reserved. No part of this book may be reproduced in any form or by any electronic or mechanical means, including information storage and retrieval systems, without written permission from the publisher, except by a reviewer who may quote passages in a review.

British Library Cataloguing in Publication Information Available

Library of Congress Cataloging-in-Publication Data Available

ISBN: 978-1-7936-2003-3 (cloth : alk. paper)
ISBN: 978-1-7936-2005-7 (pbk : alk. paper)
ISBN: 978-1-7936-2004-0 (electronic)

CONTENTS

Preface		vii
Acknowledgments		xiii
1	The God That Failed	1
2	The Power of the Present	29
3	The Power of the Past	55
4	The Shadow of Truth	83
5	Erotic Power	109
6	Metaphoric Power	137
7	The Solemnity of the World	163
Bibliography		191
Index		193
About the Author		197

PREFACE

Whitehead is usually included among those termed "process philosophers" because he proposes a radically temporalist metaphysics, one that gives primacy to temporal change. His basic units of reality are finite actual entities, events that come to be and perish. All else are features of actual entities. Enduring entities, for instance, are complexes that endure by stabilizing the character of the temporal sequence of the momentary actual entities comprising them. However, in *Process and Reality* Whitehead makes two exceptions to this ontology: he identifies possibilities as eternal, and posits an actual entity that is both eternal and everlasting.

My first aim in this book is to argue that these exceptions render Whitehead's metaphysics incoherent. My second aim is to show how what remains in *Process and Reality* after eliminating the notions of eternal objects and God can readily be reshaped into a coherent radically temporalist metaphysics. My third aim is to indicate how this reshaping can be furthered by what is found in *Adventures of Ideas* and *Modes of Thought*.

Whitehead famously remarks that "the safest general characterization of the European philosophical tradition is that it consists of a series of footnotes to Plato" (1978, 39). According, I take my cue from what he says is the key to Plato's mature thought, found in *Sophist* 247e where, in Jowett's translation, the Eleatic Stranger says: "My suggestion would be, that anything which possesses any sort of power to affect another, or to be affected by another, even for a moment, however trifling the cause and however slight and momentary the effect, has real existence; and I hold that the definition of being is simply power" (quoted Whitehead 1967, 119–20). Or as Whitehead paraphrases it: "The essence of being is to be implicated in causal action on other beings" (120).

I want to underscore two fundamental features of this text. First, note that the Eleatic Stranger's definition of power is a suggestion. He proposes it as a way to escape the dilemma posed by materialists who claim that only things we can see and touch have real existence, that ideas are either reducible to physical things or they are figments of our imagination. Figments they may be, says the Stranger, but that does not mean they do not have power to affect and be affected by other things. We cannot touch an idea but we can feel its impact on our lives, in the wild dream, for instance, that leads to the demolition of an unjust law or the carefully hedged hypothesis that results in an important new medical therapy. Insofar as we are persuaded by the Stranger's suggestion, its power will also be manifest by its altering how we think and act, a power compelling not by its physical impact but by its allure.

Second, the Eleatic Stranger goes on to say, *Sophist* 248e–249a, that "being as being known, is acted on by knowledge, and is therefore in motion, for that which is in a state of rest cannot be acted upon" but remains "in awful unmeaningness an everlasting fixture." Whitehead's gloss on this is that "'action and reaction' belong to the essence of being: though the mediation of 'life and mind' is invoked to provide the medium of activity" (1967, 120). In other words, the power of affecting and being affected, which is the reality of being, is teleonomic: oriented toward an outcome, although not necessarily consciously. To really exist is to act, and to act is to be an actualizing process, neither an eternal nor an everlasting fixture. Or to put it another way, the form of real existence is the form of agency, which is to be oriented by virtue of a possibility into fashioning something that makes a difference with respect both to what is given and to what is possible.

In keeping with the Eleatic Stranger's suggestions, as recommended by both Plato and Whitehead, this book is a metaphysical essay about the fundamentally temporal character of power, of the teleonomic powers that make realities that become and perish, emerge and decline, create and destroy. I will explore the hypothesis that everything that exists has been made, that every maker has itself been made, and that everything made is finite and therefore eventually unmade. It follows that the power to make, which is also the power to unmake, is expressed in possibilities sought and ends achieved that are values which are functions of what exists, therefore values that are vulnerable: always at risk, always in need of replenishment, repair, or replacement.

I find this radically temporalist ontology in the metaphysical perspective developed by Alfred North Whitehead, and so the form my exploration will take is to deploy that perspective as adequately and coherently as I am able. Because this ontology is obscured by some of Whitehead's own key notions as well as by those of a great many of his interpreters, my task is a contrarian's: to recover what has been obscured by arguing that it's about time we took Whitehead seriously in his request that we take time seriously. I am hardly alone in this role, but most of those who have been deeply influenced by Whitehead's metaphysics while rejecting his nontemporalist intuitions have not developed their criticisms. Like Don Sherburne, they have raised their contrarian banner but not sallied further forth. Or like Susanne Langer, Robert Neville, and Don Crosby, they have expressed their disagreements by developing metaphysical philosophies of their own, ones showing Whitehead's influence but in no other sense Whiteheadian.

My initial enthusiasm for Whitehead's philosophy of organism was because of his notion of a God whose powers were not absolute, who therefore was able to love, to care, suffer, change, and whose power was persuasive, luring not commanding. Over the years, however, I have come slowly to recognize that there is no way to make the radically temporalist aspects of Whitehead's metaphysics compatible with his notion of God as it is developed in *Process and Reality*. This God is an entity that changes, but never comes to be or perishes; it is actual but not finite. The pure possibilities it envisions and orders are not made but eternal. Its prehension of the achieved values of actual entities makes those achievements everlasting. These intrusions of timeless realities seem to be echoes of Plato's understanding of time as the moving image of eternity, temporal entities as dependent on what is not temporal. I want to recover a Whitehead devoid of such intrusions, to revivify his arguments for a metaphysics that inverts the Platonic relationship, a metaphysics that derives the nontemporal from the temporal, taking the imperishable to be an abstraction, an unmoving image of the perishable.

Many process philosophers, oddly enough, seem reluctant to take time seriously. They should be celebrating the primacy of becoming over being. They should be insisting that whatever entities are actual are therefore temporal accomplishments, analyzable into their component data, vectors, powers, and functions, but themselves the only actualities. They should be denying the very possibility of eternal and all other timeless realities, and likewise of substances and all other endlessly enduring realities. They should be arguing that there can be no region of reality except that made and unmade by finite perishing entities. Instead, these process philosophers are always slipping in by the back door what they say they have booted out the front door. They keep joyously discovering some sort of entity independent of and more important than the momentary achievements of which just previously they had been proclaiming all else were only features.

Why these persistent efforts to multiply entities beyond necessity? Substance ontology and the notion of a realm beyond time are resilient errors, but why should they plague even those ostensibly committed to their denial? The reason might be simply because the foundational character of temporality is obscured by the residues of old metaphysical beliefs, including those embedded in our most archaic habits, in our languages, maybe even in our genetic structure. Perhaps. But one reason substance thinking never seems to go away is because too many thinkers fear the consequences of taking time seriously. It's not just that process is often obscured but that process philosophers are too often the obscurantists, attempting purposefully or otherwise to hide the full force of their ontology's implications. I hope to brush away what keeps being obscured, to let those implications once again shine forth.

In the pages of this book, I am not attempting to defend my truths against others' errors, for what I am developing is a speculative hypothesis not a dogma, an adventure into open water not a mooring in some safe well-guarded harbor. As Whitehead says, "the true method of philosophical construction is to frame a scheme of ideas, the best one can, and unflinchingly to explore the interpretation of experience in terms of this scheme" aware that in doing so "the merest hint of dogmatic certainty as to finality of statement is an exhibition of folly" (1928, xiv). Metaphysical statements are suggestions, having to do with processes not results, concrescings not satisfactions, yet they are expressed, as they must be, as results, as systems of interpretation. For any adventure worth its salt seeks results: strives as best it can to arrive at some destination, to find a better way toward a better outcome. Open-water journeys require more than enthusiasm, however. They require well-made boats and sails, careful attention to waves and wind, skill in pulling off timely reaches and close hauls. And they require above all the ability to make do with whatever is at hand in order to devise workable responses to the unexpected. What they don't require, because they know not ever to expect it, is safe harbor.

The adventure on which this book embarks is one on which I am inviting you also to embark, and so I hope as you read you will be alert not only to my arguments but also to how I am attempting to be faithful to an ideal of bounded openness. Perhaps thereby I will enhance the lure for you of a way of doing metaphysics and of metaphysics thus done that is thoroughly and gloriously timebound. When you finish this book, if you have been reading well, and have soldiered on despite your disagreements, or hopefully because of them, you will have entertained a suggestion about interpreting Whitehead that frees you from dreaming of a time when there will no longer be any stormy seas to navigate, no longer any need to find your way through uncharted waters. May you with Whitehead's encouragement be eager to navigate the wine-dark sea, not settling for any final result, any definitive interpretation, any sort of Ithaca—except it serves as a brief respite from which soon to set your sails once more for open water and the next stage of your journey after the unattainable, that most human of all our possibilities.

ACKNOWLEDGMENTS

The origin of this book is a paper I read at the Sixth International Whitehead Conference in Salzburg the summer of 2006, titled "A Nontheistic Whiteheadian Cosmology." It was expanded two years later into an article in *Review of Metaphysics*: "A Functionalist Reinterpretation of Whitehead's Metaphysics." A number of philosophical colleagues sent me comments on my talk and/or my article. Their criticisms and words of praise, but most importantly their suggestions for improving my argument, were exceedingly helpful, encouraging me to continue with my project. I would like to thank them: Randall Auxier, Donald Crosby, Lewis Ford, William Hamrick, Donald Schindler, and Jan van der Veken.

My understanding of Whitehead's metaphysics, its strengths and its weaknesses, has been influenced by some of my teachers at Grinnell College, Union Theological Seminary, and Yale: Paul Kuntz, Henry Nelson Wieman, Daniel Day Williams, William Christian, and Robert Brumbaugh. I would also like to thank other colleagues, Whiteheadians and otherwise, who have stimulated my thinking by their divergent assumptions, approaches, and achievements: Frederick Ferré, Merle Allshouse, Malcolm Evans, John Bennett, Melvin Woody, Pamela Crosby, Joseph Bracken, Pete Gunter, Donald Sherburne, Robert Neville, Nancy Frankenberry, David Hall, Joseph Grange, Patricia Cook, George Lucas, and Brian Henning.

Another kind of thank you: to the Whitehead Research Project's book series on Contemporary Whitehead Studies, edited by Roland

Faber and Brian Henning, for considering my manuscript—and accepting it. I appreciated the comments of the anonymous reviewer used by CWS, who strongly underscored the strengths of my manuscript while sharply criticizing a number of weaknesses and omissions needing to be corrected. A thank you, repeatedly, to Jana Hodges-Kluck, senior acquisitions editor at Lexington Books, her assistant Sydney Wedbush, and production editor Jacques Plante for shepherding me through the process from submitted manuscript to printed book. Their clarity and knowledge combined with their patience made them a delight to work with.

And also a special thank you to my best friend and companion, Sally Martin, who has suffered through my multitude of attempts to restate in non-technical terms one or another point in my manuscript in the hope she would find it at least intelligible and maybe even interesting enough to converse with me about. Sometimes she did; somethings she didn't. I learned a lot about stylistic niceties and their relevance to even the most technical of ideas through our conversations. To her, I dedicate this book.

1
THE GOD THAT FAILED

In *Process and Reality*, Whitehead identifies four metaphysical reasons for including God in his cosmology, the first three of them associated with the primordial nature, the fourth with the consequent nature: [1] God is needed to account for an intrinsic bias in natural processes, a bias toward the actualization of the most suitable of whatever possibilities are available; [2] God is needed as a receptacle for all possibilities, and for their organization into the ordered system on which cosmic order depends; [3] God is needed as the agent able to relate possibilities relevantly to the need for novelty in the creative advance of the cosmos; and [4] God is needed as a long-term evolving constraint on such novelty, in order to provide the stability that undergirds the creative advance.[1]

My aim in what follows is to explain how each of these metaphysical functions provided by the notion of God is deployed in *Process and Reality*, underscoring why Whitehead thinks his metaphysics needs that function. I then raise problems with both the how and the why, arguing that the godly function discussed fails to resolve the systemic difficulty it was designed to address. I contend that these functions exacerbate those difficulties instead, rendering Whitehead's metaphysics incoherent. Hence the aim of this chapter is negative. The exploration of an alternative that achieves the needed metaphysical coherence, readily available within the pages of *Process and Reality*, will be the task of chapters 2 and 3.

THE SUITABILITY BIAS

Whitehead's reason for including in his metaphysics an entity with a primordial nature is most clearly explicated in his brief account of scientific prediction in the last four sections of *Process and Reality*, Part II, chapter IX (1978, 199–207). Although the discussion is about a complicated scientific method for devising and testing theories, the data which the theories interpret are empirical matters of sense perception. Metaphysics, for Whitehead, is a speculative flight that should originate and terminate in such matters, so Whitehead's justification here for God is experientially grounded. God is introduced so that his metaphysics can be adequate, so that it can account for one of the most pervasive features of the world as we understand it: our sense of the intrinsic temporal continuity of things.

Whitehead begins by asking a metaphysical question: "What is there in the nature of things, whereby an inductive inference, or a judgment of general truth, can be significantly termed 'correct' or 'incorrect'?" (199). Inductive inferences are the bread and butter of our daily life. We pass people on the street, some of whom smile at us, others of whom scowl, most of whom simply ignore us. None do us any harm, and so we assume anyone else who we pass will also do us no harm. Without giving it any thought, we infer from the behavior of a handful of people that all others will behave similarly. We make a hasty inductive generalization. A more careful consideration would likely lead us to a more cautious judgment: that it is very likely the next few people we meet will pass us by without incident, but that there is of course a small chance one of those people will put us in harm's way. Trusting people to behave peaceably in a stable law-abiding community is a reasonable judgment for us to make. To imagine that every stranger we meet is somehow a threat to our well-being would be thought wrong-headed, an irrational or paranoid response.

Whitehead's question is whether there is something about "the nature of things" that justifies these seemingly rational judgments, that assures us they are not arbitrary. Is there an objective basis for thinking that what has been the case will usually continue to be the case? Whitehead's answer is that "the philosophy of organism provides two distinct elements in the universe from which an intuition of probability can originate. One of them is statistical" (201), and it is to a consideration of that element that we will first turn.

He uses "railway time-tables" to illustrate our commonsensical statistical intuitions. We believe that timetables for prior months "represent the facts as to past running of the trains, within certain marginal limits of unpunctuality, and allowing for a few individual breakdowns" (199). And we believe timetables for the upcoming months will also represent the facts with similar accuracy. We assign these beliefs a "high probability" of being correct. Were the time-tables about high and low tides, we would think their accuracy even more probable, but were they about the weather, we would downgrade the probabilities of their accuracy.

Our confidence in the accuracy of both prior and upcoming railroad timetable information is based on an induction we make from some particular past events we know from our own first-hand experience: Yesterday I saw the 10:30 a.m. train arriving at precisely 10:30, although the 11:20 train didn't arrive until 11:21; to the general claim that the trains coming to our station are quite likely to arrive when scheduled, tomorrow's train will leave the station right at 10:40, so don't be late getting there or you'll miss it. "There is a conformity to matter of fact which these judgments exhibit, even if the events concerned have not happened, or will not happen" (200), and the justification for this belief is statistical. For every scheduled train arrival, it is possible the train will be on time and possible it will not. Past data show it is on time far more than not—let's say nine times out of ten—so we infer that there is a 90 percent likelihood that any future arrival will also be on time.

We can think of situations, of course, where this sort of confidence in the statistical analysis that grounds our prediction of train movements can prove to be unjustified. For example, an unexpected once-in-a-lifetime storm, such as a category 5 East Coast hurricane similar to Katrina or Maria, or a suddenly explosive midwestern tornado or derecho, would disrupt the trains for hours or days. Whitehead mentions "the unprecedented Mississippi floods" that occurred in May and June 1927 and wreaked havoc with the accuracy of the state's railway timetables (200). However, because the floods occurred only in that one state, Vermont residents had no concerns in July about the accuracy of the timetables for their own state. Nor would they have been justified on the basis of the punctuality errors in Mississippi timetables to predict similar errors in future Vermont timetables—even though unexpected November 1927 floods in Vermont did in fact result in just such errors (200). Our confidence in statistical predictions based on inductive inferences from what we know lessens not only due to unexpected variations in what we take to be normal, but also when what we know is scant, concerning for example "some scientific conjecture as to the internal constitution of the stars, or as to the future of human society after some unprecedented convulsion" (201).

Obviously statistical predictions increase in accuracy as the relevant database is enlarged, but where the relevant data have become practically or actually infinite, sampling methods become crucial. There are more train schedules and more data on their accuracy than we could reasonably check, so we select a small amount of that information as representative of the whole potential database. The standard method for securing a representative sample is for the sampled items to be chosen randomly: for example, every tenth item in an alphabetical list, the same percent of ethnic minorities or women or registered voters in the sample as in the database.

However, "no sample is 'random'; it has only followed a complex method" and hence "will give a statistical result entirely dependent" on that method (203). If the only grounds for the claim that a database is adequate, that it includes all relevant data, are the same grounds for the method by which a statistical sample of that database is determined, then there is no way that the method can predict a novel result. An outcome different in kind from those contained in the database will not be considered a datum, and so will not be included in any sample on the basis of which a prediction is made. If the sampling method is numerical, the database of items from which the sample is created will be numerable, and so a random sample of community assets will not include any information about its moral stature or adherence to traditional values. If meaningful propositions are thought to be necessarily truth-functional, then aesthetic judgments will be excluded from any sampling of factual information about the nature of things. If only white males who own property have the right to vote, then women, African Americans, Hispanics, and Asia Americans will not be sampled in a poll of political preferences.

This generates what Whitehead calls a "famous dilemma." Suppose an inference is made from a finite sample of a database to the existence of a novel kind of particular entity. Either the prediction will be thought "irrational, futile, useless," and so discarded, or it will be justified only after additional information has been secured, by expanding the database (203). If the prediction is still thought to be inadequate, perhaps biased because of its continued exclusion of a certain kind of datum, the sampling method will be faulted, the judgment said to be biased because its database is biased. So there will need to be an "appeal to a wider meaning of probability," and hence to a more suitable database that the sampling method makes possible (201). But "it is arguable that this wider probability is itself another statistical probability" with some as yet unacknowledged bias (201). Which, because it would therefore still be inadequate, would require justification by a similar appeal to a yet more encompassing method. We would be caught in an infinite regress.

The only way to stop an infinite regress in the justification for the confidence we have in our probability analyses, says Whitehead, is to "reach a 'ground' which is not selected for any reason of probability. It must be selected because it is *the* 'ground' presupposed in all our reasonings" (201). Whitehead points to a "natural method of sampling" to which we can appeal, a method "rooted in the nature of the case and not arbitrarily adopted" (206). Statistical sampling presupposes the continuity of past and future, a "tacit presupposition" that the "future is derived from the present by a continuity of inheritance in which this condition is maintained," that there is a "close analogy" between the "general social environment" that grounds past cases and the environment that grounds future cases (204). How well the train company has been managed in the recent past—how frequently its locomotives and train tracks were serviced, how rigorously its crews and their managers were trained, how carefully its timetables were constructed—is how well we presume they will be managed in the near future. Our confidence in this analogy increases the more the continuity is physical rather than cultural, a matter of seasonal weather patterns and local terrain stability rather than human decisions and institutional practices.

Whitehead's metaphysics provides an ontological justification for this belief in continuity: "It is evident that the ultimate 'ground' to which all probable judgments must refer can be nothing else than the actual world as objectified in judging subjects" (203). His appeal is to "the actual world," to the nature of things. But this is not a world apart from we who seek to find it as an ultimate ground for our judgments. Instead, it is a world objectified in us, a world of which we are products—a world of which judging subjects are an integral part. Its ontology is what *Process and Reality* hypothesizes: a world of the coming to be and perishing of actual occasions. An actual occasion, Whitehead reminds us, is "essentially social" in two ways: the "outlines of its own character are determined by the data which its environment provides," and these data "constitute that display of the universe which is inherent to the entity." Hence "the data upon which the subject passes judgment are themselves components conditioning the character of the judging subject" (203).

So the "close analogy" between general past conditions and future predictions of individual cases is explained by Whitehead's ontology of how perishing actual occasions determine the outlines of the actual occasions that arise from them. The character of an actual occasion is a concrete display of its social environment; the social environment is an approximate display of the individuals to which it gives rise. We are like our ancestors, as our descendants will be like us; the physical processes shaping the cosmos moments after the Big Bang are like those shaping it now. Whitehead sees this ontological claim as an "enlargement of the premise in ethical discussions: that man is a social animal. Analogously, every actual occasion is social." So the persistence of types of actual occasions presumes the existence of analogous types of environmental societies, and hence of "the laws of nature in operation throughout the environment" (204).

Hence Whitehead develops a little syllogistic chain, a sortes, regarding inductive inferences. It goes like this (205):

1. Premise: $Eao_f \approx Eao_p$—the environment of a predicted future event "contains a society of actual occasions" that is "analogous to a society in the present" environment;

2. Premise: if $(ao^1 \approx ao^2)$ then $(d^1 \approx d^2)$—"analogous societies require analogous data for their several occasions";

3. Premise: if $(d^1 \approx d^2)$ then $(E^1 \approx E^2)$ —"analogous data can be provided only by the objectifications provided by analogous environments";

4. Premise: if LN^1 then Eao^1—"the laws of nature are derived from the characters of the societies dominating the environment";

5. Thus: $Ln^f \approx Ln^p$—"the laws of nature dominating" the predicted environment "have some analogy to the laws of nature dominating the immediate environment."

Whitehead then carefully underscores the importance of the terms "analogous" and "dominance" in his sortes, because they introduce crucially a "margin of uncertainty" (205). The dependence of the emergent individual on its surrounding social environment is not absolute. The causal power of the environment dominates but does not determine the character of what it makes possible. The character of the past is a necessary but not sufficient condition for the character of the present. The accuracy of tomorrow's timetable of train arrivals in Montpellier is analogous to the accuracy of yesterday's, not precisely the same. Children are analogous to their parents, not their spitting image. Furthermore, "the laws of nature are the outcome of the social environment" (204). So it is not only that the power of the laws of the natural environment to shape us is not absolute, but also that the laws change as the environment changes. Persistence is always only approximate. And hence inference from past to future is a "baffling mixture of certainty, ignorance, and probability" (205).

We should note also that the past which dominates the present emerging from it is not the whole past, not even the whole of the cosmic epoch in which it comes into existence. The dominant past is "the relevant portion of the cosmic epoch" (206), a limited region important because of its specific causal influence. Hence "the relevant objectifications, forming the relevant data for any one occasion, refer to a finite sample of actual occasions in the environment" (206). Although each actual occasion prehends in some manner all the actual occasions in its environment, the relevant portion of that environment is "a finite region of the extensive continuum, so far as adequate importance is concerned in respect to individual differences among actual occasions" (206). This finite region is a sampling of the whole, justified by its importance for the actual occasions prehending it. The environments of each of these actual occasions are analogous, different but not importantly so, because their prehensions overlap so extensively. Our samplings are not arbitrary but grounded in the way things are:

> Accordingly our knowledge of the external world, and of the conditions upon which its laws depend, is, through and through, of that numerical character which a statistical theory of probability requires. Such a theory does not require that exact statistical calculations be made. All that is meant by such a theory is that our probability judgments are ultimately derivable from vague estimates of 'more or less' in a numerical sense. We have an unprecise intuition of the statistical basis of the sort of way in which things happen. (206)

It may seem like weak tea, this "unprecise intuition" of the natural continuities underlying the statistically-grounded laws of nature. However, it is quite robust because it is grounded in ontologically fundamental features of our cosmic epoch. However, Whitehead does not think it robust enough. Let us turn therefore to the second of the "two distinct elements in the universe from which," according to Whitehead, "an intuition of probability can originate" (201): our intuition of "an alternative non-statistical ground" for our probability judgments (206). And this brings us at long last to God.

In addition to the statistical ground, says Whitehead, "another factor" is required to ground our probability beliefs (207). To account for the continuity of environments over time, for their stability, something more than approximate repetition is required. In an ever-changing world, adaptive innovation is crucial for an entity to endure: changes that adjust a person or an amoeba or an actual occasion to the environing changes of which it must take account, that preserve the entity by modifying it. Trains arrive on time or fail to do so, and a statistical analysis of a relevant sample of past timetables and actual arrivals allows us to predict the likelihood of the next train arriving on time. Incidental novelties with regard to when a train arrives and the reasons for its variance from what was predicted can be ignored, as we did for instance in dealing with the Mississippi and Vermont floods. However, technological innovations such as more efficient kinds of engines or computer-controlled train speeds need to be taken seriously. Properly understood and adopted, they could increase the accuracy of the on-time predictions of train arrivals and departures by minimizing both mechanical and human error. Indeed, it is precisely by taking advantage of such novelties that the train companies were able to survive as viable transportation systems when faced with the novel competition first of private automobiles and then commercial airliners.

We are not surprised by the success of new ideas, even though we are well aware that most novelties are worthless because they are impractical and that most successful ones have a short half-life—as many train companies eventually discovered. For we sense that innovation is the key to survival not merely in particular enterprises like transportation companies but also in human endeavors more generally: in the Darwinian survival of the fittest organisms, and in the survival of inanimate objects, including even the supposedly everlasting mountains and the eternal stars. We have, and here Whitehead outruns this data, "an intuition of probability respecting the origination of some novelty" (207), a sense that more is going on than mere chance when seemingly random deviations from the statistical mean occur. We have "an intuition of an intrinsic suitability of some definite outcome from a presupposed situation," an outcome for which statistical predictions cannot adequately account. Some novelties are not simply novel but are suitably so. We feel that a "preferential adaptation" of selected possibilities occurs, involving their "graduated 'intensive relevance'" to the novel alternatives the situation permits (207).

This intuition is not just that some realizable novelties will in fact be actualized but that those novelties will be biased toward outcomes conducive to new sorts of stability more adequate to changed conditions and to the enhanced values such adaptive success provides. The bias is toward the better, toward the environmentally adaptive stability requisite for improved individual achievement. Just as new engineering and computer technologies increase opportunities for developing more effective railway services, so also with all matters from the concrescing of actual entities to the character of the cosmic order of things: the novelties are suitably meliorative.

The suitability is not simply a statistical result, because it deviates from established probability distributions. "It depends upon the fundamental graduation of appetitions which lies at the base of things, and which solves all indeterminations of transition" (207). It is an intuition that there is a reason in the nature of things for why the possibilities available for effecting transitions from established to altered actualities are ordered with an optimal bias rather than randomly. This sense of a firm constant ground for meliorative change, Whitehead argues, is due to "the prehension by every creature of the graduated order of appetitions constituting the primordial nature of God" (207).

Whitehead calls the agency "God" but then carefully empties the term of its standard religious meaning. In no sense is this a religious intuition, he insists, for it lies "at a far lower level of experience than do the religious emotions" (207). Yet neither is it merely an intuition of an inexplicable bias toward the intrinsically more suitable. The intuition is metaphysical, a sense that this bias is due to an agency at the base of things, influencing the character of temporal transitions. Whitehead then adds, a bit defensively: "the secularization of the concept of God's functions in the world is at least as urgent a requisite of thought as is the secularization of other elements of experience" (207). This agency, its function secular not religious, purely metaphysical and primordial, is "the ground of all order and of all originality" (108). It is a notion of an intelligent designer. Not an imperial designer of this world or even of an ideal best of all possible worlds, but rather a designer of the tools by which the world's finite agents can shape their various situational conditions for the better.

Whitehead's intuition is fourfold: that novel possibilities emerge constantly in the course of things, that there is a bias in their character toward the actualization of greater value, that this bias is the result of their graduated relevance to that outcome, and that this grading is effected by a primordial agency. Any of us would affirm the first aspect of this intuition: that novelty is an intrinsic feature of the cosmos. Many of us might even affirm the second and third aspects of Whitehead's intuition: that these novelties are meliorative. But whence comes the seemingly gratuitous addition of the fourth aspect of his intuition: that the bias is due to the work of a metaphysically fundamental agency? Why does the cosmic order require not only a ground for the stability and the originality it manifests but also an agent effecting that ground?

When Whitehead talks of intuitions, he is making an appeal to direct experience, to the felt reality of inescapable causal efficacies, apart from the analyses and generalizations by which we interpret such feelings. For instance, the ultimate notions of "concrescence" and the "production of novel togetherness," captured in Whitehead's idea of Creativity as the Category of the Ultimate, "are inexplicable either in terms of higher universals or in terms of the components participating in the concrescence" (21). "The sole appeal," says Whitehead, "is to intuition" (22). But intuitions are slippery things. All too often what seems inescapable—a self-evident truth, a brute fact—turns out, embarrassingly, to be a prejudice. Our direct experience is ofttimes blinkered by self-interest or group conditioning, our intuition a belief which the passage of time, the cooling of emotion, or an enlargement of perspective shows for what it really is. Where the sole appeal is to intuition, there is no way to criticize a belief. *De gustibus non disputandum est* may be a proper claim with regard to whether hominy grits taste good, but it is inappropriate in matters scientific, moral, or metaphysical. Are we without rational recourse when confronted by a putative intuition that humans of a different color or culture or sexual preference than the speaker's are intrinsically inferior, or on the contrary that all humans are created equal and endowed with certain intrinsic rights? The appeal to intuition leaves metaphysics with no traction, and so should be suspect.

Whitehead has a reason, however, for his claim that God is the source of a bias in the creative advance toward the better. For it is not God that he intuits but the suitability bias. God is a theoretical entity, a notion posited out of a metaphysical need to account for the bias. And Whitehead's reason is that the gradation of possibilities constituting the bias requires a graduator. A meliorative design requires an innovative designer, but the designer can be innovative only if novel possibilities are both relevant and accessible, and such an opportune selection requires an opportunistic selector. The argument is Thomistic: whatever is created or designed needs itself to be created or designed, and this sequence of effects and their causes cannot go on endlessly but must terminate in an uncreated creator, an undesigned designer. The necessary condition for a meliorative order is an ultimate meliorative orderer. To understand why Whitehead thinks this is so leads us to the second of the four reasons he gives for including God in his cosmology.

THE ETERNALITY OF POSSIBLES

The suitability bias in the creative advance of our cosmos is a bias among possibilities, and it is because of how Whitehead understands possibilities that he needs God for there to be such a bias. He calls possibilities "eternal objects." They are *objects* because they can be objectified, concretized as specific features of actualized entities. For instance, blue is an eternal object, a color possibility that can be a feature of something material. A bolt of bleached cotton cloth could be dyed almost any color, but when I dye it with indigo tin the possibility of blue is the one actualized; it is objectified as the unique color feature of a unique piece of material. This immature blueberry is red, but as it matures it becomes blue; the blue that was its possible color becomes the specific color feature of this specific matured berry. Standing outdoors near my Cumberland Valley home, I look up on a sunny day not at a generic blue sky but at the specific blue of that day's Cumberland Valley sky.

Eternal objects are *eternal* because they can be objectified not just once but endlessly, as features of an indefinite number of different actual entities and complexes of actual entities. An actual entity comes to be and perishes, occurring only once and uniquely: this bolt of blue fabric, this blueberry, this morning's sky as seen from my porch. An eternal object need never be actualized, but should it be it may then recur: first as an actualized feature of one specific entity, then of another, and then another, but nonetheless remaining, always and everywhere, a potential feature for any subsequent entity. There is the blue of this fabric, the blue of that berry, and the blue of the sky above, three actualizations of the same blue, one reality objectified multiple times. Blue was never born nor will it ever die. Thus when Whitehead lays out the Categoreal Scheme of his metaphysics in *Process and Reality*, he identifies two basic kinds of existence: actual entities and eternal objects, what occurs and what recurs, agents and their objective features. Although he lists six other categories of existence, these two "stand out with a certain extreme finality," the other types having "a certain intermediate character" because of their dependency on the basic two (1978, 22).

The formal definition of eternal objects is that they are "Pure Potentials for the Specific Determination of Fact, *or* Forms of Definiteness" (22; Category of Existence 'v'). Later on this gnomic definition is explicated by stipulating that "any entity whose conceptual recognition does not involve a necessary reference to any definite actual entities of the temporal world is called an 'eternal object'" (44). Thus to conceive of an eternal object is not thereby to learn anything about the actual world.

The possibility that the stagecoach from Yuma will arrive this afternoon at 3:10 is a real possibility that will become a specific feature of the situation of the Yuma stagecoach stop at ten minutes after three when the team of horses brings it to that destination at that moment, although the possibility will never be actualized if the stagecoach is delayed by some unexpected material happenstance, like a fallen tree or a band of robbers. It is possible that my blueberry may not have turned blue by the time I eat it, in which case the possibility of eating a blue possibility at that time will be unactualized. The sky above is bright blue, then it clouds over and the sky is dull gray, but the sun comes out and the sky again is brightly blue—the possible blue sky during the period when the sky was grey is a possibility that was not and can never be actualized.

In each of these cases, the possibility is anchored to a temporal event, so it is not repeatable. If the coach is late, that possibility is irretrievably lost. But the possibility of that same stagecoach arriving at Yuma some other time could be actualized many times, perhaps each subsequent day at 3:10. And many more times if the possibility has to do with any stagecoach at any town, and indefinitely many times if the possibility is of any human conveyance arriving on time at any specified location. For eternal objects to be eternal, they must be unanchored from the actual world, treated apart from any of their actualizations. An anchored possibility, such as the stagecoach for Yuma arriving at 3:10 that particular day, is not an eternal object as such. It is a possibility about a feature of a possible occurrence. Occurrences are unique; they cannot recur. So any possible feature of the occurrence ceases to be possible if the occurrence is actualized without that feature as an actualized feature. It is not the possibility of blue that is anchored but the possibility of this cloth, this berry, or this sky being blue in that place at that time. Blue as such is not anchored; its reality is not dependent on any temporal event of which it might be a feature. That's why Whitehead calls eternal objects "pure potentials" having no "necessary reference to any actual entities in the temporal world." Yet what then are possibilities that are temporally anchored?

Whitehead's difficulty comes primarily not from this claim that possibilities are eternal in the sense that they can recur, but from his further claim that their eternality entails they are essentially self-contained. He characterizes them as an infinite plurality of isolated possibilities, a "barren inefficient disjunction of abstract potentialities" (40) having no internal—no intrinsic, no essential—relatedness to one another, much less to the actual world. "An eternal object, in itself, abstracts from all determinate actual entities, including even God" (256), and as such it has no defining characteristic as its individual essence, no essential manner of relatedness to other eternal objects, nor any inherent relevance to any temporal realities. It lacks agential power.

Defining characteristics are features of what Whitehead calls societies: nexūs with social order, which include in particular enduring objects, kinds of complex entities that, unlike eternal objects, come into existence, persist for moments or centuries, and eventually perish. Whitehead uses the term 'defining characteristic' to refer to "a common element of form illustrated in the definiteness of each of its [a society's] included actual entities," a form arising in each entity because of "its prehensions of some other members of the nexus," those prehensions imposing "that condition of reproduction by reason of their inclusion of positive feelings of that common form" (34). Societies are individual facts of the togetherness of actual entities, the definition of which is due to their forms.

Whitehead likens a defining characteristic to Aristotle's substantial form: the stable continuity underlying the flux of a thing's accidents. Except that for Whitehead a defining characteristic changes; it is not permanent, but simply changes more slowly that the other features of that thing. It is the power which past actual entities exert on the nascent actual entities prehending them that determines the extent of the "likeness" among the successive entities comprising an enduring object. "How each individual actual entity contributes to the datum *from which* its successors arise" and "*to which* they must conform" to it (56) decides the extent of its survivability. The forms of which an enduring object's common element of form is composed are anchored eternal objects. When the common element is altered in response to changes in the enduring object's inheritable environment, some of its eternal objects become unanchored, replaced by different eternal objects newly anchored, in an attempt to alter its defining characteristic in ways more likely to sustain the enduring object it defines.

Enduring objects endure because they are able to change, their member actual entities able to adapt to emergent threats to their continued togetherness. They cease to endure when their adaptations are inadequate. Some of the blue fabric is made into a blue tunic worn frequently by a woman from the time she purchases it to the time when it has been worn thin and is turned into cleaning rags. Its defining characteristic is composed of actualizations of eternal objects including the color blue, but the perpetuation through the years of the tunic is due to the sequence of actual entities that prehend positively their predecessors' actualizations of blue, thereby actualizing it again and yet again, eventually less and less effectively, the fabric fading and its fibers weakening, until the tunic's defining characteristic is no longer transmitted, the fabric no longer a blue tunic.

The individual essence of an eternal object is that it is what it is, which means it is not capable of definition. Its reality is a matter of "mere isolation indistinguishable from nonentity" (257). It follows that they must all be what they are primordially, from before the coming to be and perishing of things, before the creating of any temporal world, any cosmic epoch. If eternal objects are not themselves essentially ordered, however, they need to be brought together with other eternal objects in a specifically organized manner, and that must be done primordially. It cannot be caused or created, cannot occur at any temporal moment, because it is the precondition for cosmos of any sort, including the current spatiotemporal cosmic epoch. Their ordering requires an orderer, and if that order is primordial, then its orderer must also be primordial. Moreover, the primordial orderer must be an actual entity because according to the "ontological principle," the eighteenth category of explanation (24–25), "all real togetherness is togetherness in the formal constitution of an actuality" (32). Furthermore, eternal objects have no reason for being what they are since according to the ontological principle, "actual entities are the only *reasons*" (24), and "a reason is always a reference to determinate actual entities" (256).

Therefore, eternal objects as an ordered system of possibilities must be an aspect of the formal constitution of an actual entity. Not just any actual entity, however, but one with the capacity for an "unlimited conceptual realization of the absolute wealth of potentiality" (343). The primordial order requires a primordial orderer, and since that ordered system has categoreal conditions that are the "timeless source of all order," of "the ultimate, basic adjustment of the togetherness of eternal objects on which creative order depends" (32), its orderer must also be ultimate; which is to say: timeless.

God as primordial does not order the eternal objects by doing something to them, by the purposeful imposition on them of a structure. Doing, purposing, imposing are temporal actions and the primordial order is timeless. Say rather that God as primordial is the "complete envisagement of eternal objects" (44)—that is, the primordial nature *is* the complete envisagement. God so understood is "deficiently actual," in the sense both that God's "feelings are only conceptual and so lack the fulness of actuality" and that therefore "apart from complex integration with physical feelings, are devoid of consciousness in their subjective forms" (343).

What Whitehead needs is an ultimate actuality to provide ontological location for the infinity of possibilities required for a metaphysical account of the creative advance, of an actual world of enduring entities both stable enough and flexible enough to support a dynamic cosmic order. Whitehead thinks that God as primordial suffices for that task. There are problems, however. Since God is an actual entity, God is able to give the eternal objects a reason by relating them in all the various ways possible. But the primordial nature of God is "deficiently actual" because only conceptual, and so at best only in a Pitwickian sense able to order eternal objects, providing them with a reason, since reasons must be referable to "determinate actual entities." And not only relating all possibilities in all possible ways, but doing so primordially! Which is surely impossible to do in a world characterized as a continually creative advance into novelty.

A primordial actual entity is an oxymoron, since the essence of actual entities is that they come to be by a process originating in physical prehensions of predecessors, which is not the case for anything primordial. Whitehead thus proposes an actual entity that is an exception to the rule, quite literally a *deus ex machina*, the metaphysical justification for which is to solve a problem by *ad hoc* means: the problem of where possibilities could possibly be if eternal rather that features of temporal agencies.

So we now have two reasons for why Whitehead introduces the notion of a primordial entity he calls God. First, to account for a suitability bias in the possibilities that give rise to the stability crucial to the creative advance of the cosmos. And, second, to identify those possibilities as eternal and to give them, indeed give any possibility, a primordial location within the creative advance. It is not enough to stop there, however. A third reason for God, according to Whitehead, is to make eternal objects relevant to the creative advance, and relevant in a way biased toward their suitability.

THE EFFICACY OF POSSIBLES

Eternal objects do not become features of actual entities by their own power. There is nothing in their nature that links them to temporal actualities. They do not ingress; they are ingressed. "The many eternal objects conceived in their bare isolated multiplicity lack any existent character. They require the transition to the conception of them as efficaciously existent by reason of God's conceptual realization of them" (1978, 349). God's primordial conceptual realization of eternal objects not only provides them an ontological location but also evaluates their relevance to the creative advance. Despite its independence from temporal particularity, God's primordial nature has "immanence in the world." As our intuition of bias implies, it is explicitly purposeful: "an urge toward the future based upon an appetite in the present," an evaluation of the worth of "an immediate physical feeling combined with the urge toward realization of the datum conceptually prehended" (32). This urge toward achieving an end must be primordial, a feature of a primordial actual entity, because only through having such an active purpose can there be a reason for it to relate novel possibilities, possibilities never before realized, to the concrescing of temporal actual entities and the creation and sustenance of enduring objects.

This is a shift from considering eternal objects as having only an "individual essence" to having a "relational essence" as well (115), from understanding them as "pure potentials" to considering them as "impure potentials" (22), as having "proximate relevance" (46) to the actualization of a possible matter of fact—as efficacious. Whitehead's God creates the universe in the sense that this primordial appetition "is the basis of all order" (347) and hence of all temporal processes, but it is not antecedent to those processes since antecedence is a temporal relation. Nor is it directly related to the course of history since it is primordial and so does not presuppose what has or will be actualized. God "is the unconditioned actuality of conceptual feeling at the base of things," an actuality that not only makes eternal objects relevant to the world but provides "an order in the relevance of eternal objects to the process of creation" (344). This ordering of relevance "is a free creative act untrammeled by reference to any particular course of things." It presupposes nothing about "the *particularities* of the actual world" but only "the *general* metaphysical character of creative advance" (344). So

God's primordial valuation of eternal objects is what makes them accessible to actual entities, and God's primordial appetite favors the efficacy of the more suitable of them.

Whitehead's claim is surprising, because it shifts to God what one might presume belongs to Creativity. The first of the categories, the Category of the Ultimate, encompasses a triad of notions—"many," "creativity," and "one"—or in other words, "disjunctive diversity," Creativity as "the principle of novelty," and "the advance from disjunction to conjunction." All other categories presuppose this ultimate triadic condition: that "in their natures, entities are disjunctively 'many' in the process of passage into conjunctive unity" (21). After all the categories are named and their functions described, however, Whitehead turns to "some derivative notions," where he asserts that "Creativity is without a character of its own" (31). God's primordial nature provides that character, or rather *is* "the acquirement by creativity of a primordial character" (344). It sets primordially the conditions for how Creativity thereafter functions, the conditions that make possible the endless sequential streams of actual occasions coming to be and perishing, enduring objects thriving and failing, the conditions for the emergence of our cosmic epoch and of its successors. God's primordial nature is that by reason of which there is a creative advance. Yet the Category of the Ultimate identifies Creativity as "the universal of universals characterizing ultimate matter of fact," the "principle of *novelty*" by which "the many, which are the universe disjunctively, become one actual occasion, which is the universe conjunctively" (21). Hence "the 'creative advance' is the application of this ultimate principle of creativity to each novel situation which it originates" (21).

So which is it by which there is the creative advance: Creativity or God? I suspect that the reason Whitehead shifts from Creativity to God is that the introduction of novelty means the introduction of hitherto unactualized possibilities, of eternal objects that have no agency themselves, that need an agent with the power to introduce them into the reiterating concrescent process by which the many things of this world become one new thing. But Creativity is a principle and therefore not an agent, and prior actual entities can't be a source of novel possibilities because novel possibles are not inherently temporal, not features of the past, and so not accessible. Except by the one agent able to access what is eternal: an entity that is itself both actual and eternal.

Once an ordered universe exists, God is not necessary for an eternal object to be efficacious. When a nascent actual entity physically prehends a past actual entity, the physical feeling carries with it an associated conceptual feeling which, because it has already exhibited its relevance by being included in that past actual entity's satisfaction, can be accessed by the nascent actual entity, treated as a realizable possible, and incorporated in some relevant manner into the emerging new actuality. However, eternal objects that are not available through the physical prehension of past actual entities remain unavailable to nascent ones until God makes them available. Without God as an "agency of comparison" able to disclose the "definite relevance" of possibilities never before actualized in temporal events, those possibilities would be unavailable to a present actual entity's concrescing decisions (31).

The immanence of God's primordial nature means that it can be prehended, but since that nature is not a physical actuality it can be prehended only conceptually. God's conceptual feelings of eternal objects are available for prehension as valuationally ranked by an appetition with respect to their relevance to the realization of more suitable matters of fact. These are feelings of impure possibilities but not limited to ones previously determined. Because they are directly accessed as possibilities by a nascent actual entity without requiring the mediation of physical prehensions of prior actual entities, they can include possibilities having no physical location, novel possibilities that have no history of prior relevance shaping their seeming worth. They are not novel, however, in the sense of being fanciful pie-in-the-sky what-ifs and dreamy might-have-beens. For "the conceptual feelings, which compose [God's] primordial nature, exemplify in their subjective forms . . . valuations determining the relative relevance of eternal objects for each occasion of actuality" (344). God selects from among the infinity of novel—not previously actualized—possibilities those especially relevant to each new situation.

Hence God as primordial "is the lure for feeling, the eternal urge of desire. His particular relevance to each creative act, as it arises from its own conditioned standpoint in the world, constitutes him the initial 'object of desire' establishing the initial phase of each subjective aim" (344). Novel possibilities must be offered to an occasion by an agent able to judge that novelty as relevant for the actual entity in its acquiring a desirable subjective aim and a repertoire of fresh ideas helpful in achieving that aim. Relevance is a determination that some members of a group, in this case of the totality of all possibilities, are comparatively more useful to what might emerge from a given situation than are others. Their ingression in a concrescing actual entity would likely be more conducive to its achieving optimal intensity of satisfaction than other possibilities.

Remember, however, that God's primordial nature is primordial, so the relational relevance of an eternal object to the concrescence of a specific actual entity, where its relevance is its novelty, its alternative to the possibilities inherited from its past, is primordial. According to Whitehead, God envisions all possibilities, all eternal objects, in their individual essences and in their relational essences to all other eternal objects. Also primordial, therefore, is God's valuation of the relational relevance of any possible relational essence that is a novelty, a creatively fresh possibility for a specific nascent actual entity. Consider a temporally anchored possibility such as the stagecoach to Yuma arriving at 3:10. Perhaps the individual essence of one of the eternal objects is the pure possibility of temporal conjunction. Its relational essence could then be all the potential ways in which things could come into conjunction, and even more specifically all the times and manners in which the Yuma stagecoach could arrive at a specified station along its route. Each potentiality of relationship would then be a complex of eternal objects and actual entities, but timelessly so, a possibility the reality of which is not conditional upon there ever being a place called Yuma or a stagecoach to Yuma. It would be a possibility relative to an actual situation before such a situation had been created.

However, if the product of an actual creativity is novel entities, it is unclear how such novelties could be eternally possible. Temporally anchored possibilities are contingent potentialities of relationship, potentialities that involve a relationship or kind of relationship that was created by a process in no sense necessary. The potentialities integral to the Yuma stagecoach cannot have been essential relational features of a timeless possibility. Even if the Temple at Jerusalem or the Second Person of the Trinity might plausibly be said to have been realities anchored to the spans of their temporal manifestations from the foundation of the world, surely not the Yuma stagecoach arriving at 3:10. To say of unique contingent achievements that their possibility is primordial is to presume that there is nothing new under the sun, that not merely this current cosmic epoch but the totality of all cosmic epochs, those previously having existed and those that might eventually exist, comprise a closed temporal system, a system the possibilities for which are all there from its first moment to its last. Included among those *a priori* possibilities would be the relationally relevant possibility of the stagecoach to Yuma arriving at 3:10, which involves an enduring object, the defining characteristic of which is that of a stagecoach that happens to be the one used on a particular day in the late nineteenth century for moving passengers and merchandise from points west to the town of Yuma. Surely for anyone who takes time seriously, as Whitehead claims to do, the possibility of this 3:10 event, including all the contingent contextual events and enduring objects that give it meaning, cannot in any sense be thought primordial.

It is not enough, however, that God be the primordial location for eternal objects and the primordial source of the novel possibilities by which actual entities are lured toward the more suitable of the available outcomes. Whitehead has a fourth reason why a nontemporal actual entity is metaphysically required.

THE RELEVANCE OF PERMANENCE

Relevance is a long-term as well as a short-term matter. If what is suitable in one moment is a threat to suitability in another moment, if an actual entity's good is irrelevant to its successor, an enduring order will not be possible but only chaotic flux. The "primordial permanence" of God is that whereby the creative advance "ever re-establishes itself" (1978, 347). It is not enough to provide the necessary conditions for the temporal emergence of a cosmic order, and to provide the novel possibilities necessary for actual entities to optimize their determinate satisfactions. It is crucial as well to provide for the originality necessary both (a) to sustain that cosmic order as a stable background for more intense but also more ephemeral modes of order such as human beings and their civilizations, and (b) to effect when needed a viable transition from a failed cosmos to its successor.

In developing his account of our intuition of a suitability bias, Whitehead was content to explain the stability of the creative advance in terms of "the prehension by every creature of the graduated order of appetitions constituting the primordial nature of God" (207). At the end of *Process and Reality*, however, he limits the relevance of the primordial nature to short-term achievements. God as primordial is "the principle of concretion—the principle whereby there is initiated a definite outcome from a situation otherwise riddled with ambiguity" (345). God's relevance to long-term stability requires that "the *particularities* of the actual world," not just "the *general* metaphysical character of creative advance," be in some sense necessary to God's nature (344). "God," says Whitehead, "as well as being primordial, is also consequent" (345). Because all temporal things are related, there must be "a reaction of the world on God," and the only way that can occur is for every actual entity to be "objectified in God as a novel element in God's objectification of that actual world" (345). The objectification is by means of physical prehensions, of finite "physical experience derived from the temporal world," and the "weaving of God's physical feelings upon his primordial concepts" is the work of the consequent nature. This marks the "completion of God's nature," so that "analogously to all actual entities, the nature of God is dipolar" (345).

Therefore, we can speak of an actual entity's objectifications in other actual entities not only as its slowly fading influence on successors but as "the completion of each fluent actual occasion by its function of objective immortality, devoid of 'perpetual perishing,' that is to say, 'everlasting'" in God's consequent nature (347). Here too, as with the suitability bias, Whitehead grounds his argument in an intuition, this time a "civilized intuition": that the problem of temporal change and timeless worth, finite achievements and infinite perfection, cannot be resolved by denying the reality or even merely the relative significance of either. Our philosophical, religious, and scientific systems that do this "have the common character of starting with a fundamental intuition which we do not mean to express, and of entangling themselves in verbal expressions, which carry consequences at variance with the initial intuition" (347). Whitehead's God resolves the problem by reconciling eternality and process as "elements in the nature of things" that are "incorrigibly there" as "the active self-expression of its own variety of opposites," a reconciliation that is "this incredible fact—that what cannot be, yet is" (350).

The intuition is the problem of reconciling flux and permanence. The concept of God is Whitehead's theory for resolving the problem without denying or subordinating one of the polar opposites to the other. The permanence of the creative advance requires aims more far reaching that an actual entity's immediate need for achieving determinate completion, long-term aims that can be achieved only by successors of the actual entity having that same aim. Actual entities must act not for themselves but for future generations. Such aims can lure an actual entity's feelings only if it understands itself as including not only its subjective immediacy but also its influence, an influence that is not merely a momentary extension of its momentary concrescence but forever. A yearning for objective immortality is needed to motivate such aims. Only an actual entity that is both primordial and everlasting can justify that yearning by exhibiting its own reality as everlasting and the actual entity's reality as everlastingly an element in that reality.

So Whitehead makes the necessary adjustment in his theory: actual entities are objectified in God's consequent nature "in which the many are one everlastingly, without the qualification of any loss either of individual identity or of completeness of unity" (350–51), and that objectification then "passes back into the temporal world, and qualifies this world so that each temporal actuality includes it as an immediate fact of relevant experience" (351). God's influence is thereby not just abstractly generic but also temporally specific, a "particular providence for particular occasions" (351). The aim that begins our brief attempt to make something concretely valuable from an inheritance of determinate fact and ideal possibility includes an inchoate sense of how the efforts of past actual entities have made our inheritance and of how what we do merges with what they did as a continued unending resource. Our "insistent craving is justified—the insistent craving that zest for existence be refreshed by the ever-present, unfading importance of our immediate actions, which perish and yet live for evermore" (351).

An insistent craving that our immediate actions have unfading importance is not a sufficient reason, of course, for claiming they actually do. Especially since it requires affirming a contradiction: that our actions both perish and do not perish, die and yet live forever after. Whitehead acknowledges that such an affirmation is incredible because it means reconciling the unreconcilable: an impossibility and its actuality. The notion of God's consequent nature has the same difficulty as the notion of God's primordial nature. It is an attempt to rescue an ontological dichotomy from incoherence. Or to put it in the vernacular, to have one's cake and eat it too. Eternal and temporal are flat out incompatibles, and philosophers who attempt to give ontological status to both end up denying either the reality or the ultimate value of one of them. Or they create a hierarchy that subordinates either the reality or the value of one while affirming the other's superiority, its ultimacy.

Everlasting and temporal, on the other hand, sound like they might be compatible, but only if one denies that temporal means coming to be and perishing. Forevermore is not a temporal notion, however, precisely because it chops off the perishing. The everlasting importance and the eternal importance of our action both go on and on, worlds without end, the latter because what was temporal is transformed into what is without temporality, the former because what is temporal is transformed into what is without perishing—which is to say, without temporality. The incoherence is blatant, and putting lipstick on it won't help.

Whitehead says that the theory of God's primordial nature is a "secularization of the concept of God's function in the universe" (207), God as a secular agency, its function purely metaphysical. God's consequent nature is explicated using similar language about its metaphysical function and to this extent it also is God as a secular agency. But Whitehead uses religious language as well in the last chapter of *Process and Reality*. He explicitly contrasts his concept of God with Buddhist ideas, and with ideas about "the ruling Caesar, or the ruthless moralist, or the unmoved mover," which he finds endemic to the theistic philosophies of Christianity, Judaism, and Islam (342–43). All of these he rejects, of course. Instead, he associates his notion of God positively with "the Galilean origin of Christianity" (343). And in noting that his theory offers "nothing here in the nature of proof," he says "any cogency" it has is grounded in "religious and moral intuitions" (343). He speaks of God's "necessary goodness" (345), of God's "tender care" that "loses nothing that can be saved" (346), of the idea of God's everlastingness as the "vision upon which the finer religions are built" (347). And with metaphorical exactitude, Whitehead ends by describing the consequent nature as "the kingdom of heaven" into which "the love in the world passes" and from which it "floods back again into the world," justifying our understanding of God as "the great companion—the fellow-sufferer who understands" (351). These explicitly religious ideas are obviously of considerable importance and, with respect to Christianity in particular, potentially transformative. But they are not our present concern, which is about the viability of the secular metaphysical functions Whitehead assigns to God.

METAPHYSICAL INCOHERENCE

Every possible possibility—thereby presumably excluding a round square, backward time travel, or subjective immortality—is timelessly so, says Whitehead. But in accord with the ontological principle, each must be a feature of some actuality. Actual entities, however, are momentary occurrences and so cannot play that role. For there to be an actual cosmos, a temporal and coherent system of occurrences, these pure possibilities must be interrelated, organized into a system of possibilities that can function as relevant options for actualization and as a limit to what is actualized so that there can be a continuity to its character. Cosmic continuity requires continuity in its relevant possibilities, which requires a continuity in the agency that accounts for that relevance. This agent's continuity must be a continuity informed by the specific actualizations comprising its continuity, how it is and gives specific shape to the relevant possibilities that give shape to how the cosmos endures as a coherent system of actual achievements. So in addition to actual entities that come to be and perish, there must be an actual entity that neither comes to be nor perishes. It must be the primordial location of eternal objects and the agency of their general relevance to the cosmos, and must also be the everlasting location of the temporal achievements of all actual entities and the agency of their specific relevance to its evolving character. I have argued that this is simply incoherent. Whitehead insists there are no exceptions to the ontological principle, then introduces a notion of God that is obviously an exception.

Whitehead gets into difficulty because of his presumption that possibilities must be essentially eternal and self-contained, having no essential relatedness to either the actual world or one another. Given this understanding of eternal objects, Whitehead is forced to populate his cosmos with a primordial agency able to bridge the metaphysical chasm between their timelessness and the world's temporality. Actual entities and eternal objects are both atomic but in polar opposite senses, one essentially temporal the other essentially nontemporal. This polarity is akin to Descartes' two mutually exclusive kinds of substance: one unextended and immaterial, the other extended and material. Neither has it in its power to effect a relationship to the other. Therefore only a reality that is neither can bring them together, an objective entity that can encompass aboriginally all possible forms of definiteness, and a concrescing agent that because it does not perish can relate these forms without beginning or end to the actual entities that do perish, and in this uniting of the two polar opposites make possible a world of temporal creatures and their creations.

Whitehead's notion of God is not a part of the Categoreal Scheme, which is composed of "the primary notions which constitute the philosophy of organism" (1978, 18). Rather, it is the first of the Derivative Notions that comprise the chapter following it. Whitehead, it would seem, added the non-primary notion of God in order to assure the coherence of the primary notions by making sense of how "possibility which transcends realized temporal matter of fact has a real relevance to the creative advance" (31).

The result is quite the opposite of what was intended, however. Whitehead says that "God is not to be treated as an exception to all metaphysical principles, invoked to save their collapse" (343), but the notion of a nontemporal actual entity is such an exception, an oxymoron that renders Whitehead's metaphysics incoherent. Actual entities are events, but God in its primordial nature does not come to be and in its consequent nature does not perish—God is an event, but one that does not actually occur. The possibility of a temporal cosmos must be timelessly primordial since nothing can come to be unless the conditions for its doing so are already in place, and yet "the acquirement by creativity of a primordial character" is "a free creative act" that "exemplifies and establishes the categoreal conditions" for temporal achievement (344)—a primordial agent that must logically and temporally precede the categoreal conditions for agency. The relevance of eternal objects to whatever the forms and contents of actual worlds might be, their graded intensive relevance to each nascent actual occasion, must be timeless because primordial, but the future is open and cannot be fully anticipated—a primordial God in an open universe, knowing in advance of the creative advance the ways in which it will need relevant novel possibilities.

If coherence is to be restored to Whitehead's system, it must be purged of the unfortunate addition of a God responsible for the primordial tasks assigned it in *Process and Reality*. We should cleanse the philosophy of organism of its secular deity so that Whitehead's system can regain the full power of its radically temporal metaphysical vision.

NOTE

1. This chapter is an elaboration of section II of my article "A Functionalist Reinterpretation of Whitehead's Metaphysics," *Review of Metaphysics* 62 (2008): 327–54. Used with permission, all rights reserved.

2

THE POWER OF THE PRESENT

In his contribution to an American Philosophical Association symposium on the philosophy of Alfred North Whitehead, John Dewey complains that *Process and Reality* attempts to combine a method of philosophizing based on the mathematical sciences and one based on the natural sciences.[1] He argues that the two methods are not compatible, however, and that the result is an unfortunate series of bifurcations between "a succinct system of independent definitions and postulates" on the one hand and, on the other, corrigible distinctions arising from "experimental observational inquiry." Whitehead's metaphysics is an incoherent mix of "morphological" and "genetic-functional" generalizations (Dewey 1937, 174).

Dewey illustrates his claim by noting the relation of Whitehead's eternal objects to actual occasions is one of "ingression." This term "suggests an independent and read-made subsistence of eternal objects" that then requires "the conception of God" as an agency able "to act selectively in determining which eternal objects ingress in any given immediate occasion" (176). Whitehead's ontology involves two different kinds of reality, one eternal and one temporal, one a consequence of his mathematical method and one a consequence of his empirical method. These two contrasting kinds of reality then need a third to relate them. Dewey thus implies that Whitehead has the same problem of ontological incoherence as Descartes, and solves the problem in the same unsatisfactory manner: by the addition of a divine agent.

Dewey's solution to this incoherence is to propose, unsurprisingly, that Whitehead abandon the mathematical method, that he construe eternal objects in terms of the genetic-functional method. Were Whitehead to take this approach, "the egression of natures, characters, or universals" would be understood as resulting from "the necessity of generalization from immediate occasions that exist in order to direct their further movement and its consequences" (176). Eternal objects—that is, possibilities "which are 'eternal' in the sense of not being spatio-temporal existences"—would "emerge because of the existence of problematic situations," as "suggestions" which could then be "operatively applied to actual existences" in an attempt to resolve those problems (176). Experimental intelligence would replace God as the agency needed to relate actual existences and eternal objects, the latter now understood to be emergent rather than timeless.

Contrary to what Whitehead seems to think, *Process and Reality* is quite able to account for novel possibilities and the conditions necessary for their actualization, and to do so in a genetic-functional way. After all, Whitehead himself says that the Categoreal Scheme "embodies the generic notions inevitably presupposed in our reflective experience" (1978, 18). The philosophy of organism, without benefit of divine agency, can be transformed into a metaphysics both adequate to experience and internally coherent, because it is devoid of essentially timeless entities, which are made relevant when needed by experience rather than actually derived from experience.

In this chapter, I explore this resource, guided by Whitehead's injunction that a metaphysics "should be 'necessary,' in the sense of bearing in itself its own warrant of universality throughout all experience, provided that we confine ourselves to that which communicates with immediate matter of fact. . . . There is an essence to the universe which forbids relationships beyond itself, as a violation of its rationality. Speculative philosophy seeks that essence" (4).

CREATIVITY

The keystone in *Process and Reality* to a genetic-functional interpretation of eternal objects, and hence a recovery of the radically temporalist foundations of the philosophy of organism, is "Creativity." Creativity is the Category of the Ultimate, which Whitehead defines as "that ultimate principle by which the many, which are the universe disjunctively, become the one actual occasion, which is the universe conjunctively" (1978, 21). Note what Whitehead then says, as he immediately restates this ultimate principle: "It lies in the nature of things that the many enter into complex unity," its unity a novel achievement "diverse from any entity in the 'many' which it unifies." Thus, "the 'creative advance' is the application of this ultimate principle of creativity to each novel situation which it originates" (21).

It lies in the nature of things that there are processes of concrescence and that they must have an outcome. It lies in the nature of things that the many occasions of the past must be felt such that they will be compatible for entering into a unique unity. It lies in the nature of things, not in the nature of God, which is a Derivative Notion added onto the ontology defined by the Categoreal Scheme. "The sole appeal" in defense of this claim about the nature of things, says Whitehead, "is to intuition" (22). Creativity thus rests on an intuition more fundamental than the intuition Whitehead posited in the prior chapter of an agency-caused tendency toward suitable outcomes. It is the intuition that there must be an outcome, whether or not it be suitable.

If taken as an agency other than these concrescing events, Creativity would become a transcendent being, a Power behind the screen of the ontological processes of actualization that saves the world by insisting that the perishing occasions have successors. Whitehead argues alternatively, in the chapter on Derivative Notions, that "Creativity is without a character of its own" (31). It requires God to provide its "primordial character" in the form of "the categoreal conditions" (344). Hence "Creativity is always found under conditions, and described as conditioned" (31). This alternative, crediting God as the source of Creativity's power, having God provide the creative advance with the novel possibilities requisite for the development and sustaining of Creativity's character, would seem to be saying that without God Creativity would have no creativity. Which is silly, just one more indication of the incoherence plaguing Whitehead's insistence that novelties cannot be invented by finite creatures but only retrieved from necessarily timeless resources.

In the definition of the Category of the Ultimate, however, Whitehead insists that Creativity is nothing except the power of the actual entities themselves, the particularizing drive of the multitude of concrescent processes, their subjectivity. It refers to the efficient causes of the makings that are the actual entities comprising the cosmos. It is the urge of their makings toward the made. An artist's creativity, for example, is not an externality that has come to inhabit her. Rather, it is her reality as an artist, the fact that her efforts are not random gestures but the transformation of raw materials in a specific manner with respect to a developing purpose, resulting in a particular outcome. The lure of the result, the challenge of the methods and tools available, and the constraints of the medium, are together the awakening of the efficient condition, which is thus the coordinating of the other conditions into an actuality, a new particular good, a novel achievement.

"The 'production of novel togetherness' is the ultimate notion embedded in the term 'concrescence'" (21). It is "inexplicable either in terms of higher universals," like a First Cause or Primordial God, "or in terms of the components participating in the concrescence," like possibilities imported from an eternal storehouse or everlasting accumulation (21). Neither of these alternatives makes sense because only agents can do anything. To treat Creativity either as a Power intrinsically or as a Power so imbued by God is to commit the fallacy of misplaced concreteness. Creativity is not a Power, but rather a Principle: an abstract generalization of the myriad of agential energies comprising the creative advance. Creativity is not an agent that works through us. It is us. To treat a general notion as though it were a specific entity is one of the banes of philosophy, as though a species were another of its members, as though *Canis familiaris* could bark. Or like the tourist in the myth, who having seen Balliol, All Souls, and a host of other colleges, ask when he'll be able to see Oxford University. Whitehead, of all people, should be careful when explicating the notion of Creativity not to commit the fallacy of misplaced concreteness.

The necessary conditions for agency, for the power to turn multiplicities into unities—the necessary conditions governing the creative energy of concrescing processes—are specified by what Whitehead calls "Categoreal Obligations." There are nine of them. In his outline of the categories by which his speculative scheme is constructed, Whitehead says that "every obligation should be a specific instance of categoreal obligations" (20). An obligation is a constraint, which insofar as it is generalizable can be thought of as a rule governing a certain kind or range of processes. As with Creativity, here also we need to resist the temptation to think of a law as pre-existing the particular processes of which it is a generalization. The categoreal obligations, indeed all of *Process and Reality*'s Categoreal Scheme, are a conceptual model, like a map or diagram. That the obligations oblige, that the rules govern, that the conditions stipulate, are illuminating metaphors not agential forces. The conditions canalizing a particular process of concrescence, or governing any particular process by which enduring objects are formed and unformed, should be understood as specifications, appropriate to that specific context, of one or more of nine general conditions.

Whitehead's list is a somewhat inelegant mishmash of these conditions, however. His ninth obligation says that "the concrescence of each individual actual entity is internally determined and is externally free" (27), but this is only Whitehead's way of emphasizing, redundantly, that the conditions shaping a concrescence do not predetermine its specific accomplishment. It is a descriptive statement about the consequence of Creativity being constrained by the other eight conditions rather than a condition itself. These remaining eight categoreal obligations can also usefully be grouped into three kinds. Borrowing from Duns Scotus (and James Bradley 1994; 1996), I will refer to these kinds as 'transcendental' because they are categoreal obligations that take categoreal obligations as their values. I hope to make clear not only why they are generalizations of the necessary conditions for whatever is to have become what it is, but also why together they generalize the sufficient condition.

THE ARISTOTELIAN TRANSCENDENTAL

One of these necessary kinds of conditions governing Creativity is that it has a vector character, that the essence of process be the process of becoming, a transformation of potentialities into an actuality. I will call this feature of the nature of things an 'Aristotelian transcendental' because of the way it focuses on the dynamics of natural processes. It is the requirement that concrescence issue in a concretum.

Whitehead needs four categoreal obligations to articulate this feature of process. The Category of Subjective Unity (Category i) stipulates that the initial diversity of data, physically prehended in an actual entity's process of concrescence, "the many [physical] feelings which belong to an incomplete phase in the process of an actual entity," are prehended so as to be "compatible for integration by reason of the unity of their [concrescing] subject" (1978, 26). The Category of Subjective Harmony (Category vii) applies this constraint to conceptual feelings as well: "The valuations of conceptual feelings are mutually determined by the adaptation of those feelings" so as to be "congruent with the subjective aim" (27). The other two categoreal obligations, Objective Identity (Category ii) and Objective Diversity (Category iii), ensure that the outcome will contain no indeterminates by demanding that any element in the final synthesis be unique and that it play a unique role. "There can be no duplication of any element" in the final "'satisfaction' of an actual entity"; and also "there can be no 'coalescence' of diverse elements" in that satisfaction (26). In short, for there to be a definite outcome to concrescence, the many must become one, must achieve a fully determinate unity out of its diverse elements. This means that each element has to play a unique role in the resulting unity, has to have "one self-consistent function, however complex" in the resulting unity, which entails that no two elements can be "exercising an absolute identity of function" (26).

More is required, however. A novel actual entity, in the sense of a new unique addition to the creative advance of the cosmos, must make novel decisions regarding its inheritance if it is to satisfy these four basic categoreal obligations. Pure repetition is impossible in an evolutionary cosmos. Things change. Wind and water wear mountains down, while volcanic fire and shifting geological plates lift mountains up. The old ways become uncouth and youngsters dream new dreams. And even where things seem to have been the same time out of mind, it is the case nonetheless that a successor's world differs from its predecessors' at least in having what the predecessors cannot have: those predecessors as its inheritance and itself as a living present. To assure that the necessary novelty is available to a new concrescence for dealing with these novel features, a further categoreal obligation is needed.

The Category of Conceptual Valuation (Category iv) states: "From each physical feeling there is the derivation of a purely conceptual feeling whose datum is the eternal object determinant of [exemplified in] the definiteness of the actual entity, or of the nexus, physically felt" (26, repeated 248 except for bracketed change). In keeping with the standard empiricist dictum that "mentality originates from sensitive experience" (248), Whitehead affirms the primacy of physical prehensions but then allows direct derivation from them of conceptual prehensions. The immediate past is physically prehended by a newly emerging concrescence as a definite datum felt with the insistent power of its availability for replication. The eternal object characterizing this definiteness is abstracted from it and entertained in its own right. It is a possibility for exemplification extracted from an actual exemplification.

For instance, I like sandwiches, and so I have tended to fix one each morning to take with me for lunch. When it comes time to fix the next day's lunch, the habit of repeating what I fixed yesterday is strongly felt, and because I haven't even had a cup of coffee yet, I accede to its pressure and unthinkingly go about making the same sort of sandwich I did yesterday and the day before. If I've already had some coffee, I might pause to consider other possibilities, but even then my proclivity will be to do again what I have done before. After all, I like sandwiches.

The manner in which a possibility is felt by a nascent actual entity, the subjective form of its prehension, is not necessarily how it was felt by the actual entity from which it is derived. "The subjective form of a conceptual feeling is valuation," which "introduces creative purpose" into that feeling (248). The subject, in breaking the eternal object free from its prior ingression, can value it more or value it less than it had previously been valued, and it does so as a function of its own developing effort to achieve concreteness. This conceptual feeling, felt with a novel subjective form, is then reintegrated with the physical feeling. The past datum is not only prehended as being what it is, but appreciated or depreciated with respect to its likely value, its functional utility for the concrescing actual entity's effort to achieve a new determinate outcome. Yesterday I thought it obvious that I should fix a sandwich for lunch, but today for some reason that doesn't seem all that imperative. I make my sandwich, but do so mainly because I always do, and because come noon I will want to have something to eat.

The brute facticity of the impinging past is inescapable: "The deterministic efficient causation is the inflow of the actual world in its own proper character of its own feelings, with their own intensive strength, felt and reenacted by the novel concrescent subject" (245). But an actual entity is a process of self-determination, which "is always imaginative in its origin." Its concrescence involves not only "conformation to pattern" but also "subjective valuation," which is "the work of novel conceptual feeling" (245). These conceptual feelings are novel because they are functions of the emerging actual entity's existential situation, its unique standpoint, and the unique decisions thereby required in order to achieve a determinate outcome. "In proportion to its importance, acquired in complex processes of integration and reintegration, this autonomous conceptual element modifies the subjective forms throughout the whole range of feeling in that concrescence and thereby guides the integrations" (245). The valuations are novel, their use an autonomous exercise. "Each creative act is the universe incarnating itself as one, and there is nothing above it"—nor before it, neither metaphysically nor temporally—"by way of final condition" (245).

So I may come to feel that what's important is not making a sandwich but having something to eat for lunch. There are probably alternatives to making a sandwich every morning, after all, and although I fix my sandwich as usual, I'm beginning to wonder if it might be easier just to buy one at the deli near where I work, or to substitute something else in place of any kind of sandwich. Were only blind habit to govern my behavior, my realization one morning that there's no bread left would send me into a frenzy of anger or despair—why didn't I get more bread, will I go hungry into an important upcoming work event. But the empty bread drawer might become instead the catalyst for devaluing sandwiches and taking seriously the possibility of a different sort of lunch that day.

The categoreal condition identified by Conceptual Valuation is the requirement that although the concrescence of an actual entity begins with the massive influence of its immediate past, the ideas derived from this inherence, although also inherited, are evaluated by the inheritor in terms not only of their prior relevance but also of their relevance to the inheritor's new situation. An emerging present is never fully determined by the causal objectivity of its impinging past because its initial response is to reassess the potential value of that objectivity in the light of its own situational needs. No bread, but fixing a sandwich isn't all that important anyway. The valuation may be negligible, but when the inheritance is complex enough the power of valuation is enhanced and the usual dim glimmer of novelty becomes the "flash of autonomous individual experience" (245). I've just decided that today I'll have not only a sandwich for lunch but also soup, which I'll purchase at the diner.

Whitehead says that the valuation of conceptual prehensions is "the subject determining its own ideal of itself by reference to eternal principles of valuation autonomously modified in their application to its own physical objective datum." With respect to this function of its mental pole, the occasion is "out of time" (248). These references to the timeless and the eternal do not imply any reality independent of temporal becoming and perishing, however. Creativity is the only ultimate and it asserts the primacy of temporal process. The principles by which each new quantum of that temporal process modifies its inheritance and its aim in order to make something of itself are those of the categoreal obligations, which together describe the constraints on the emergent quantum that it be creative enough to instantiate Creativity, to add a successor space-time quantum to the one now perishing. Autonomous valuation is out of time because it is a concrescence function, an aspect of the process that fashions what is temporal.

My sandwich example is not about the concrescence of actual entities, so it goes without saying that not only is the physical demand to have a good lunch temporal but so is the working out of a solution to my discovery that there's no bread today with which to make my sandwich. Concrescence, however, the process of creating a new unit of time, of making a new actual entity, cannot be in time, since it is the making of what is temporal. This seeming ontological incoherence, a bifurcation between the temporality of temporal units and the nontemporality of their making, is a significant problem, but it is not the incoherence discovered in chapter 1 between the eternity of eternal objects and the temporality of actualities. The possibilities involved in conceptual prehensions and the valuation of those prehensions are situational: temporal not eternal, particular not universal. The making of a sandwich is a temporal process; it takes time to accomplish, and likewise making an idea about having lunch at the diner into actually having that lunch takes time. Making new actualities, with the help of possibilities and their valuations, that comprise an enduring object such as a sandwich or an action, is not yet those facts but how they come to be.

The categoreal obligations comprising the Aristotelian transcendental govern a teleonomic process by which an inheritance of physical and conceptual feelings is made compatible for a uniquely determinate integration. But these conditions cannot be fulfilled unless some degree of novelty in the available possibilities is introduced. It must be in the nature of things that there be available in the inheritance of an emerging actual entity a sufficient range of exploitable possibilities for it to adapt its inheritance to its unique situation so that it can become one actual thing.

This is a minimally necessary but crucial constraint. It stipulates nothing except that as the indeterminate energy of any concrescing entity is given increasingly determinate shapes, these determinations cannot include irreconcilable differences. Constraints on the multiplicity of inherited physical facts and the multiplicity of the possible forms for their reconciliation cannot make it impossible for some sort of concrete unity to emerge. Any kind of sandwich must begin with ingredients that are suitable for making it, and the process of doing so must trace a sequence of actions that eventuate in that kind of sandwich. The "ought" of the obligation to make something out of what is given implies "can" because what is given is necessarily given as somehow compatible.

Therefore what Whitehead says of the Categories of Subjective Unity and Subjective Harmony—that they "jointly express a pre-established harmony in the process of concrescence of any one subject" (27)—is true only if it is expanded to include the Categories of Objective Identity and Objective Diversity, and therefore the Category of Conceptual Valuation. The harmony that is pre-established is that the constantly repeating transformation of Creativity into a newly specific creative vector, whatever that be, must be such that it can culminate in a concrete actuality, and that this requires that process to be creative enough to be able to adjust the inherited value of available possibilities sufficiently to do so.

THE LEIBNIZIAN TRANSCENDENTAL

It is not sufficient that the many must constantly become one, however, because this demand is compatible with the decay of value, with a loss of complex structure and contrastive intensity. The creative process must involve not simply the attainment of value but of enhanced value. The aim of a concrescing entity, says Whitehead, must be at "maximum depth of intensity of feeling, subject to the conditions of its concrescence" (1978, 249). The multiple actual instances of the Creativity principle are vectors toward the best of the outcomes possible for each of them. I will call this necessary feature of the nature of things a Leibnizian transcendental.

We have already glimpsed this transcendental condition when I explicated the suitability bias, Whitehead's claim that there is a bias in the character of the novel possibilities constantly emerging in the creative advance. The problem with this claim, I argued, was not the bias but Whitehead's argument that it could only be accounted for by an ultimate agency able to bring it about. The necessary condition for their being a meliorative order, he insisted, is that there be a meliorative orderer, an agency that Whitehead calls the Primordial Nature of God. It was the burden of chapter 1 to show that such an entity renders Whitehead's cosmology incoherent. The aim of this chapter is to show why there is no need for such an entity, that Creativity as limited by the Categoreal Obligations suffices.

Moreover, Whitehead justified his belief in the suitability bias not by any statistically grounded empirical evidence but by appealing to "an intuition—in general vague and unprecise" of its likelihood (207). As I argued, however, appealing to intuition is a weak crutch on which to lean with any confidence because so easily countered with a counter-intuition claimed by equally confident opponents. Whitehead is on surer ground in his Categoreal Scheme because there he makes the more sensible move of formulating a metaphysical hypothesis about an ultimate principle and its universal conditions. Among those conditions is the requirement that an actual entity's aim be at the optimal intensity possible given its various constraints. The truth of the Leibnizian conditions lie in their contribution to the adequacy and coherence of Whitehead's ontology, not to an intuition that might have motivated him in developing those conditions as he did. Intuitions are for mystics, hypotheses for metaphysicians.

Two clarifications are worth adding. First, the best is an aim, not a result. It is an outcome sought but not assured. Second, the aim at the best possible is a particular aim of a particular concrescing actual entity toward a particular outcome, not a cosmic aim toward a cosmic outcome. Hence this constraint on Creativity is Leibnizian only in a limited, if not a Pickwickian, sense. Whitehead is claiming that aims are always and everywhere local, the best of all possibilities for a specific situation and therefore an individuating outcome. There is no aim at the best of all possible worlds. Creativity is a principle regarding vectors; it itself has no vector. There are only the parochial vectors of the multiple concrescences that at any moment comprise the world.

The goal of any concrescent process must be optimal intensity—the value that constitutes the best of the worlds possible for it. It takes Whitehead two categoreal obligations to express this requirement. The first of these is the Category of Subjective Intensity (Category viii), which stipulates that "the subjective aim, whereby there is origination of conceptual feeling, is at intensity of feeling (α) in the immediate subject, and (β) in the *relevant* future" (27). The stipulation clarifies for the sake of what the best is sought, by doubling it.

The alpha condition is that it be for the immediate subject. The aim of a concrescing actual entity should be to enhance the intensity of its own enjoyment, which means to achieve an outcome intrinsically more valuable than what it has inherited. Self-fulfillment is the fundamental goal of every creative effort, making in the concrete moment, the specific here-and-now of its emergence, something not only worth doing but, insofar as any achievement is partial and so to some degree inadequate, worth doing better. It's not enough simply to make another sandwich, but to sense an improvement that might be possible and then give it a try. We grow restless with the same-old-same-old, and look for an interesting variation on our routine.

The beta condition to Subjective Intensity complicates the task by requiring that the enhanced enjoyment sought be expanded to include not only the present moment of achieved value but also the value of successor moments insofar as they are relevant. Of course, what those future values will be is unknowable until they have been created, so what is being stipulated is that the process of present creation take account of its likely subsequent influence. The worth of an achievement must factor in a sense of its consequences, the likelihood that the value being fashioned can be sustained beyond the present, indeed further enhanced, and that features of the concrescing process that would likely undermine the replicability of what is being sought be inhibited.

That it is in the nature of things that the aim of a concrescing actual entity must be at optimal intensity for the long run as well as the short run makes its task far more difficult. What is best for the moment may be likely to be bad for the moments that will follow. The adjustments that need to be made now in order to take account of what might happen next will be minor if the situation is traditionalist, if a subsequent actual entity is likely to replicate the current entity's replication of its predecessor. The more novel the present achievement, the less clear its likely impact will be on the specific constraints and opportunities with which the next entity must come to terms. The more creative the concrescing, the more problematic the requirement to take the immediate future into account. And the more problematic what needs to be done, the more problematic how best to do so.

I've always included a slice of cheddar cheese in my ham sandwiches, switching from medium to mild or to sharp cheddar on occasion for the sake of variety. But when the grocery store is out of cheddar one day, I need to buy another cheese. I opt for blue cheese which I've never eaten but of which I was attracted by its unusual look. I'm excited by the possibility that blue cheese and ham will prove to be the basis of an even better sandwich than cheddar and ham. I rationalize my radical move by thinking that it will at least be as good, but I'm concerned that my abrupt departure from the familiar might result in a sandwich I won't like as well or might not like at all.

If a possibility selected as the subjective aim of a nascent actual entity, or as the subjective form for the actualization of that aim, cannot find an argument able to yield a determinate value, some alternative possibility will have to be substituted. For the Aristotelean constraint requires that some value result from the process of concrescence, that it produce a concluding transformation that is fully, irreversibly, actual. But this substitute process may well yield a value of lesser worth than the one initially sought, a less successful integration of the breadth of components with the depth of each one's difference from the others, because, in accord with the Leibnizian rule, the substitute aim would otherwise have been selected in the first place.

The Aristotelian demand for an immediate result thus puts pressure on the Leibnizian search for the best result, quite likely forcing the concrescing entity to settle for an integration based on some readily available least common denominator. That achievement would probably replicate prior achievements if the values by which they are inherited are fairly uniform and simple. But when things are even slightly complex and changing, the replicators are likely not to be fully compatible, and so the concrescence will need to settle for some lesser achievement. In the absence of novel patterns for actualization, novel functions for determining the end and means of vector processes, the quest for the better good will lead, ironically but inevitably, to a worse good. Some sort of novelty is needed that goes beyond adjustments in the relevant importance of the values inherited from the achievements of predecessor actual entities.

If value is to be enhanced, or even sustained, in a cosmos where mere re-enactment entails decay, more novelty is needed that can be achieved by Conceptual Valuation, by appreciating or depreciating inherited values. Hence Whitehead postulates another categoreal obligation, the Category of Conceptual Reversion (Category v): "There is a secondary origination of conceptual feelings with data which are partially identical with, and partially diverse from, the eternal objects forming the data in the first phase of the mental pole. The diversity is a relevant diversity determined by the subjective aim" (26), which, as Whitehead later clarifies, is an "aim at attaining depth of intensity by reason of contrast" (249).

Diverse physical feelings yield diverse conceptual feelings, but when the diversity is extreme enough, when incompatibilities become incommensurable, a concept of their reconciliation needs to be more inventive than the adjustments conceptual valuations provide. A new kind of possible unity needs to be introduced, by interpreting the divergent conceptual feelings as versions of a more general or more fundamental possibility. "The positive conceptual prehension of relevant alternatives," of "proximate novelties," invites an "enrichment of subjective forms, both in qualitative pattern, and in intensity through contrast" (249). A novel possibility does not ever come out of nowhere, as some sort of bewildering surd. It comes as a variation on the familiar, a shift in emphasis or point of view, as a refreshing alternative to the usual way of characterizing the established order. So a new concept is derived from the initial conceptual feelings, responding to the difficulty in how they might collaborate in actualizing the nascent subject's aim. It interprets the clashing values as neighbors rather than strangers, as proximate rather than distant alternatives—and therefore as reconcilable. They are taken to be children of the same parents, branches from the same trunk, the same melody played in different keys, complements rather than opposites, contraries rather than contradictories. Provolone cheese would have been a better choice than blue cheese as a substitute for cheddar because it looks similar and might therefore taste similar. There are still risks in making a shift away from what is traditional, but when a shift is needed it makes sense to operate on the principle that similar kinds of possibility will tend to have similar actualizations. Tend to have, however; not will have.

Whitehead says that Conceptual Reversion is "the category by which novelty enters the world; so that even amid stability there is never undifferentiated endurance" (249). As we have seen, conceptual valuations also introduce novelty. The difference between valuation and reversion is that the latter kind of novelty, unlike the former, presents a challenge to the extant system of relevant possibilities rather than reaffirming it. The emergence of a conceptual reversion in the process of concrescence destabilizes established forms of possibility by opening the possibility of improving on them. Instead of eliminating differences as discordant, it provides an affirmation of their value by encompassing them within a wider or deeper unity. The new is taken as an improved version of the old, completing it rather than repudiating it.

THE HOBBESIAN TRANSCENDENTAL

Actual entities are not isolated dynamic systems; they "involve each other by reason of their prehensions of each other" (1978, 20). Any such "togetherness among actual entities is called a 'nexus'" (20). A nexus can be linked together with other nexūs to form a more complex nexus, which in turn can be an element of a yet more complex nexus. Any nexus can be the source for some of the conditions shaping the concrescences of other actual entities and nexūs of actual entities. The most important sort of nexus is a 'society,' a "nexus with social order." An 'enduring object' is "a society whose social order has taken the specific form of 'personal order'" (34). Social order has three intertwined features: a "defining characteristic," which is "a common element of form illustrated in the definiteness of each"; because of "the conditions imposed upon it by its prehensions of some other members of the nexus"; "by reason of their inclusion of positive feelings of that common form" (34). In a nexus with social order, if the characteristics that governed the determination of the predecessors to the actual entities which are current elements of that society have a privileged place among the data they prehend, because the conditions governing the nexus include that of attempting to perpetuate the characteristics comprising its common element of form by reiterating them in a number of actual entities simultaneously and sequentially, then the society also has personal order and is thereby an enduring object. "The nexus forms a single line of inheritance of its defining characteristic" (34). These enduring objects "are the permanent entities which enjoy adventures of change throughout time and space" (35).

Thus a new kind of transcendental condition makes its appearance. It applies its constraints to the concrescent process of each of the actual entities that are members of an enduring object, but it does so for the sake not of each entity but of the interrelation among them, for the sake of the nexus. The condition this transcendental imposes is that one of the aims of the new actual entity emerging within a nexus be that it replicates the character its predecessors have in common. Because it governs a process for ensuring the continued survival of a kind of nexus, I shall call this third transcendental condition 'Hobbesian.'

The Hobbesian constraint rescues the other two transcendental constraints from entailing an inexorable temporal decline in achieved value. For it stipulates that there be a method for an actual entity to reach beyond its own familiar but endangered good in order to acquire some alternative better good. The Leibnizian condition orients the actual entity toward the best possible concrescent result available to it under the immediate exigency of fulfilling the closure demanded by the Aristotelian condition. The Hobbesian condition enlarges this orientation so that the good the actual entity seeks is not found exclusively in the intensity of its own immediate achievement combined with the anticipated future relevance of that intensity. It is found as well in the value a number of concrescing entities have collectively actualized for it and the value its actualization has for what a number of other actual entities might henceforth actualize.

To accomplish this, Whitehead identifies yet a further categoreal obligation: a mode of conceptual modification of both physical and conceptual feelings, governed by the Category of Transmutation (Category vi). Where the concrescent process has derived the same conceptual feeling from a multiplicity of physical feelings, "the prehending subject may transmute the *datum* of this conceptual feeling into a characteristic of some *nexus* containing those prehended actual entities among its members, or of some part of that nexus" (27). Transmutation is "the way in which the actual world is felt as a community, and is so felt in virtue of its prevalent order" (251). It is how the Hobbesian condition is implemented, its demand fulfilled that values be actualized that transcend the immediate concerns of the individual members of a nexus and thereby enhance the values they each are able to attain. The viability of the Leviathan rests on the greater good its members are obliged to seek as the condition for fulfilling their own best interest.

Conceptual valuation is a sufficient method for discounting the clashing diversity of the multiple aims and achievements of the members of a nexus, taking them as a single datum organized by the single conceptual feeling they in fact all exemplify. In conceptual reversion an alternative possibility is derived from that single concept, a version of it that will allow the unifying datum to retain more of the diversity present in the initial multiplicity, not discounting the diversity as seriously as conceptual valuation would. Transmutation is bolder, permitting the organizing concept to have a looser relationship to the datum it is interpreted as characterizing. This organizing concept is derived not from all the members of a set of physical feelings but from only some of them, or—even more radically—from physical feelings that lie outside the set. "In such a case the objectification may introduce new elements into the world, fortunate or unfortunate" (251).

For example, we see a pattern of blue and red dots as a uniform splash of purple, their sharply contrasting differences organized by an eternal object that none of them exhibit, by a purple quality that is neither blue nor red but the result of combining them. A state of the United States whose citizens, year after year, cast a clear majority of their votes for Republican candidates may be said to be a "red state" even though millions of its citizens vote Democratic "blue," and even though those in any election who vote one way are only in part those who vote that way in the next election. Likewise for blue. Red and blue thus indicate reversions, statistical generalizations that justifies using a feature of a portion of the whole to characterize the whole. Purple indicates a transmutation of these generalizations, a concept imported from outside the universe of red and blue in order to describe a statistical distribution that justify using neither a red portion nor a blue to characterize the whole. A map of voting colored by state-wide results for a particular election will be a polka dot pattern of reds and blues, but if the map is to show multiple-year election results it would be appropriate to use red even for a state that sometimes is blue, and vice versa, reserving purple to color states that during the specified time period have nearly half the time gone Republican and nearly half the time Democratic.

The importance of transmutation is that it permits inventive simplifications by means of which vast congeries can be integrated into a single well-functioning whole. Epistemologically, transmutation is how such complexities are made intelligible. "We can only understand by discarding," says Whitehead. "Apart from transmutation our feeble intellectual operations would fail to penetrate into the dominant characteristics of things" (251). We need to overlook detail in order to see important patterns, to find the statistical slope—the tendency—in the seeming cacophony of particulars, to avoid missing the forest because of the trees. To understand is to identify an organizing principle, to formulate a law the events exemplify. Apples fall randomly from trees and planets trace errant pathways across the sky, but Newton's gravitational laws allow us to explain both these very different events as exemplifying the same dynamic pattern, from which therefore the subsequent behaviors of both can be predicted. Nor need our understanding be certain. We often fashion a rule exhibiting a pattern that although inadequate to the particulars is nonetheless a near enough approximation that, when it suits our purposes, we can take it as adequate, as good enough for government work. Or, as a working hypothesis reasonable for us to use unless additional data disconfirm it. Of course, this strategy is open to abuse, as when spin doctors take a minor change in voting pattern as a significant shift and therefore as a mandate for their candidate.

One kind of existent in Whitehead's cosmology is "propositions, *or* matters of fact in potential determination, *or* impure potentials for the specific determination of matters of fact, *or* theories" (22, deleting capitalizations). These are relevant possibilities, an "objective lure" resulting from a "discrimination among eternal objects introduced into the universe by the real internal constitutions of the actual occasions forming the datum of the concrescence under review. This discrimination also involves eternal objects excluded from value in the temporal occasions of that datum, in addition to involving the eternal objects included for such occasions" (185).

What is excluded for the sake of understanding is not eliminated; the cosmos is always far more than what we take to be the nexus comprising it and to be their defining characteristics. The rule by which we order experience into a stable meaningful world involves transmutation: vast multiplicities of detail characterized by means of a single idea, often one exemplified by only a portion of the detail or by none of it. So our understanding focuses on some eternal objects while neglecting others, excluding them from value, hiding them in an endless expanse of unimportance. And yet they are there, neglected but not gone. The discrimination of a neglected or hidden possibility, its entertainment as a proposition for enactment, has transformative potential. This radically new possibility, this surprising alternative to the familiar ones, is not a subjective but rather an objective lure because the possibility it discloses is derived from physical feelings even if obscured by reversions and transmutations.

Cosmologically, transmutation is the way by which the creative advance is able to foster and sustain relatively intense and long-enduring complex forms of order. Creativity encompasses not only vectors toward some determinate outcome and toward an optimal intensity of outcome but also vectors toward optimal endurance. Vast ranges of various particulars need to function as though they were one thing, comprising a stable background able to support the salient transformations occurring in the foreground. Actual entities need to be organized into hierarchies of enduring objects, into complex nexus the more enduring of which provide a predictable foundation upon which the less enduring ones can strut and fret their hour upon the stage. The birth of a solar system or the burst of a supernova depend on the stability of a background continuum of space and time permanent enough to be taken as though everlasting. The historical odyssey by which the idea of human freedom has come to be embedded, tenuously but genuinely, in the practices of some human communities requires a structure of civilized order that has persisted long enough to be presupposed by generation after generation of its constituent members as obviously the way things should be.

In a cosmos of actual entities constantly adding their novel uniqueness to the creative advance, such systemic stabilities require constant adaptive readjustments in which limited subordinate features can rapidly be added, subtracted, or altered without harming the more general features. Likewise, the effective transmission of the conditions for actualizing significant value intensities means that actual entities must subordinate their immediate individual goods to the enduring environment of hierarchically ordered systems necessary for the subsequent emergence of similar or greater individual goods. The function of a government in human societies is to undertake initiatives that serve the general good even if doing so means transmuting particular goods, devaluing the members of the group and their individual achievements to some extent or another for the sake of the whole group, treating them as components with finite utility rather than as unique individuals with a worth beyond price. Rare the actual entities or persons who would suffer this deferred or denied gratification gladly. Without the offices of Leviathan imposing juridical, social, and political constraints on those under its hegemony, the viable possibilities for creative achievement would all be nasty, brutish, and short.

A scholar with a new theory poses a threat to older theories and their adherents, exposing their inadequacies, denigrating their continued importance. It is appropriate that the older theories be defended, but in a manner that gives advocates of the new theory opportunity to make their case. The vilification or suppression of scholars and their theories that those in authority find threatening can undermine the authority and hence the long-term viability of the scientific enterprise, as in notorious examples such as the Soviet Union's Lysenkoist genetics and the Discovery Institute's intelligent design. The Hobbesian transcendental permits but does not celebrate authoritarian forms of social order, for a nexus is all its members, and the more the upper reaches of a hierarchy suppress the individuality of its lesser-order members the more likely the social order will falter.

The advance of science requires, although it does not always get, scholars able to adjust their own particular achievements and professional ambitions to accord with the shifts in paradigms that successfully vetted transmutational theories create. Similarly, social groups need, although they often fail to get, leaders who are able to set policies that serve the long-term viability of the society, leaders who are adept at shaping attitudes and framing laws in terms of communal rather than individual needs. This skill is best exercised when it includes reversions as well as transmutations, when it includes the ability to see not only possibilities to which narrow individual perspectives are blind but also ones that disclose courses of action that can reconcile conflicting individual interests and parochial factions rather than intensifying their incompatible aims, that can serve the whole without sacrificing too much of the particular. The key to effective reversion and transmutation is fostering an enduring object's defining characteristic in a way that lets it function as simultaneously a source of stable continuity and disruptive innovation, nurturing distinctive individuals whose differences serve the general good by continually testing its adequacy and then repairing replacing, or renovating whatever inadequacies it is shown to have.

Whitehead offers the Battle of Waterloo as an example of how transmutation functions by providing the transformation potential of possibilities lurking in the shadows of the world as we know it. This complex historical event resulted in the defeat of Napoleon, "but the abstract notions, expressing the possibilities of another course of history which would have followed upon his victory, are relevant to the facts which actually happened." What happened entails what could have happened but did not: "hypothetical alternatives," comprising "a penumbra of eternal objects, constituted by relevance to the Battle of Waterloo" (185).

Perhaps these alternatives are entertained by "imaginative historians" and explicitly examined for the insights they provide into the actual course of things. Perhaps they are dismissed out of hand, although even then they are thereby recognized as relevant enough to have been noticed and as needing to be dismissed. More typically, these might-have-beens are felt more than thought, admitted by some into "effective feeling" but "for others the ideas float into their minds as daydreams without consciousness of deliberate decision; for others, their emotional tone, of gratification or regret, of friendliness or hatred, is obscurely influenced by this penumbra of alternatives, without any conscious analysis of its content" (185). This penumbra of hypothetical alternatives, more typically sensed than analyzed, is the resource for the transformative ideals harbored by actual fact, haunting both the best laid and the worst laid plans of mice and men.

Transformative possibilities are akin to errors: they are at odds with what is accepted as truth, with what conforms to the established structures and the normative rules governing them. They are wrong but not useless, for they are ideas about how we might be able to change the world—therefore ideas by means of which we change it: "The conceptual feelings entertained in any nexus modify the future role of that nexus as a physical objective datum. . . . What is conceptual earlier is felt physically later in an extended role. Thus, for instance, a new 'form' has its emergent ingression conceptually by reversion, and receives delayed exemplification physically when the other categoreal conditions permit" (253). The ideal is parent of the actual. Unless a different order of things is first conceivable, it cannot be taken as a goal to be made actual.

We often act blindly or impulsively, the relevant possibilities for actualization not recognized or only felt at levels below consciousness. Insofar, however, as we dream of something better or entertain a working hypothesis or develop a plan of action, we take one of the penumbra of alternative possibilities surrounding the actual world as an objective lure drawing us toward a world never before actualized, a world until then barely conceivable, one that can arise often only at great cost, at the sacrifice of present values and their proximate supports.

Often, of course, it is not always we who take the transmuted alternative possibility as an objective lure; it can take us. We are grasped by the opportunities the transformative ideal promises, finding ourselves enamored by its beauty or its goodness, resonating to the new truth with which it rings, ready to stand athwart the barricades or to ride into the valley of death so that it might be actualized—if not for us, at least for the generations after us. And in its service, behold all things become new. Or so we hope, and strive to bring about, and the new world that emerges is indeed a transformed world.

Although it is not necessarily a better one, for sometimes the ideal is enemy of the good. Unless the established order of things provides a sufficiently stable background for the objective lure to be alluring and for the resulting creative effort to actualize it, the contrast between the ideal and the actual can fracture the actual. The stability of the background, of the taken-for-granted traditions that have made the novel possibilities possible, can be too great. The transformative ideal can require the neglect or negation of far too much of the inherited past, destabilizing what remains. The French Revolution upended far too many of the *ancient régime*'s stabilizing features, so that even the days of the week and months of the year were given new names. Voltaire's demand that the infamy be destroyed was achieved, and it seemed almost all things made new. But the new order could not stabilize what it had attempted to establish, and the Republic became an Empire. The ideas of liberty, equality, and fraternity led all too soon to Napoleon and the corpses strewn across the fields of Waterloo.

The Hobbesian transcendental identifies the conditions that allow for an enlargement of the scope of the possible, allowing a society to adapt its traditional ways to the needs of a changing world. This transformative gain in resources for accomplishing the quest for a better order of things demanded by the Leibnizian transcendental makes it possible. However, it is possible for the aim to end up betraying itself. The effort at its actualization, the need to deal with the insistent demand of the Aristotelean transcendental that the actualization not be delayed, can result in a world worse than what was. Even the shift from the narrow focus of actual entities at maximizing their own immediate good to the wider concern for contributing to the continuity of an enduring common good does not mean that the world, as Whitehead's metaphysics describes it, is progressive. The categoreal obligations identify the necessary conditions by which the actual entities comprising the cosmos seek always the better. But there is no necessity that the cosmos will thereby grow better.

THE VALUE OF ADAPTIVE CONTEXTS

This chapter has been about the power of the present, the capacity of actual entities to achieve through their concrescing a spatio-temporal order of enduring significance because both rationally stable and transformatively flexible. Thus whereas chapter 1 undertook the negative task of showing that the notion of God that Whitehead includes in *Process and Reality* renders his metaphysics incoherent and inadequate, chapter 2 has undertaken the positive task of showing that the Categorical Scheme in *Process and Reality*, which makes no mention of God, suffices to account for an adaptively stable cosmos, the world as we find it. My argument can be summarized this way:

The Aristotelian transcendental describes the constraints on the initial data available for a nascent actual entity to prehend in a manner that permits their integration into a determinate unified actuality. It thus identifies the coherence and consistency that are a necessary condition of any systemic structure: the requirement that its elements be compatible and well ordered. The Leibnizian transcendental indicates as a complementary necessary condition that this aim be for the best outcome possible, that a nascent actual entity's inherited data be relevant, that they be applicable to the creation of its own immediate value and to the value of its impending future. The Hobbesian transcendental extends the Leibnizian constraint spatially and temporally, indicating as a third necessary condition for any systemic structure that the aim be not only toward an entity's own individual value but also toward values exhibited by the enduring objects to which it belongs, that its aim be at an encompassing adequacy of societal and ultimately cosmic attainment. These constraints on Creativity echo, appropriately, the constraints Whitehead says govern the creation of any meaningful speculative philosophy: "that it be coherent, logical [consistent], and in respect to its interpretation applicable, and adequate" (3).

Simply in order for an actual entity to instantiate Creativity, for it to be a manner by which "the many enter into complex unity" (21), its initial subjective aim and the subjective forms of its initial prehensions must be oriented toward a best available outcome. The relevant eternal objects able to constitute that aim and the manner of its realization are therefore inherent "in the nature of things" (21), as features of the governing functions implicate in the achieved values of the perished actual entities initially prehended. There is nothing further needed, no possibilities for determination required except those necessarily available at the actual entity's origin.

Thus "the gradation of the relevance of eternal objects to the concrescent phases" of a nascent actual entity, including those hitherto "unrealized in the actual world" (31), can be achieved by a creative manipulation of what had previously been relevant. No primordial actual entity is needed for our refreshment or our comfort, neither to harbor novel forms for us to entertain nor to determine their relevance to our struggles to achieve worthwhile ends. The ideal of a better way is always an implicate feature of the given, and the actualization of new givens with enhanced value enhances accordingly the ideals for value actualization that those new givens harbor.

The categoreal obligations frame the way that value is secured and perpetuated by the recurrent stimulation of each of us and all our cousin entities, actual and enduring, to search among the ruins of past achievement for ways to effect a better achievement. Thus is the wild appetition of those activities tamed, Creativity rather than Chaos made the useful general term for their dynamic drive, individual urges transformed through abstractive generalization and alternative instantiation into the achievement of more-intense values. Thus has nature evolved from a confusion of stochastic flashes of achievement to a cosmos of enduring material objects, to the emergence of organismic life, and recently to the formation of self-conscious human organisms.

This autocatalysis of our cosmos and of ourselves, and the constant quest for its betterment, are the result of the interplay of the three transcendentals, the three kinds of fundamental constraint canalizing Creativity. That the achievements of concrescence have taken an upward course—or that they will continue doing so—is a temporal contingent fact, however. It is an achievement that need not have been as it was, nor need it be continued. But the urge upward, and the possibility for that urge to be realized, have been ever-emergent durable features of our cosmic epoch, shaping its creative advance in the ways described by the principles Whitehead has speculatively proposed for our consideration in the Categoreal Scheme chapter of *Process and Reality*.

NOTE

1. This chapter is an elaboration of portions of sections I and III of my article "A Functionalist Reinterpretation of Whitehead's Metaphysics," *Review of Metaphysics* 62 (2008): 327–54. Used with permission, all rights reserved. The basic idea of section III was first stated but not developed in section II of my article "Whiteheadian Recollection," *Journal of Speculative Philosophy* 15 (2001): 214–27. Used with permission, all rights reserved.

3

THE POWER OF THE PAST

At the opening of the Platonic dialogue bearing his name, Meno asks Socrates whether virtue can be taught.[1] The answer, it would seem, is "no": virtue comes only "as a gift from the gods" (1997a, 99e). Because it is not an item of knowledge, there are no rules for acquiring virtue that a teacher can impart and a student learn. So those who possess virtue—and at least a few among the citizens of Athens are in fact virtuous—must have acquired it in some nonrational, non-pedagogical way, perhaps by genetic inheritance or dumb luck, but more likely by the intervention of transcendent benevolent powers.

This last possibility would seem to be precisely the one Whitehead proposes in *Process and Reality*. An actual entity cannot be taught by its predecessors how to be virtuous, how to optimize its value opportunities; nor can it figure this out on its own. Unless a nascent actual entity receives the initial aim for its concrescence as a gift from God, Whitehead argues, that aim cannot be upward, cannot achieve an outcome better than, or at least as effective as, what its predecessors were able to achieve.

What is true of individual entities is presumably also true of complexes of entities such as we human beings. The achievements of the past are an insufficient resource for teaching us how to acquire and then actualize a novel vision of social enhancement—a more just community, a lasting peace, a better order of the ages. Nor can they provide even the novel strategies necessary to perpetuate those past achievements. This innovation, says Whitehead, can come only from a primordial actual entity that aims endlessly for the better and so intervenes in the becoming of all its cousin actual entities, especially those composing the regnant nexūs of conscious organisms, inspiring them with new possibilities for attaining something better than they could ever have managed on their own. "He does not create the world, he saves it: or, more accurately, he is the poet of the world, with tender patience leading it by his vision of truth, beauty, and goodness" (1978, 346). Without God, the way of the world would lead necessarily toward the degradation of enduring achievement, toward the irreversible loss of whatever truth, beauty, and goodness there might happen to be.

I reject this claim of Whitehead's. The notion that a special entity, God, is required so that there might be a source for the novelties by which creatures are creative and worlds saved is redundant, and redundant on Whiteheadian grounds. I shall argue that an actual entity's initial aim need not be supplied by God, that the resources for novelty in an actual entity's initial aim are amply provided by its inherited past.

INITIAL AIMS

The structure of concrescence is necessarily teleonomic. The task of every emerging actual entity is to integrate the disparate plurality of its inheritance into a unified outcome. It cannot fail to do so. Whatever the means undertaken, whatever the emphasizing, negating, merging methods employed, it must be oriented toward an achievable outcome which in some fashion it achieves. In chapter 2, I call this constraint the Aristotelean Transcendental: the requirement, to put it in Aristotle's language, that an actual entity's efficient cause be controlled by its final cause. The emerging entity begins with an inheritance and a requirement, with raw materials and an initial aim to make of them a single concrete fact. The power of actualization, of turning a goal into an achievement, is solely that of the emergent process. Once begun, concrescence is closed to external influence. As becoming, it is not yet an objective fact and so cannot be the object of any other entity's influence. How its initial aim will be achieved only it can determine.

Therefore, if God is to have any influence on what happens in the making of particular actual entities, and hence have an influence on the cosmos in general which they comprise, it will have to be right off.

What is just beginning needs a goal to guide it, an initial aim to orient it. Where could such an aim come from, except from an already existing agent? But not just any goal is requisite. The freedom to choose whatever one wants and to pursue it as one wishes can lead to unfortunate outcomes. Unrealistic, ambiguous, self-defeating, or silly goals—pursued with inadequate consideration of relevant difficulties, available resources, and unexpected consequences—usually end in failure, in degradation of an inheritance rather than its enhancement. "Apart from the intervention of God," Whitehead therefore argues, "there could be nothing new in the world, and no order in the world. The course of creation would be a dead level of ineffectiveness, with all balance and intensity progressively excluded by the cross currents of incompatibility" (1978, 247). The simple fact of an ordered world in which changes for the better are possible even if obviously not assured is evidence that "originality in the temporal world is conditioned, though not determined, by an initial subjective aim supplied by the ground of all order and of all originality" (108).

The mechanism for God to transmit an initial aim is the hybrid physical feeling. An aim is not a physical fact but rather a possibility, an end in view, an idea about what should be the outcome of a process. The only way an aim can be acquired, therefore, is by a conceptual feeling. Conceptual feelings, however, are necessarily "derivate from physical feelings" (247), in keeping with "Hume's principle of the derivation of conceptual experience from physical experience," a principle that Whitehead says he embraces "without any exception" (250). It is possible for a concrescing subject, having a physical feeling of an immediately past actual entity, to then have a conceptual feeling derived from that physical feeling. These are called hybrid physical feelings: "the prehension by one subject of a conceptual prehension, or of an 'impure' prehension, belonging to the mentality of another subject" (107). A hybrid feeling is indirect: a conceptual feeling by one agent of a predecessor's conceptual feeling, derived from a prior physical feeling of that predecessor.

Whitehead then makes the astonishing claim that a nascent actual entity secures its initial aim by a direct feeling of God's conceptual feeling: "the primary phase [of a concrescence] is a hybrid physical feeling of God, in respect to God's conceptual feeling which is immediately relevant to the universe 'given' for that concrescence" and that "reproduces for the subject the data and valuation of God's conceptual feeling" (225). A direct feeling of God obviously cannot be a *physical* feeling, however, since God is a subject endlessly concrescing, never completed, and therefore never able to be the object of a physical feeling. So any prehension of God has to be directly conceptual, not hybrid. It would seem that for Whitehead Hume's principle has an exception after all.

The exception is fundamental. Whitehead says that God is the originator of each new actual entity by providing it with an aim, its value lying in its relevance to the best outcome available, or at least to a range of the better outcomes, in the context within which the new entity will emerge. "Each temporal entity, in one sense, originates from its mental pole" (224), which makes it reasonable to say that God is "the creator of each temporal actual entity" (225). This doesn't mean, Whitehead assures us, that "the ultimate creativity of the universe is to be ascribed to God's valuation." God is "the aboriginal instance of this creativity, and is therefore the aboriginal condition which qualifies its action" and therefore qualities the actions of all other actual entities (225). Yet every actual entity is uniquely creative in how it shapes its initial conditions into a uniquely determinate outcome, for there are always "indeterminations awaiting its own decisions" (224).

These indeterminations are seriously constrained, however. Only God can envision all possible possibilities, the realm of pure eternal objects, and so only God can envision those from this totality that are best suited for expressing an aim best suited for realizing the best outcome possible within the physical constraints comprising the context for any specific actual entity's emergence. God knows what's best; the concrescing subject has no choice except to aim for what it is told is best, and to implement that aim as best it can. There may be a small range of equally suitable aims for the emergent subject to choose among, and there will be alternatives that in different ways are equally worthwhile moves to make to resolve intermediate obstacles. But there is no room for argument over the end to be sought and the means for seeking it, since only God can know for sure what, in the most concretely situational way, is best. A temporal subject is not an automaton. It has real choices to make, but they are limited by tight constraints not open to debate, most importantly by the stipulation imposed on it by its initial aim.

As to how the content of these aims can be characterized, Whitehead says that "the primordial appetitions which jointly constitute God's purpose are seeking intensity, not preservation." God is "unmoved by love for this particular, or that particular; . . . indifferent alike to preservation and to novelty" (105). This is so because "God's purpose in the creative advance is the evocation of intensities." His aim is only at "depth of satisfaction [for each actual entity] as an intermediate step toward the fulfillment of his [God's] own being" (105).

This is about God's primordial nature, of course. When Whitehead in the closing pages of *Process and Reality* gets around to the consequent nature he will talk of God's love, the "tender care that nothing be lost" (346). However, it is difficult to reconcile these two natures: one devoid of love, indifferent to particulars; the other tenderly caring for particulars, patiently saving whatever can be saved. We must set aside the consequent nature from consideration, however, because it is the primordial nature, "the ground of all order and of all originality" (108), that alone creates the world by instilling in each actual entity its character, its sense of purpose and the drive for realizing it. The world is as it is because of God: a world of particular interests seeking to maximize the worth—that is, the intensity—of what they achieve. Actual entities are not concerned with the preservation of past achievements out of love for their intrinsic worth but rather with their preservation or destruction for whatever instrumental value they might have for the entity's "clutch at vivid immediacy" (105).

This seems to make of God a surprisingly selfish entity, setting the conditions for the emergence of actualities so that the result is the fulfillment of God's own being. Or if not a selfish God then perhaps a "remorseless" one, whose "ruthlessness" is its "inexorable" insistence on "valuation as an aim towards 'order,'" toward vivid immediacy no matter what the carnage (244). Whitehead in the last chapter of *Process and Reality* makes it clear, however, by means of an Aristotelean twist, that both selfishness and remorselessness are misinterpretations of God's purpose. God "is the lure for feeling, the eternal urge of desire" that "constitutes him the initial 'object of desire' establishing the initial phase of each subjective aim" (344). It isn't that God desires an increase in the intensity of every particular achievement, but rather that a nascent actual entity desires that intensity for itself by feeling God's relevant conceptual feeling. The entity's conceptual feeling is moved by its feeling of God's conceptual feeling, as Aristotle claims when arguing that "thought is moved by the object of thought," which "moves without being moved, being eternal" (344; quoting from *Metaphysics 1072a*, tr. W. D. Ross). The notion of an indifference of eternal perfection—"untrammeled by reference to any particular course of things" and "deflected neither by love nor by hatred, for what in fact comes to pass" (344)—is difficult to reconcile with a metaphysics of process, much less with the accessible God who tenderly seeks to save the world by fostering actualizations not only of truth and beauty, but also of goodness.

The question is not whether novel possibilities are crucial for the initial aims of actual entities, since they are. Nor is it crucial whether the source of these possibilities is random or directed, since the discovery or invention of novelties of any sort require a directing agency. The question is whether that agent is an actual entity or whether it is God. I am arguing for creative self-determination and opposing the need for divine determination. The vaunted freedom of the actual entity becomes oddly Pickwickian when it is limited to accepting or rejecting God's suggestions, never being able to originate anything on its own. The temporality of things, their occasionalness, can only be taken seriously by affirming that all there is to reality is the recurrent vectors of transformation running from indeterminacy to determinacy, from possibilities to their actualization. This is the plain, and I think univocal, meaning of the ontological principle that "everything in the actual world is referable to some actual entity" (244). We should resist the temptation, even if Whitehead himself failed to do so, to construe it as permitting realities that do not become and perish.

There can be no actual entity other than those that come to be and perish because to be actual is to become a determinate fact, although a momentary one only. Every actual entity is an actualization process, an activity resulting in a product that is neither more nor less than its process, the two inseparably and immediately one. The functions qualifying temporal realities recur, to be sure, but they recur only because they are characteristics of perishing realities that can be appropriated by their successors. A function or characteristic has no independent actuality, however. It is a contribution to the shape of an event, a condition in the contouring of its trajectory. There are no shapes as such, only shaped events; no functions as such, only vectors functioning in certain ways to affect features of those shapes; no possibilities as such, only pathways by which functions can transfer one shape into another.

Whitehead has insisted that possibilities must be essentially timeless, and therefore without relation to any particular temporal reality, except as relevant "in the primordial mind of God" who provides them to an actual entity as its initial aim (46). Instead, I propose that we understand a possibility as an inherent feature of a temporal process, a finite function of the particular spatio-temporal context that comprises its ambient. All relevance is proximate relevance; a possibility's local relevance constitutes its essence. Possibilities are ordered intrinsically with respect to the actual world they qualify. Their relatedness is internal to their temporal context, nor something imposed on them by a nontemporal orderer. The ontological principle is satisfied because every possibility exists as a characteristic of some determinate nexus of actual entities. A possibility is never nowhere, but always embedded in an ambient where it is available for prehension by the situated agents emerging as the successors of that context. Possibilities, like actualities, come to be and perish.

Interpreted as functions of actual spatio-temporal environments, novel possibilities are then inherently available to a presently emerging actual entity because they are already inherent in its past. The possibilities to be found in any actual entity's past are of three sorts: previously actualized possibilities, possibilities previously entertained but never actualized, and possibilities never before entertained. They are all available, potent characteristics of the realities impinging on the present, accessible resources for a concrescing entity in its struggle to become a concretely potent actuality. Their use is not simply a matter of plugging them in to a process of actualization as though they were preformed modular units. As possibilities take on functional roles in an actual entity's concrescence, they become increasingly particularized: specified, merged, adapted, construed, distorted. Actualities are all achievements resulting from temporal processes that involve the transformation of disparate physical and conceptual elements, by means of functional reshapings within categoreal constraints, into an integrated whole. These inherited facts and possibilities, tailored to function optimally within the limitations imposed by idiosyncratic local expressions of the generic constraints, are what make the making of new things possible. They are themselves made possible by previous localizations of generic possibilities and generalizations of previously localized possibilities. What is newly made closes off some resources for subsequent relevance while opening up others, expands the influence of some while shrinking the influence of others. As the things that are made change, so also the available functions, facts, and possibilities for making them change, and likewise as these alter so also what gets made alters.

It is difficult to believe that all these possible transformations—creations out of what has, is, and will be given and possible, inherited and invented, in all the shifting contexts of the creative advance—reside primordially in some receptacle entity, ready for whatever use any one of them might turn out to have. Whitehead treats possibilities as though they were like numbers, which because of their abstract purity are individually unique, collectively infinite, and timeless. Whatever possibilities are, however, they are surely not mathematical abstractions, but are rather finite ever-shifting features of contingent processes, elements that have themselves been made and that are involved in the making and unmaking of all the entities that comprise the actual world.

Human beings, for instance, become persons. We develop character, a sense of identity that shapes how we respond to what we have experienced, and our character changes as a result of those experiences and responses. As adults we are not who we were as children nor who we will be when elderly. Although there are continuities, there is nothing unchanged about us because, as we change, the conditions of our selfhood change as well. As members of a social order, we together with our family, neighbors, and fellow citizens are governed by commonsense conventions, everyday practices, governmental edicts, and constitutional laws that stipulate the conditions under which we can pursue our varied purposes. Making our way thusly through life, the what, the why, and the how of our makings alter those governing conditions at all levels. Governments come and go, nations rise and fall, the generations pass. Because of what we and our parents did, we live in a world different than our grandparents' world, and because of our actions and our children's, our grandchildren will inherit a world different than ours.

These same processes also characterize biological evolution. The environmental and genetic conditions governing phenotypic development and reproductive success change constantly, resulting constantly in new variations of organism, new species, new genera, new phyla. Generalizing these personal, cultural, and biological histories, Whitehead speculates about changes even in the conditions governing the space-time processes constitutive of the universe itself. He proposes that other cosmic epochs will eventually succeed our own, as they have already preceded it (91, 288). Whitehead takes his metaphysical hypotheses as limited not only because they are made by a fallible human being but also because they could be accurate, at best, only for our current epoch in which, as he claims, actual entities are the ontologically basic modes of existence.

We can treat Whitehead's notion of an actual entity as a model for this complex dynamic of relationships, treating it as a model not just for the basic constituents of space-time but for any sort of making. Actual entities are concrescences, processes by which varied antecedent conditions are worked up into something new. The content, manner, and character of a newly emerging actuality—its material, formal, and final conditions—are derived from prior makings. These past entities are appropriated by the newly emergent entity as data for integration. They are objectified for it by means of various selections of their concrete features, which thereby set limits to the scope and character of what will result but also provide possibilities for determining the degree to which that result departs from those of its predecessors.

In the prehension of its immediate past, the present entity acquires its orientation, its resources for determination, and its structural and procedural boundary conditions. The past that determines the fundamental conditions, the shape and content, of the world we inhabit, is also a source of possibilities that allow us to alter these conditions in novel and incrementally fundamental ways. Reality is a continual sequence of prior makings turned into new makings, of transitions in which there are no originations that were not once destinations and no destinations that do not become fresh originations. Everything comes from conditions that precede it, including those conditions; *ex nihilo nihil fit*. Values temporally made are objective achievements. They are the work of natural processes, whether the result of blind causal transactions or of open-eyed cognitive and actional purposes. And these objective value achievements are comparable and rankable. There are warranted reasons for locating them on a spectrum that runs from better or worse, from usable to irrelevant, from obstacles to opportunities. Neither values nor their sources need to be universal, necessary, and eternal in order to be objective, incontrovertible, and significant.

PHYSICAL PURPOSES

If nothing can come from nothing, and if there is no God to provide a nascent actual entity with its initial aim, how can that aim ever arise? The nascent entity would be like Locke's *tabula rasa*: a blank slate on which an actual outcome is to be inscribed. Initially the entity so understood would be without an aim, naked of any orientation, needing tools it knows nothing of to fashion a result of which it is totally ignorant. If there is no initial aim, however, there is the past, the perishing predecessors from which the nascent entity emerges. Locke was mistaken: the slate is never blank. Because it is not a slate but a ground: the fruits of the entity's antecedents that in their perishing provide fertile soil for the growth of new fruitions.

This transition from one growth to another can be found in the notion of 'physical purposes' as these are explicated in what Lewis Ford calls Whitehead's "penultimate theory of concrescence" (2008, 316). Ford identifies Whitehead's "ultimate" theory as this earlier one plus precisely what I am objecting to: the addition of God's Primordial Nature as the necessary source of initial aims and novelties. I think that physical purposes are a sufficient resource for explaining how a nascent subject can form its own subjective aim and devise novel approaches to its actualization without the need for a *deus ex machina*. Let me explain why.

As Whitehead develops the notion (1978, 248–49; 275–80), a physical purpose occurs in the initial phase of concrescence as the transition from an inherited past to that past as relevant to a determinate outcome. The perishing of the subjectivity of one actual entity is succeeded by its objectification for the subjectivity of its immediate successor. The subjective form of this physical feeling is one of re-enaction in its successor. From this physical feeling is derived a conceptual feeling of the eternal objects exemplified in it, the subjective form of which is one of positive or negative valuation. How the physically prehended past is conceptually prehended is the subject's necessary addition to the initial data of its concrescence, an addition that gives Creativity a freshly existential expression by transforming the subject's inherited data into relevantly possible resources for its own determination. These two feelings, physical and conceptual, are then integrated by means of a "generic contrast" between the physical drive for replication and the conceptual judgment of its worth. The conceptual feeling "closes in upon" (276) the physical feeling, valuing it not simply for what it is but also for the specific relevance of what it is to what the new subjectivity might make of itself. This integration creates a physical purpose.

Were a conceptual feeling only a "conceptual registration" (248) of the eternal objects found in its associated physical feeling, devoid of any distinctive subjective form expressing how positively or negatively those eternal objects are felt, the present would merely replicate the past. The argument for why there is a need for interposing a conceptual feeling of God's conceptual feelings seems to be based on the presumption that this would be the case: the assumption that without an infusion from elsewhere of fresh possibilities with regard to the whats and hows of ends and means, all an actual entity could do would be to register past possibilities, and therefore its concrescence could do no more than replicate that past. However, a conceptual feeling has a subjective form provided by the concrescing subject, its manner of prehending that feeling, one that involves a valuation of what was felt physically. The nascent actual entity not only registers the possibility but also judges it. It thereby "endows the transcendent creativity with the character of adversion, or of aversion" (276).

Because these adversive and aversive judgments are applied to physical feelings from which the now-evaluated conceptual feelings were derived, how those physical feelings are henceforth felt is as possibilities worthy of actualization. They are felt as relevant or irrelevant, significantly so or trivially, to an outcome. "Creative purpose" thus emerges in the actual entity's initial prehendings. How it acquires subjectivity is through becoming "a determinate of its own concrescence." It determines "its own ideal of itself" by means of the "eternal principles of valuation" described in the categoreal obligations, in the generic conditions of Creativity which it has "autonomously modified" by giving them an existential application, thereby transforming a generic aim into a subjective aim (248).

This emergence of an autonomous self, a subject with its own aims, involves physical purposes of "the first species" (276). These aims are minimal. Their main function is to provide the sort of adaptation to local conditions needed for a successful outcome under conditions unavoidably different than those of the entity's inheritance. In chapter 2, I referred to this kind of physical purpose as the instantiation of an Aristotelian transcendental, the existentializing of conceptual valuation, of the categoreal condition that the concrescence have some kind of specific outcome, that its possibilities give rise to a unique determinative event—that the many become one.

The "second species" of physical purposes continues to involve not only valuation up or valuation down, but does so by the introduction of novel possibilities through reversion (277). Reversion involves a "secondary origination" of conceptual feeling, one involving eternal objects "partially diverse" from those involved in the primary phase of concrescence: "proximate novelties" felt as "relevant alternatives" (249).

An attempt at mere replication is a recipe for stasis and hence for eventual failure because reproduction under the aegis of conceptual valuation can only adjust to minimal fluctuations in the stable ambient supporting the possible emergence of an actual entity's successors. It cannot adapt to abrupt significant alterations in that ambient, nor can it do better than its predecessors, nor improve the likely success of its successors. The introduction of "the more remote alternative possibilities" (278) allows the emergence of outcomes that are more complex and sustainably so, and hence valuationally superior. Enduring objects are such outcomes. They reproduce over time a consistent pattern of achievement, most primordially and most fundamentally a vibratory rhythm in which the constituent moments vary in a manner that integrates those variances into nondivisive contrasts which intensify the value of the enduring whole. This "consistency of physical purposes explains the persistence of the order of nature" (276).

Reversion "is the category by which novelty enters the world; so that even amid stability there is never undifferentiated endurance" but rather both "*a ground of identity* and an aim at contrast" (249), which is to say an aim at "balanced complexity" as the key "condition for intensity" of outcome (278). Creativity is thus the generalized notion of vectors of concrescence as not only oriented toward a determinate outcome but also toward an improvement in the scope of what is included in that outcome and the intensity of its integration: "the urge towards" maximal realization of available possibilities under "conditions of contrast" (278). In order to existentialize this generic urge, a concrescing entity needs to revert its conceptual feelings. It needs to discern specific proximate alternatives to its specific inheritance if it is to enhance the quality of its own specific achievement and of its relevant ambient, as well as contributing to ongoing collective enterprises of sustained value achievement. I referred to this in chapter 2 as a Leibnizian transcendental, because it stipulates that the generic aim of any actual entity is always at the best of the possible worlds available to it.

Whitehead's penultimate theory of concrescence provides in the notion of two species of physical purposes the requisite wherewithal for actual entities of any sort to create both their own individuating aims and the novel possibilities needed to actualize them successfully. Physical purposes are an inherent capacity of actual entities, their power to be original, to devise novel aims and novel methods for their actualization. When Whitehead adds God to his theory of concrescence, he shifts the primary source of originality from the actual entities to God. The concrescing actual entities become subservient agents carrying out their master's commands, creative in working out in the most effective way the instrumental details of the reconciliation process, but for the master's sake, not their own. By identifying the power of physical purposing as exercised in devising the initial phase of a concrescence, the actual entity can be understood as creating itself for itself. To be is to be becoming, and becoming is a process of self-formation.

VAGUE POSSIBILITIES

Fundamental to Whitehead's insistence that an actual entity's initial aim must be provided to it by God is the presumption that eternal objects are specific: essentially in "complete disjunction" from each other, a "barren inefficient disjunction of abstract possibilities." It is solely by means of their "primordial valuation" by God that they are ordered relative to temporal realities (1978, 40). For every event or feature of an event, there is an eternal object that is the possibility it has actualized. The more complex the event, the more complex the eternal object, and for every event that could have happened or yet could happen there is an eternal object, the multiplicity of them infinite in number and timelessly extant in God's primordial nature. Hence all the specifically possible satisfactions available to a nascent actual entity at the initiation of its concrescence are timelessly available to God, and although many have already been actualized and so are also present in that entity's physical prehension of its immediate past, a novel particular possibility by definition is only available to God. For if it is novel, it has not already been actualized and so has no temporal location unless made temporally available by God. Whitehead's requirement that any novel initial aim must be given to an actual entity by God is thus an unavoidable consequence of his claim that possibilities are essentially both particular and eternal.

I argued in chapter 1 that there can be no place for eternal objects in a process metaphysics, and that Whitehead's attempt to include them renders his metaphysics incoherent. I have been developing in this chapter the notion of possibilities as temporal, as functions of temporal situations, and therefore features of the inherited past that are inherently relevant by virtue of their direct impingement. But these features impinge by being prehended, and prehension is always with the nascent entity's assessment of its relevance. Possibilities are not entities but pathways available to processes, most basically to processes of concrescence. What is possible changes, as shifting conditions alter old pathways slightly, although sometimes closing old ways or opening new ones.

There is a crucial additional feature of possibilities that I briefly mentioned earlier but which needs more elaboration, one that is key to how the past can be both the source of an actual entity's novel initial aim and a continuing resource for how that aim is creatively actualized. What is fundamental to possibilities functioning as final causes is that usually they are initially vague but become less and less vague as concrescence moves toward a determinate outcome. As the possibilities become more precise, more clear and distinct, they may transform the pathway they traverse in unexpected ways. The end achieved is going to differ from the end initially envisioned, not only because of its greater specificity but also because of an alteration in its pathway, achieving what had not originally been envisioned.

Let me return to Lewis Ford who, having helped us see the significance of what he calls Whitehead's penultimate theory of concrescence, rejects it on the grounds that it cannot supply the concrescing actual entity with a specific initial aim. "I recognize," says Ford, "that creativity is essential for concrescence as supplying the activity to make it possible. But without a specific goal it is insufficient to direct the various prehensions to a concrescence's particular unity. . . . Neither creativity nor the categoreal obligations alone can supply that specificity" (2008, 310).

Ford is arguing that an actual entity's initial subjective aim specifies its goal, and that only in the light of such a specification can the emerging entity achieve a determinate outcome. Because an entity's subjectivity is only generic at the initial phase of concrescence, it cannot be the source of anything as specific as the goal of its own initial aim must be. Creativity supplies the energy for concrescence, argues Ford, but its vector character requires from the first a specific end which can be provided only by a reality, indeed a prehensible actuality, other than the nascent entity. That is, by God.

This argument makes sense if initial aims are like travel destinations. We must first decide where specifically we want to go before we can determine the best way to get there. Having picked Chicago as our goal, and having determined that the Indiana Turnpike is the best way to get there, we can be on our way. We could get to Chicago by other routes, those best for other reasons such as their scenic beauty or their being less congested, or we could perversely decide to drive to Buffalo instead. But our degrees of freedom are pre-formed by the relevant specifics of available goals and transportation routes. If we have only a vague idea where we want to go and no sense of what we think might be the best kind of route to take, we will either never leave home or our trip will quite likely be an unsatisfactory ramble arriving eventually at a destination that could just possibly be a good one but more than likely will be disappointing.

Ford is echoing Whitehead's argument, but as is often the case Whitehead is his own best critic because his analogies for concrescence are not of this thoroughly specified sort. He typically is thinking not of Google Maps and similar recipe-driven enterprises but rather of artistic endeavors. "The subjective aim is seeking width with its contrasts, within the unity of a general design. An intense experience is an aesthetic fact, and its categoreal conditions are to be generalized from aesthetic laws in particular arts" (1978, 279). A creative artist's initial aim is relatively vague. One painter, for example, may hope to capture the play of late afternoon light on a cluster of birch trees, while another wants to express serenity through geometric shapes in primary colors. Certain generic aesthetic conditions immediately become relevant for both painters, as constraints or opportunities. Differing tonal values of the same color will yield for the one different representations of the presence of sunlight, while it will provide the other with ways to calm the clash of juxtaposed primary reds, yellows, and blues.

As these artists begin to translate their aesthetic conditions into paint on canvas, their original ideas become clearer. Successful decisions about what to do in fashioning their creations lead to developments that build on those decisions, providing increasing specificity not only to what they are accomplishing but also to what they are hoping to accomplish. This specifying creates unforeseeable problems, however, difficulties that appear only as unique features of the growing specificity. The increasing quantity of the dark tones the first painter has introduced is obscuring the importance of the gently curving tree trunks for the structural balance of her picture; the second painter's massive use of bold colors is undermining what he wants to be a complementary mass of bold shapes. The solutions to each of these problems may be less than satisfactory, weakening the aesthetic quality of the final objects, but they might evoke fresh insights instead that transform the character of the artists' paintings in unexpected but powerful ways. The subtle shifts among small dabs of dark-toned shades may provide the one painter with a more profound balance than the elongated whites of the birch trunks, not so much evoking the pastoral emotions of a forest at dusk that she had originally sought as conveying instead an unsettling sense of the unavoidable approach of death. The other painter's finished canvas may have abandoned geometry altogether as he lets the colors through the very sharpness of their contrasts establish an unexpected sense of a persisting benign order.

Similarly, one of the clichés of novel writing is that the fictional characters take on a life of their own, that the artist cannot anticipate the implications of the interplay of events, personality, and context as those elements are translated from chapter outlines into a specific narrative. Likewise, I had no idea before I wrote the prior paragraph that my note to illustrate Whitehead's quote about the aesthetic character of concrescence with an example from painting would result in two sharply different examples, the specifics of which I would then try to narrate as the development of different kinds of Whiteheadian contrasts, contrasts that serve not only to enhance the scope and intensity of my invented artists' two paintings but also to enhance my aim for that paragraph. Whitehead's understanding of the function of art gives a metaphysical bite to this otherwise psychological account of how an artist—and by generalization any actual entity or nexus of actual entities—develops a vague initial aim in ways that transform it into an unexpected concrete result.

The account of Art spread episodically across the pages of *Adventures of Ideas* interprets its function in civilization as similar to Plato's notion of the Socratic horsefly. Its role is to unsettle our established ways of seeing, thinking, and doing by puncturing the systemic envelope that defines and sustains them. We are blind to what lies outside the world of meaning that envelopes us until a work of art pulls us beyond that world's confines, confronts us with aspects of a reality too diverse in scope and rich in qualities to all fit into any one coherent and consistent systemic whole. Art exposes us to what from the perspective of our established ways seem to be unbelievable facts, impractical methods, and incomprehensible possibilities, and suggests how a new system might be devised that would include these previously unknown—neglected, forgotten, misconstrued—novelties. It fosters open ambients.

The adventure that leads to the disclosure of such realities and to the creation of a new world that gives them meaning is how civilized order is able to sustain itself and how simpler forms of order can give rise to more complex ones. The adventure lies in the fact that the novelties are disruptive because by definition we do not at first know what to do with them. The lure of their beauty, however, and the lure of the beauty of their possibly refreshing, possibly transforming integration with the old familiar ways, motivate our search for a path along which we might venture in an attempt to turn them into the truth of a new and more adequate world. The story can never be written in advance of how a way is found and whether it leads to victory or defeat, or leads more likely to a bittersweet mix of partial success and partial disappointment. One way or the other, it is a story that will be recorded afterwards as a part of the meaning of the new order that has resulted.

ALTERNATIVE POSSIBILITIES

If the past is to be interpreted as a sufficient source of possibilities relevant to the aims of an actual entity and a society of actual entities, if it is to be understood as having an analogous function for individual humans and communities of humans, as well as for civilizations, historical epochs, and cosmic epochs, then more needs to be said about why the past plays such a central role in the ways we are. In what follows, I will tend to focus on human societies but the analogy among kinds of societies and between societies and actual entities is robust and should be presumed.

The inherited past is a finite landscape of settled and unsettling features organized systemically. It is a world: most generically, the world of our cosmic epoch; more specifically the physically prehended immediately local predecessors of an emerging actual entity; and somewhere betwixt these extremes, the world of us humans. Key among the features of this world are its governing rules, the established conditions that comprise its horizon, that delimit what is possible about what ends can be pursued and which of them ought to be. A rule is an ideal, a final cause orienting an actual entity's endeavor to become a thing or a community's effort to endure.

Things are ordered into a system when they are related by means of an authoritative rule. Four lines of equal length are ordered into a square by the mathematical instruction that they be connected by a right angle at each end to one of the other lines. A collection of ingredients is arranged into a casserole when combined and cooked in the manner and sequence stipulated by a culinary expert's recipe. A bunch of people arrange themselves into a service club or a political action committee when they agree to a common statement of purpose and a set of bylaws for how they are to go about fulfilling that purpose. In these examples, the normative ideal is abstract—a concept, a rule, a plan of action. It functions as the way in which existents ought to be organized into a more complex existent, a whole of which they are the components. First the ideal; then the actual system that instantiates it. However, this dynamic can be inverted. A complex actual existent contains as its defining feature the formal structure that is the condition of its existence. Enjoying a casserole, I might ask the cook for its recipe so that I can understand how it is made, why it tastes as it does. British civil and governmental practices predate the common law rules by which they function. First, the actual system, then the pattern that measures its value and the components into which it can be analyzed.

Either sense entails the other: the regulative ideal and the actual practice are coimplicates.

The physical reality of the ideal instantiated is not a mirror image of its conceptual reality, however. What actually is the case necessarily falls short of what would ideally be the case. The four lines comprising a square and the rule for composing them in that way are strictly equivalent because mathematical entities are purely conceptual. The ideal is the actual. A square tabletop made of oak, however, does not perfectly replicate the formula for its construction, just as my effort to make the casserole I enjoyed at a friend's dinner party might very well result in one that fails to taste exactly the same.

This slippage between the ideal and the actual is all the more obvious when the existents comprising the system organized by the rule are free agents, agents who need to understand the rule in order to follow it, and who often have reasons not to follow the rule even when they understand its normative authority. The atoms may blindly run in accord with Newton's laws, but the citizens of a nation must choose whether or not to run in accord with its legislative statutes and their bureaucratic implementation. A citizen's choices are limited by the extent of the coercive power the government can legitimately use in order to enforce its laws, by the habits and customs in which they unthinkingly find comfort and guidance, and by the institutional structures—the physical buildings and roadways, the landscaped parks and cultivated fields, the costuming and pageantry—they inhabit. A citizen's choices are constrained, but not determined. The range of difference between the actual result of a rule's institution and the ideal result, the result that would have replicated the rule, identifies the various ways in which the system could have deviated from its actual course, its manner of functioning, while still being an expression of the rule defining it. Amid the possibilities of deviance, those who continue their allegiance to the ideal even if they continue to fall short of it can be said to be guided by "conformative ideals." Which is how we go about our lives as brothers at arms, part of the sisterhood, reliably responsible citizens, loyal followers, committed advocates.

In biology, these various ways are the possibilities for mutational deviation between an organism and its offspring. A random mutation is a possible actualization of a genetic strand that has for the first time been actualized, occurring not as the result of some purposive agent but by chance. In human societies, deviations from conformity to the established rules and acceptable practices are also often unintentional minor modulations in belief and practice that go unnoticed. Just as often, however, deviances from the societal norms are intentional acts. The trespass of the law may be a temptation we could not resist, a challenge to which we rise, a gratuitous expression of our independence. Any of these deviations are possible because they are all obvious correlatives of the rule they violate. 'Thou shalt not' entails 'thou canst.' Our awareness of the rule entails the possibility of violating it. The permissible identifies the impermissible as also possible, and both sorts of possibilities are thus essential features of the social order governed by the rule that has sorted them into conformal and deviant kinds.

Deviations, however, need not be simply negative actions in violation of an ideal. The penumbra of alternatives surrounding any normative ideal also suggests something positive: viable variations to its regimen. The law may be modified by a legislative amendment or a bureaucratic interpretation. A new strategy for winning a game or fighting a war might prove successful, an innovation in dress or verbal expression might go viral. There are also the alternatives that had or still have their advocates, but that have never been actualized. A welter of such variations is always strewn across the cultural landscape—lost causes and failed dreams, neglected paradigms and marginalized perspectives, ends we have not pursued but that still might surely be worthy of our commitment. Let me call these variant possibilities "reformative ideals." In affirming them, in taking one of them as an ideal worthy of our loyalty and diligent pursuit, we are no longer merely deviating from an established rule. We are proposing that a better version of the rule replace it.

The ways in which we can modify the landscape of our inheritance by inventing new versions of its features to replace ones thought inadequate will never exhaust the ways we could have modified it. To arrive at something determinate, we may need to exclude and subordinate versional possibilities that some may think deserve inclusion, or else this recurrent opportunity for revision will likely never reach completion. The reformative ideals relevant to a given world are an inexhaustible source of novelty, giving rise over time to an indefinite sequence of revised versions of the world, adaptive worlds always capable of reformation.

And yet governments fall, civilizations collapse, and even cosmic epochs come to an end. The landscape of our world sometimes can change so significantly that the result is no longer a version of the old but something more radical: a new kind of world. A revolutionary government overthrows the old regime; a new civilization with a very different cultural sensibility arises from the ashes of its predecessor; a transition to a wholly other cosmic epoch takes place. We can cantilever our possibilities by analogies and metaphors, by abstract generalization and imaginative extrapolation, until we find ourselves imagining what was before unimaginable. On such occasions, we find ourselves considering as a viable alternative what had once been not merely speculative or foolish but downright inconceivable. We find that we can stretch our hands beyond the boundary fences of our world and touch, ever so tentatively yet so electrifyingly, a "transformative ideal."

Transformative ideals are the ones Whitehead mentions in *Adventures of Ideas*, ideals that beat "like a phantom ocean" against the shoreline barriers of our world, wave after wave, "sapping the base of some cliff of habit" (1967, 19), until the ocean breaks through, the old order is washed away, and out of the rubble a different world with different normative conditions emerges. The constituents may be similar or even the same; much of the rubble may be salvageable. Nonetheless, a new kind of world has now been established, with its own new kind of horizons and barriers, a new landscape of what is possible and what permissible, of what is imaginable and what conceivable. This world, however, will in good time undergo modulation into its own distinctive versions through an exploration of its inherent possibilities. These reformative adjustments will continue to be made, until fissures of a fundamental sort emerge and the waves of some fresh transformative ideal which those adjustments also implicitly contained come crashing through the world's seemingly permanent retaining walls. And thereby a yet newer kind of world arises, and this goes on, kinds of worlds without end. Transmutation is the category by which that adaptive novelty is extended so as not only to sustain balanced complexity but to increase the scope, intensity, duration, and flexibility of that complexity. I have called the conditions that structure changes of this sort a Hobbesian transcendental, because it stipulates that an actual entity's or enduring object's aim must take account of values broader and more enduring than those relevant to its own immediate fulfillment.

Human societies are complex systems dominated by sophisticated agents able to imagine deviations from established rules and established patterns of their actualization. Less complex systems have the same dynamic form: an inherited order fraught with the possibility of its reiteration, but containing also deviant processes without which repetition of the particular achievements of actual entities and variously more complex societies of actual entities would lead to stultification and eventual decay. The decaying of a social order can be reversed, however: the decline slowed and then stopped, the system stabilized, its capacities renovated and even transformed, without a loss of continuity.

This dynamic of systemic achievement and decay is at every moment contingent, the capacity for strengthening values also a capacity for diminishing them. Sometimes stability is a glorious accomplishment, a triumph over the chaotic confusion of a period of continual dislocation; sometimes the stability is the result of an increasing inadequacy of well-established ways, and so is the source of an impending collapse. Neither progress nor decline are inevitable. The discovery or invention of novel possibilities are key to either alternative course of things. The choice of which ideals ought to be affirmed and by what means they should be pursued seems best left to the entities directly involved in the processes and values concretely in play for the situation at hand. On metaphysical as well as pragmatic grounds.

THE FINAL CAUSE

This chapter has been about the power of the past, which means it is about the importance of order over will. It argues for the primacy of ideals, which means it argues for the primacy of entities able to discover what should be amid the overweening pressure of what is, and then able to act on its behalf. If actual entities are to be more than servants of a transcendent guiding agency, they will need to make some choices of their own. Or rather, much more than that: they will need to be able to fashion some of the choices among which they then choose. If they have the capacity to innovate at all, however, then there is no a priori justification for claiming they lack the capacity to innovate regarding their own aims and the manner and methods of their actualization, to be their own source of their final cause. So this chapter has celebrated agencies—occasional or enduring, individual or societal—that are at once the creators and creatures of their cosmos.

I have criticized Whitehead's notion of God as the agency by which Creativity becomes particularized, the timelessly constant source of the initial aims by which actualization can occur. However, the notion of such aims has been expanded in this chapter from final causes initially specified to ones initially too vague and so only slowly specified, and then further expanded to include final causes reformed and transformed, requiring and creating novelties initially ignored or not yet comprehendible, possibilities not yet possible. Whitehead is alert to the implications of this expansion by expanding the role of God to include not only the provision of actual entities with their initial aims but also with determining the conditions under which those aims are actualized. "The primordial nature of God is the acquirement of creativity of a primordial character," says Whitehead. God's "conceptual actuality at once exemplifies and establishes the categoreal obligations" (1978, 344). God is made the source of the Categoreal Obligations rather than Categoreal Obligations being the constitutive conditions to which all agencies, including God, must conform. He makes abstract order primary, with specific purposes judged by their adherence to its constraints. For each individual entity and for the systems of social order they comprise, not only are their proper goal pre-established but also the conditions for the proper pursuit of those goals. In place of a cosmos of constantly reworked forms of systemic order created by multitudes of finite entities with variegated finite powers and interests as the final authority, the metaphysical foundation of the cosmos, he substitutes the will of a single entity with special transcendent powers. My critique of Whitehead's notion of God in this chapter has thus been a metaphysical insistence on the ability of temporal momentary events to originate and sustain their cosmos, and therefore to obviate the need for some grander kind of entity to do it for them.

The Categories of Obligation are not timeless universals. Like any abstraction, like the Creativity of which they are conditions, they are generalizations of particular facts and their functions and features, of the concrete ways in which available possibilities have been actualized in the past. They are transcendental abstractions because they identify the most generalized features of the creative advance of finite comings to be and perishings, an ongoing temporal process without origin or end. Categoreal obligations are the lessons of our past available as normative guides for choosing how best to contribute in our brief moments to what and how the world is becoming. The ordered system that is our cosmos is the actual implicate of the Categories' ideality. They together, the past of actualities and the possibilities from which they developed and to which they can give rise, are the final cause of all agency, both mentor and judge of whatever is being made.

The value of recognizing the importance of the past, of paying attention to systems and the ponderous ordering of things they entail, is that it encourages us to be realistic in our embrace of ideals, to avoid the willingness to sacrifice the rich lode of past accomplishments for the sake of an impossible future. Whitehead thinks that without God, as the source of the ability for anything from actual entities to human beings to be innovative, decay would be unavoidable. But he also thinks that without God providing the necessary constraints, those actual entities and persons would be excessively innovative, undermining the conditions for enhancement and so leading unavoidably to decay. However, the past understood as a heritage of enhancings and decayings is itself the source of both the needed well-founded constraints and imaginatively relevant innovations. The lessons of the past, generalized as normative and then applied with creatively adaptive skill, are as good a guide as any god. As they are also a more coherent, practical, and beautiful metaphysical hypothesis about the ways of the world.

The access to novel variants of an experienced quality suggests a schema of increasingly divergent novelties that leads from these conformative variations to reformative variations in which the abstract possibility itself is varied, and then to transformative variations in which the kind of possibility is modified. The divergences comprise a schema because each possibility involves only a slight alteration in the ones contiguous to it. Each modifies a single feature of the instantiation pathway of relevant possibility while leaving other features of the pathway intact. Novelties that make a difference effect minor alterations in the inheritance from which they were derived, the accumulation of such modest efforts resulting eventually in significant change, for better or for worse.

Values are concretely actualized possibilities that can be de-concretized by generalization, by undertaking an archeology of their origins. A value leads back to the function of which it is a value, and the function once recovered can then be actualized by any of the other values that satisfy its conditions, many if not all of which have never before been actualized. A new value actualizing a familiar function is an imagined possibility at last made concrete, a long-held hope finally realized in flesh and blood or stone and mortar. Our world is transformed by this new value, maybe from horizon to horizon, but it remains the same basic world, a world governed by the same function. There has been a new pressing of grapes, but from established varietals in order to make a familiar wine for the same old bottles. Occasionally, a new value actualizing a familiar function expands the horizon of our world, however, opens us to previously unimagined possibilities and undreamt means for their actualization. The proper recollection of the past, discerning amid its irrevocable thereness the conditions for the conditions governing that achievement, is our engine of self-transcendence. A rediscovery of the functions inherent in the past is our way to make new varietals of grape and new bottles worthy of the new kind of wine their harvest will actualize. Ah, brave old world, that has such new worlds in't.

For every system, then, there is a normative structure by which the functioning of its subsystems and the actions of its individual members can be assessed. Beneficial deeds and upright character, fair laws and their equitable application, take their cue from that system's moral order. Such a normative framework can itself be subjected to moral assessment, however, by appeal to the system's reformative and transformative ideals. Such ideals are transcendent to the conformative framework of the system because they are grounded not in the system in question but in its wider contextualizing system. But this transcendence is a function of the relationship holding between the two systems; what is transcendent for one system need not be for another.

It follows that for any system there must be a contextualizing system the framework of which constitutes its transcendent values. Yet this progression need not have, indeed cannot have, an end. Nor are the transcendent norms changeless. Since they are a function of the system for which they are transcendent ideals, changes in that system—and changes in the varied other systems that as predecessors, successors, or contemporaries share the same contextualizing ideals—lead slowly but surely to changes in its normative character and then lead, more slowly but just as surely, to changes in the character of its transcendent ideals.

Thus, on the one hand, it is true that we cannot see beyond the horizon of our world, where that horizon includes not only a structure of ideals located in its normative framework but also a more vaguely sensed yet still discernable structure of transcendent regulative ideals. Certain ideal possibilities for thought or action will not even be conceivable, given a particular cultural world, and it would be anachronistic for us, if we live within a culture that makes them conceivable, to condemn those from another culture for not having such thoughts much less not having institutionalized what they imply. "You ought to do it" implies not merely "you can do it" but also, and as its precondition, "it is imaginable."

On the other hand, however, it is also true that changes in a worldview come about as the result of thoughts and actions, operating within the constraints of the horizon of that worldview, that alter its subsystems sufficiently to require adaptive adjustments at the most general level. Those changes mean a change in the cultural horizon and may as a consequence reveal new aspects of its nested wider contexts, may make it possible to imagine possibilities before undreamt of, to grasp ideals never before conceived, including even presuppositions about its ontological foundations. In the dialectic of actual worlds and their ideal norms, neither has pride of place. Concrete choices in commitment and practice can change our ideals; our ideals can change the shape of our convictions and our deeds.

Hence from any novel quality of an occurrence or nexus of occurrences a string of possibilities can be traced, each similar to its neighbors, leading to prior prehendable actual features of the world. No matter how novel the novelty might seem, how radical the revolution or cataclysmic the upheaval, no matter how distinctively different it is from some ancestral entity or quality to which it is compared, a pathway runs between them that traverses a landscape of incrementally differing conceptual valuations, reversions, and transmutations—a landscape of conformative, reformative, and transformative variations. There are no gaps because the realm of possibility and the realm of actuality together comprise a single matrix of connectivity. Were there a gap, nothing could follow. *Natura non facit saltum.*

The past is a resource because it is not dead. Its constant closures are never final. What is settled brute fact is not opaque, but shows its origins. It tells us the story of its coming to be our past, which is a story of the multitude of the stories about what others before us have sought and what they achieved, stories about what wasn't achieved, what they failed to achieve, what was lost, cast off, or compromised. The story which we have made our story guides us by its abstract conditions for how we ought and often must conduct our search, and why some pathways are ugly, false, or wrong while others are beautiful, true, and good because of how they go or where they lead.

Our story is not an item of knowledge providing us with answers to all our questions, indeed not even to a single one of them. It is not our teacher because it has no theory to propose, nor a catechism for us to follow. Nor is it a divine monarch, obedience to whose commands will save us. There is just the story, which is many stories, and when we make our story a part of it, we walk with those who have preceded us, accomplishing, as they did, whatever we can manage in the days we have, in the world as we find it. And so, we and our story become of that story an integral everchanging part.

NOTE

1. This chapter, in the sections "Physical Purposes" and "Vague Possibilities," draws from my article "In Defense of Secularizing Whitehead," *Process Studies* 39 (2010): 319–33. Used with permission, all rights reserved.

4

THE SHADOW OF TRUTH

The publication of three sets of student notes from the fall and spring courses Whitehead offered at Harvard and Radcliffe in 1924/1925 afford an interesting glimpse of what he was thinking soon before his 1927/1928 Gifford Lectures, expanded and published in 1929 as *Process and Reality*.[1] In addition to his familiar critique of scientific thought as unhelpfully reductive, Whitehead offers an alternative metaphysical account that includes four notions that resonate nicely with what I have so far been arguing.

One of these notions is his insistence on the dynamic interdependence of a fundamentally atomic actuality, and the failure of science and metaphysics to articulate adequately its complexity. A second notion has to do with the open-ended character of the natural order, and the need for theories about it that echo that openness. Scientific and metaphysical hypotheses need to recognize the ragged edges to their systemic claims, the niches in the boundary walls of what we take to be established truth and acceptable behavior that suggest a need to rethink the grounds for our beliefs and practices.

A third notion is Whitehead's proposal that the coming to be and perishing of things requires a Ground that does neither: The Eternal. As eternal it cannot act and thus cannot change anything, neither itself nor other entities. Yet it can be changed because it is the Past, which is changed constantly by the perishing of present accomplishment. How this can be so leads to Whitehead's fourth notion, the shadow of time, which I will develop into an elaboration of the argument of Chapter

Three that the Past is a sufficient resource for explaining the Creative Advance.

The 1924/1925 Harvard/Radcliffe lectures, edited by Paul A. Bogaard and Jason Bell, and published in 2017, are not a text Whitehead wrote, nor are they notes for his class sessions. They are notes taken by two members of the Harvard philosophy department (W. P. Bell and W. E. Hocking) during his lectures at Emerson Hall, Harvard Yard, plus notes by a graduate student (Louise R. Heath) in parallel lectures he offered the day before or after at Radcliffe College. The notes are not transcriptions. They were created in real time, on the fly, and sometimes after late nights spent on other matters. The notes are similar enough, however, to make citations by each student's name unnecessary. The voice we hear is clearly always Whitehead's.

SIMPLICITY

During his first Harvard lecture, September 24, 1924, and in identical language two days later in the Radcliffe College version of the same lecture, Whitehead says that "Metaphysical Philosophy," the kind of philosophy he is for the first time formally attempting, is "*not* the mere handmaiden of Science," but rather stands "as near to Poetry as to Science, and needs them both" (2017, 5, 413). Whitehead's apparent reason for why metaphysicians needs to use both scientific and poetic methods is because "metaphysics is [the] critical appreciation of [the] whole intellectual background of man's life" (413). It leaves nothing out, because it seeks a critical appreciation of the whole. Hence everything is its subject matter, from one extreme to the other, from the humanities to the sciences, from poetry to mathematics.

That's true enough, but it's too trivial a reason. It's not just that metaphysics deals with everything but that everything is an interdependent whole: "Togetherness of things is *fundamental*. 'Organization' (in Biology) exists only in Relationships. There can't be any one thing (a horse, e.g.) except in certain *circumstances*. Its *happiness* too, a further dependence" (5). The togetherness of things is not a unitary lump; nor is it a heap of separable things, not even a well-ordered heap. Rather, it is a process of events internally related to all other events, "a flowing process of becoming—of *realization*" (5), where all else is the environment for each. "Every entity," says Whitehead, "expresses itself in the whole of reality & [the] rest of reality is patient of it" (416). Everything is distinctively individual but nothing self-sufficient. The world is a boundless process of emergent structures that are transitions to other structures. It is not just any whole, but an unimaginably dense whole, too dense ever to fully grasp.

Why poetry and science are so crucial to metaphysics is that they offer the tools, the methods, by which it can grasp the ungraspable. What these methods are is captured in Whitehead's remark that a "diagram is [the] mathematicians' analogue to Plato's *myth*." Whitehead says he prefers a diagram to a "long verbal statement" because he "can't make up myths!" (172), but it would be more accurate to say that he prefers diagrams to complex mathematical formulae and myths to long verbal statements. Since myths and diagrams are analogues, however, it's not just to diagrams but to myths as well that we can have recourse. To either, as a way to gain access to a world otherwise too dense to be understood.

Whitehead sometimes speaks of a diagram as a picture. It's not, however, in the sense of being a reproduction of some region of reality, because it leaves a lot out. It's a sketch, not a replica. A roadmap is a diagram that excludes everything about an area except its roads, which are enlarged and the details of their shape smoothed for easier recognition. The diagrams Whitehead draws on the blackboard are extreme in what they omit: only a few lines, indicating relationships relevant to what he is discussing, along with letters that name them. "Silly little diagram," Whitehead remarks, but "don't be afraid of being silly sometimes" (133). Besides, it's *"equally* silly to go agitate air with noises and tell people to *understand* them. Make *another* noise and say 'that's what I *mean*'" (328). The advantage of a diagram is that it *"does* preserve that scheme of relationships which are relationships *among* the internal relationships" (328). It discloses the form of the basic relationships of a complex reality while stripping away the confusing details not relevant to the analysis.

The same is true of myths, which may be thought of as verbal diagrams that "give you an easier picture," a way "more convenient, psychologically, to reason" about some particularly complicated things (26). Myths are not limited to the humanities, since they are used in science with respect to what Whitehead calls "ultimate presuppositions" such as electrons or quanta. "Electrons are mere myth," he says, "a way of stating things" (425). Calling an electron a myth, however, isn't saying it's a useful fairy tale about something that isn't there. It is useful only if grounded in verified facts and subject to a formal analysis which gives rise to further verified facts. Electrons refer to objective features of the world, but ones best dealt with in mythic terms. A certain kind of electro-magnetic field, which we call an electron, is a flux of energy that we can take as having a vibratory "character with a focal centre." This electron is not a concrete thing, however, but "that *type* of vibration with that location" (26). It's a useful way of talking about something very complicated. Like using graphs in dealing with unemployment data. The graphs are a helpful way to clarify complex trends, but they would be worthless "if there were no such thing as Unemployment in the Nation," if there were no unemployed people whose numbers were actually being totaled (26). Myths require facts but are not reducible to them, for like diagrams they make visible what the facts in their millions obscure.

"We habitually reason and think with *surrogates*" (26), of which diagrams and myths are important examples. They are our way of making sense of things, interpreting them in ways we find meaningful. We do this by abstraction: isolating a particular fact from its environment, and identifying, by how we select it, its value for us, its relevance to our aims. Abstracting a fact from the intertwined complexity of the world is not an arbitrary process. It is not, as Locke or Hume would claim, simply a matter of a mind observing "sense-data and spatio-temporal relations between them." Nor is it, as contemporary science would have it, "energies" that *are nothing but* their "Spatio-temporal adventures" (24). Both of these extreme approaches lose sight of their point of departure, substituting what they have abstracted for what they abstracted from. Whitehead wonders what has become of "ordinary entities, which in ordinary life we 'observe'—Sounds and Sights bars of iron and green trees and birds, bodily feelings of wide gradations, watches etc." (24).

He proposes a different approach, one that remains connected to the complexity of things, suggesting that there are "three types of entity" we need "to play with" in order to give an adequate account of what is involved in having an experience. First, "Observers"; second, "Things observed," which is the "Field of Display"; and third, "the

Physical Field," which is the "Field of Control" (24–25). These three types of entity are related: "The Display *is* what it *is* now; but . . . is always *for* something else. *For* an Observer," and because of conditions that have led to the Display and to its likely consequences (27). These conditions are the Field of Control, which is the background context for both Display and Observer, accounting for how what is displayed came to be so displayed and to what end. This triad of abstractions explicates abstraction by calling attention to how an abstraction is made: by an Observer, who distinguishes the immediate perceptual Display of an object by the use of contextual Controls which single out that object and explain its character, and which also provide an insight into the concrete whole from which the Observer has abstracted the Display.

Understanding this to be how an abstraction is accomplished raises the important question of its value. Why focus on certain features of experience rather than others? Because doing so is an effective tool with which to further some purpose—like validating a scientific hypothesis or creating a valuable work of art. Thus, Devices like myths and diagrams can be thought of as Controls for determining how data are selected and how organized. And if they illuminate our sensory and cognitive capacities effectively, they will have furthered our knowledge and its usefulness, its truth and its value, by allowing our imagination to see possibilities that can provide better controls and better aims, while recognizing their unavoidable imperfections, the need for constant revision. Thinking with surrogates is not merely a useful habit, it's a necessary one. "With man," says Whitehead, "it is not possible to deal with [the] universe without abstraction" (219).

A clear example that Whitehead discusses at length is the concept in geometry of a point-instant. We understand the notion of something being right here just now, but it's a quite vague notion, ambiguous as to how it might be taken. The mathematician eliminates "the prolixity and pitfalls of ordinary language" (211) by abstracting from the concrete notion of "here" until its ambiguity is purged: a point is a spatial location that has no length, breadth, or depth. It can be uniquely defined by three spatial coordinates x,y,z. The notion of "now" adds a fourth coordinate, t, indicating the point's temporal location. Point-instants are thus "very high abstractions" (267), achieving "exactment" by an "enormous simplification of thought"—by what Whitehead calls "cognitive gelding" (197).

Exactment has an additional virtue, an emotional one. It "calms the air of excited mystery" that often surrounds things which because of their complexity or beauty or novelty are felt to be marvels beyond our ken, uncanny conundrums of overwhelming significance. Scientists are trained to see things in terms of abstractions, permitting them to remain unexcited in their pursuit of what is objectively the case. As Whitehead puts it, for example, "The Scientist doesn't want his heart to 'leap up' when he beholds the rainbow." Instead, he "gets out his spectroscope" (56). Or consider the discovery of irrational numbers like $\sqrt{-1}$, which seemed to the Greeks an uncanny kind of number. It was useful, however, and so was used—although sparingly and always with a certain unease. When mathematicians finally worked out its exact meaning within a theory of numbers, its mystery was toned down enough, so that scientists—and metaphysicians—would know exactly what they were thinking about and so could deal with its ontological importance without confusion (266).

RAGGED EDGES

The problem for Whitehead is not exactment. Not only does he insist that the precision gained by abstraction is necessary in order to understanding our experiences but also that it is useful, and most importantly so with respect to the high-level abstractions of mathematics utilized by scientists in developing and testing their hypotheses. Abstraction is both necessary and useful, but it can also be dangerous if its limits are not recognized. We are familiar with what Whitehead calls the "Fallacy of Misplaced Concreteness," the mistake of confusing abstractions with the concreteness from which they have been abstracted (2017, 43). However, Whitehead notes as well the parallel problem of excessive effort to achieve exactment, the attempt to be more precise than our interpretation requires: committing the "Fallacy of Misplaced Abstractness" (473).

The art of reasoning is to arrange our abstractions "so they bring out by their very nature" what is important about what is being investigated, fashioning a sort of picture of the logical relations in their formal side (199). Effective reasoning requires being master of our techniques, exploiting them as far as appropriate, but knowing and respecting their limits. It means knowing how much exactness is worth putting in, not letting technique obscure the aesthetics of our subject matter but also not letting the aesthetics obscure the formal relationalities involved. Mathematical precision and emotive significance are "intense" ways of interpretation. Whitehead recommends, instead, "the Peacock's way" (211): distributing the intensity, as a peacock does when spreading its tail, so that contrasting or even mutually exclusive features are harmonized rather than one of them dominating while the other is discarded.

The aim of science may be at theories verified by established fact, but its key tool is the use of hypotheses, which are effective insofar as they offer what Whitehead calls a "vague apprehension of a vague sort of relationship" (242). A hypothesis pushes out *beyond* what is clearly and obviously fact," beyond exact data and tested theories. It directs attention to possibilities of connection not previously explored, ones offering thereby a wider although fuzzier grasp of things (241). A habit of formulating promising hypotheses cultivates the "vividness and delicacy of appreciation" that prepares the mind for imagining what was assumed to be unimaginable, for noticing what otherwise would go unnoticed. "You do not perceive what you're not prepared to perceive." Even what proves to be a false hypothesis, Whitehead adds, can lead to a "right type of observation" (242).

This is what poetry gladly does and that science needs to do as well. A great poem evokes a feeling that the poet "has gone beyond [his or her] own direct experience." We may eventually forget the details of the poem, but our "apprehension of wonder" that it kindled remains. Whitehead, having just said that the scientist should avoid the wondrously befuddling excitement of seeing a rainbow in order to focus on identifying its cause, now applauds experiencing the wonder of a rainbow or a skylark's song at dawn (242). But as always, it's the middle way to which we are directed. On the one hand, hypothesizing can easily be little more than fantasizing, a matter of imagination run wild. We need to be able to identify and "to have firmness of mind to discard what won't hold water" (248). On the other hand, our hypotheses can be controlled by "lazy assumptions" about the adequacy of familiar truths. We should not develop a habit of constantly rejecting new ideas because of the risk of them failing.

It helps in avoiding these extremes to take account in some regular fashion of work going on in other fields, both those closely related and those less obviously so. There is a danger in both science and philosophy of engaging in "detailed subtlety without a broad view," pursuing "a lot of niggling investigations that lead nowhere," that have "no relevance to anything" (250). There is not anything wrong with detailed subtlety, of course. When specialized efforts become an end in themselves, when we fail to understand the details of what we accomplish as having a wider relevance, our work will have limited value because done unaware of other investigations with which it is incompatible. Our results will confirm a narrow purpose while ignoring or being ignorant of conflicting purposes. Such conflicts need to be taken seriously, which means recognizing that we need to widen our perspective. You "can't get a correction" to the clash of established theories "without a wider harmony," without a hypothesis that reaches beyond what has been rationally justified and empirically verified. "You will not get something you *Know* is true. But you will get [a] *'well-grounded' hypothesis*; and you've taught yourself to be imaginative without any danger of running wild" (248). It is in the *"irrationality"* of scientific or metaphysical knowledge "that you'll find [the] best ground for revision" (248). For "when you've got *hold* of your Concept," your working hypothesis, "you'll find some things it doesn't explain—rough edges" (21) that suggest there is "something behind your symbols which when elucidated leads to something" which, because of your narrow focus, you had been unaware (250).

Get up against the rough edges of thought, Whitehead advises, although it "depends on *how* rough as to what you do." For instance, "Quantum *vs*. Wave Theory on *face* of them quite contradictory. But each [are] explaining so much that you can't believe either quite wrong" (21). You have to use "*Common sense* about judging your rough edges" (22), how in this case to reconcile the fundamental differences between these two fundamental theories, or somehow to affirm them both despite their incompatibility. Sometimes those detailed subtleties and niggling trivialities, freed from narrow-visioned understandings, can be "*Minute Clues*" to a needed rethinking of the truths we think self-evident. "Very trivial facts" can have *"enormous* importance," as for instance it was noting the "*slight* difference of atomic weights in isolating Nitrogen" that led to the discovery of Argon; it was paying attention to the "silly little shifting" in the orbit of Uranus that led to the discovery of Neptune (22). A good hypothesis, in other words, "must always allow for ragged-edges" (488).

It is a boon to our attempted mastery of abstractions when the tools we use are able to reveal their own limits, to display not only the features they are designed to emphasize but also their boundaries, the perimeter of their expertise—thereby revealing their beyond. Diagrams and myths do this fairly well because they are so obviously partial. A diagram is a sketch, calling attention not only to a formal pattern otherwise easily overlooked, but also acknowledging by its sketchiness that there are all sorts of other things that obviously had to be excluded in doing so, some of which might nonetheless justify being seriously looked at afresh. A myth is a story, a verbal account of something that begins with some event, from which it moves along to other events until it comes to the one where it ends. The story conveys more than it says, however, not only pointing to truths about those events that might otherwise be overlooked but also conveying a realization that the story goes ever on, toward unexamined consequences and further unmentioned episodes. To put it in a slightly different way, diagrams and myths are open-ended. They point beyond themselves, revealing that there is more than what they are equipped to articulate.

The creative possibilities of rough edges are ontological as well as epistemological. Rough edges are features not only of how we think, our hypothesizing prowess, but also of how the world works, how it can be a continuum of atomic individuals. On the one hand, the world is composed of finite actualities, emergent momentary events, unique particulars that are "mere flashes in the pan" (140). Now this flash; now that one; now yet another. On the other hand, the world is marked by things that are not atomic, things that endure, that are systemic, stable, well-ordered complexes that persist over time. These enduring entities remain a unified whole even as they grow or shrink or oscillate, move about and pursue ends, adapt to changing conditions or disintegrate: electrons and molecules, organisms and environments, planets and galaxies. The world is fundamentally oxymoronic: an atomic continuum, a momentary stability. In short, a reality with a flourishing of ragged edges that only myths can express adequately.

The scientific myth which can help us explore the incompatible features of the metaphysical oxymoron of atomic durations is the one about the evolution of our cosmos. For in the beginning, there were the mere flashes, the momentary achievements: emerging and perishing in bursts of actualization. Slowly, however, these kinds of entities became "self-propagating," replicating themselves in successors that in turn did likewise, fashioning links between bursts that served as a "basis for Endurance" (140). These linkages made possible longer and more expansive forms of enduring that came eventually to comprise a stable "Environment," an "Order of Nature" that augmented the likelihood of entities successfully enduring and propagating successors similar to themselves, "an order growing in its achievement of Value by its achievement of Endurance" (140). The stability of an environment is what made possible "this evolution of *Similar Things*." Early on, an "enormous number of Electrons" were propagated, and then protons, which "evolve[d] into higher types," combining in complex ways that eventually resulted in 92 basic kinds of molecules, and after billions of years in stars with planets, and on some of those planets millions of species of organisms, and on our planet a very few "types of *men*!" (141).

Enduring entities are dependent on their environment and it on them. "Each entity *takes account of* [its] surrounding field and vice versa. . . . The Entity then isn't the Entity in itself alone but in interaction with [its] Environment" (93). The atom, in other words, is not actually isolated. Its relationship to other atoms is not, as atomists from the Greeks to Newton contended, only external. Its relations are internal, such that "apart from its Environment, Entity has lost individuality." Abstract it from its "particular Spatio-temporal root," from its "anchorage in the Environment," and it has lost its uniqueness, lost that which makes it "this" entity and not a place holder for any entity with similar characteristics (115). The emergence of a momentary atomic achievement depends on what its environment allows, what the stability of its context makes possible. Yet since that context is composed of enduring entities which are composed of momentary ones, and since its emergence is the achievement of value, then "the whole of what there is in realization is things becoming of Value to one another" (71).

Environmental stability is relative, not absolute, an "Evolution toward Stability" through a slow "modification" of the environment to the benefit of the kinds of things already adapted to it (141). Were this the whole story, however, there could never be novelty because novelty requires instability, and without novelty there could be no modification, slow or otherwise, of the environment. The emergence of novelties, of new kinds of things, "takes place at an Edge between two Environments—between two fair stabilities with just enough Instability there" for novel things to be formed (141–42). Yet with just enough stability for them once formed to reproduce sufficient others like themselves to comprise a flourishing new kind of thing. "Creative Activity," says Whitehead, is "not an independent Substance but *emergent* upon occasions from *possibilities* of relationship." It emerges "by reason of the niche which is there for it in the Universe" (356). Niches, rough edges, or simply Edges: they are Whitehead's many names for pathways into what lies beyond the established boundaries of the extant world. They are faults in the stable order of things through which new possibilities arise, opportunities for new variations, or versions, or even new kinds of achievement.

The relationship of two different kinds of stable environment with their differing kinds of stable entities creates a minor instability along their adjacent edges, a niche chipped away from the continuity of their shared boundary, a slight breach creating an openness that is neither one environment nor the other. A crack of some sort in the established order of things can offer an opportunity to escape the repression of unsuitable possibilities, to be free to achieve something different, to create a novel variant that until then had been impossible. Or alternatively, it can offer an opportunity to escape any such variant if it is taken as a threat to the established order of things, avoiding it long enough to multiply sufficiently to be able to fashion a suitable environment for itself. "Translating the niche *qua* Potentiality to [the] niche *qua* Actuality" requires the "Creative Energy" for achieving definite novel individual embodiment of that energy (361) within a suitable environment, an environment "with a patience for reiteration of that [novel] Character" (362). By such inventiveness are new species of organism born, new kinds of actions taken, new physical or cultural worlds created, a cosmos transformed.

THE ETERNAL

In all that Whitehead has been arguing so far, his ontology is of a fundamentally temporal cosmos marked by creative explorations that push beyond the given in ways that preserve things as they change them. However, when Whitehead addresses the question of how the evolution from momentary atoms to enduring environments is possible, and also how stable enduring environments can be transformed into different but nonetheless still stable environments, he finds an appeal to temporal processes insufficient. We need, he argues, "some *ground* of things by virtue of which they are what they are." We need an "eternal principle which carries with it the solution (from within!) of these questions. Something self-explanatory" (2017, 55).

A flash in the pan has no awareness of any flashes occurring before it or after it. It is the present emerging out of the resources available to it, without any awareness (in the generic sense of prehension) of the specific source of any resource or even any awareness that there are such things as sources. Self-propagation, however, requires a sense of there being the possibility of more than present achievement, namely a repeat of that kind of achievement. It is not the particular flash-in-the-pan fact that recurs, because it's not possible that what is uniquely this determinate moment can reoccur. Rather, it is the kind of fact that recurs, a fact similar to the achieved fact, a successor very much like itself. This entails an efficacy of generalities: the constitutive functioning of moments as a kind, of which the present emerging moment is an instance. Achievements as a kind must be possible, particular moments occurring not simply as particular but at the same time as members of a sequence of instances of a kind. "*Whenever* you get anything general you've got something that lies *beyond* [any] particular occasion" (57). There must be something else beyond the temporal now and the particular fact therein achieved, beyond what come to be and perish, that makes possible their transformation into kinds and thereby environments and worlds. When you talk of such a reality, "you're essentially presupposing the *Eternal*" (57).

The reason Whitehead calls this source of generality "the Eternal" has to do with what its nature must be in order to carry out its function. It cannot be an actual entity, nor an environment of interlocking enduring things, because such things are finite, bounded by a particular location at a particular time, no matter how extensive or enduring. Whereas what is needed is something that is a feature of every emergent actual entity and hence every enduring complexity. Something that is "The 'Static Basis' gives the character to the process of Realization" because it is found in all occasions. "We can know nothing which is not embodied in the occasion that we are apprehending," but what we are aware of that is general "in making that occasion what it is . . . must turn up in any other occasion what is relevant to that one." If an entity "is in any way connected with" another entity, "then the Eternal of the one must be Eternal of the other" (58). Furthermore, emerging entities are not points at instants but moments with spatial and temporal volume. Because this is so, they can be organized into systems that sustain a pattern of value with spatial breadth and temporal duration adequate enough to support the coming to be and perishing of those momentary components. But the Ground that makes it possible for particular things to emerge and for patterns of their achievements to form and endure cannot be spatio-temporal because it is what they presuppose. The Eternal is therefore immortal not everlasting, not "always enduring but something *out of* Space and Time" (59).

In chapter 1, I argued that Whitehead's attempting to reconcile essentially temporal actual entities with God's eternal primordial nature is incoherent. He gives us some leeway here, however, if we do not take what he is saying literally. The only way "The Eternal" can be understood is mythically, for myth can hold contradictory claims together as a tension rather than an incoherence. To be momentary or to endure is to be essentially temporal, but to be eternal is essentially not to be temporal; the Eternal is both. Let's take this notion of the Eternal as mythic, embrace its silliness, and refuse either to reject the notion out of hand or to rush blindly into a seemingly obvious harmonization of its oxymoronic meaning. Let's rub close to this myth's rough edges and see where that leads us.

The Ground of the momentary events that comprise the world must be a general not a specific reality if it is to make them relevant to each other. It must be omnipresent if the world is to be one cosmos, an interdependent unity of finite components. But how does this account for the emergence of stable systems, of a cosmic environment, an order of nature characterized by long-enduring laws? Whitehead's answer is that how the Eternal functions is by "conditioning the processional Realization" (61). He explains that "to condition is to impose limitation," which in an environment of other entities and their possibilities "means essentially the reference to alternatives inherent in that particular occasion of Realization" It means that "what is infinite" can be "bounded by something if its own kind—the 'Alternative'" (61), which are possibilities realizable on a given occasion, and what is not realizable on that occasion is, for that occasion, impossible. "All reference to *Possibility* is a reference to some ground which is *in* the Occasion but which is not occasional – Same holds for Impossibility" (60).

Emergent moments are not arbitrary achievements, random possibilities realized while others are ignored. Such a helter-skelter process would not be processive; it would be chaotic not cosmic. For there to be an ordered process of coming to be and perishing, there must be a limit on any nascent actual entity to what is possible for it, within the confines of which a unique new moment can be made. "The how of limitation is the Eternal. How *fact does come before* us in a plurally monadic form" (60). The procession of the world is plurally monadic because the Eternal limits what is possible for an emerging moment, but does not determine what can be done with those possibilities that remain. "The 'how' of limitation" is "also the transcendence of limitation" (60). The moment made is self-made within constraints inherent in its situation. "Each [moment] emerges in respect to its *own* grounds" (93). What Whitehead will later call the Creative Advance is "not managed from Without by a stage-manager" but is "all-inclusive/self-explanatory." It "embodies in itself its own conditions, includes its own motive which can therefore be conceived as the reason for the passing, and its 'How'" (92).

The Eternal is not a stage manager because it is not an agent. Doing something is an action, a behavior, which involves orientation toward realizing a possibility. For Whitehead, teleonomic behavior is a feature not only of any organism but of any entity whatsoever. To be actual is to have been made, and making is a process directed by an agent toward the realization of a possible outcome. The Eternal is the Ground of these created things but not their creator. Whitehead's Eternal is not a Divine Creator, not a Demiurge, not even the God of *Process and Reality*, all of which are agents shaping the world as best they can toward ends they envision. But if it cannot choose the possibilities that are to be available for what emerges each moment, how does the Eternal function? It limits not by choosing but by disclosing, and what is available for disclosure yet not within the inherit capacities of an emerging moment are the facts of what have proceeded it, the context of the prior achievements that comprise the emergent's environment. That is, its past.

An event occurs, and then is no more, but if what has passed away were simply gone then there would be no limits to what in the emerging moment was possible. So the limitation of possibilities is necessary to there being a cosmos, and therefore it must be the case that what perishes does not pass away. Our intuitions, Whitehead insists, confirm this ontological fact, for we all have a "*Sense of Intrinsic permanence of the Value that has been achieved*" (72). Whitehead references Keats, presumably the last stanza of "The Eve of St. Agnus" which begins:

> And they are gone: aye, ages long ago
> These lovers fled away into the storm.

Gone, yes, but not forgotten. Fled away, yet passionately remembered, memories always there to be recalled. "The *irrevocable* Past as yet the *relevant* past" (2017, 72).

So how the Eternal shapes the course of things without being an agent is as the receptacle for actualities that were present in their moment of achievement but are now no longer present. Their actuality is nonetheless relevant to their successors because it is retained by the Eternal, included in the emerging of new actualities as limitations on what could possibly emerge. "Every definite occasion points beyond itself by enriching the Eternal," (74), thus taking "its place as an eternal truth" (75). The truth of what is past, the value of definite achievement, is a fact that cannot be avoided, that must be taken account of. The heritage of the new is the irrevocable condition for what it can become. It is a constraint, but in the form of a structure. A limit is not only a barrier eliminating certain opportunities for what might be realized again; it is also a channel affording access to opportunities previously not possible. The pathway through a dense forest constrains us to walk between narrow boundaries, but those constraints offer us a way to reach a destination that otherwise would not be possible. "A Structure is a definite limitation amid an unbounded . . . *ocean* of *possibilities*" (91). It is the shape of the process by which something can be realized—a framework that liberates by limiting. The Past, preserved by the Eternal, is the "How" of emergence, the mode of "becoming in *this* particular and definite way!" (91).

This is an argument filled with dramatic implications. Whitehead has been elaborating a concept of the Eternal as the timeless ground which is necessary for a world where coming to be and perishing can lead to stable environments capable of supporting enduring forms of achievement, including limited forms of novel achievement that make possible the stabilization of some of those novelties and so the emergence of different enduring forms of achievement. He has called this ground 'The Eternal' because it is timeless and boundless, and is thus the obvious contradictory of whatever is temporal and finite, and therefore changing. Yet Whitehead is also arguing that the Eternal changes, because it is continually being enriched by what has perished. The Eternal changes, and it does so because of what is temporal. It cannot change on its own initiative; it can do so only because of the temporal. Crucially, however, not because of the temporal as such, but because of each particular temporal individual's influence. "Value as shaped and particularized upon any finite occasion is the Eternal captured by the finite. But that's all the Eternal *can do*:—to become so captured" (71), because only agents can act and only actual entities can be agents. "Emergent Value is 'The Capture of the Eternal'—What *has* been is an eternal fact that nothing can blot out," but it is an eternal fact "held and captured there and now" by a temporal fact in the making (87).

Obviously, the next question to ask is: how can what perishes change what is not perishable? By perishing, says Whitehead. Because "*as* the Eternal *is now* for *us*," it is likewise for any past "now," for all the entities comprising it. So "the total nature of the past belongs to it" (74); the Eternal gets altered because it is constantly enriched by new facts. The total nature of the past changes each moment it is augmented by a present achievement perishing, so the conditions by which the Eternal limits the emerging present are constantly changed by the specific achievements of its predecessors. When we remember some past event, the truth of what it once was influences our remembering, changing our general sense of the past because of its particular relevance. As with memory so with all else: "Each fact of realization takes its place as an eternal truth" that influences whatever happens, altering in some way the character of its influence. Indeed, the "very laws of Nature are relevant to the past," and so altered under its influence (75).

Whitehead then draws an even more radical conclusion: "The eternal is nothing but the *Unity* of its limitations" (76). Truth is fundamentally about realization: the truth of a fact is its realization, and the eternal truth of this realized fact is its alteration of the Eternal. Furthermore, because a truth is a particular realization, the value achievement of an atomic fact, the How of its realization is "always a *particularized How*—having relevance to the particular" (87). Consequently, the character of the Eternal is thus always altered in a particular way, in a manner particularly relevant to the particular current situation, always changing in specific ways as specific new realizations become specific new eternal facts. These limits set by the Eternal are thus always context-sensitive, always located within an environment because of which the influence of those limits can endure, and thereby can contribute to the preservation and growth of the temporal value of subsequent limits.

A radical consequence of this radical claim is that change is boundless. "As Nature arose, it may decay." We need to recognize the possibility, says Whitehead, of "an Evolution of the very order of Nature," that the "Spatio-temporal system and the Sensibles" that comprise "the static ground of being in *this* order of Evolution," may be the "actual product of other orders of Evolution" (136). "Cosmology is itself an issue from something else" (461). This is not to imagine some kind of linear progression originating at "a time before there was time—which is nonsense" (138). We cannot start the evolution of the Cosmic Order from some ex nihilo "arbitrary starting point" or from some aboriginal "arbitrarily given stuff." Instead, we need to think in terms of expansions. "The Cosmic Order presupposes an Expansion which stands behind (beyond) it." But not simply one expansion. There are *"various stages"* of expansion such that our "Cosmological Stage presupposes other stages that provide [the] very ground of *Becoming* for [the] Cosmological stage." Whitehead knows he is going beyond what can be observed, but "not beyond what has been found necessarily . . . to give any rational account of Cosmological order" (136). Metaphysicians are too apt to embrace a "World-Elephant-Tortoise philosophy, but we mustn't stop with [the] Tortoise just because [our] brain doesn't want to go further" (143). Reality is an evolutionary process, without a beginning and without an end, without a least expansion and without a most.

What is temporal captures the Eternal, and as completed fact becomes itself eternal, thereby changing the Eternal. The eternal is temporal and the temporal eternal. Having said these things, and drawing a little diagram of how it works, Whitehead notes that *"this* is a *myth* too—drawn on black board" (87). We can see why metaphors are so important for metaphysics, for thinking creatively and hence for understanding a world restlessly changing, inherently evolutionary. For both metaphors and worlds create instability, by virtue of which new possibilities emerge that give rise to novel achievements—achievements initially individual but eventually collective, achievements initially a threat to the stability they eventually secure by altering it. A metaphor is a paradox, a cognitive contradiction held together because of the fresh possibilities it discloses, and thereby fosters. The cosmos is an ontological paradox, a constant clash of conflicting actual stabilities that foster the fresh possibilities from which is fashioned the creative advance that makes our actual cosmos an ongoing adventure. "What an extraordinarily *odd* fact *definiteness* of achievement is," exclaims Whitehead (361): a particular individual, momentary or enduring, emergent from a particular contextual disunity without which it could not be; a collective whole, cosmic or cultural, emergent from a radical plurality of incompatible particulars, without which it could not be. No wonder only metaphors can express metaphysical truths adequately.

ACTIVE SHADOWS

I will now turn to a particular phrase that Whitehead uses briefly but never explicates: the "shadow of truth." I think it gives us a crucial insight into Whitehead's metaphysics, exposing a niche that opens that metaphysics to new and enhancing possibilities. An account of "the shadow of truth" is, of course, a myth about a metaphor, and like any such metaphor it harbors destabilizing possibilities. Shadows are created by opaque objects intercepting a field of light, leaving a dark area behind them in an outline of their shape. A shadow is an absence. Truth is a primary feature of any fact, a feature without which it is not fact, without which it has no intrinsic value. Truth is a presence. Whitehead's myth tells us about an absence that is a presence, because it makes a difference for what has presence, and that in doing so makes a difference for what is absent because yet only possible.

At first glance, Whitehead's statements about the shadow of truth are like those we have already considered. Truth is about the process of making a unique fact. The truth of that fact is its realization, how its possibilities have issued in a particularized moment, how a specific actual matter-of-fact has been achieved. The Past is the irrevocable totality of those facts which, because of features of the Eternal ingredient in each new process of making, limit its possible outcomes. In this sense the Truth which is the Past is the shadow that falls on the emerging present, shaping its particular characteristics, the shadow that likewise falls on the Eternal, shaping its characteristics as well. "The shadow of truth" is a metaphor, however, and metaphors have difficulty holding their concepts firmly within boundaries. Unintended new possibilities keep bubbling up. The interpretation I will now sketch explores one of those possibilities.

Whitehead uses the phrase "shadow of truth" on three occasions. The first time is eye-opening. After stating that "every definite occasion points beyond itself by enriching the Eternal," he adds that this involves "enrichment of realm of Existents (=Platonic Ideas)," which is an "Essential attribute of [the] Eternal" (2017, 74). The Eternal sets limits to the emerging present not only by the constraints imposed by the prior achievements it makes present, but also by constraining the pure possibilities that are available. The whole realm of ideas "itself alters in its reference to the particular occasion as they flow by. *How* it gets altered:—the shadow of truth falls on it . . . and affects it" (74–75). What is meant by "affecting" is soon clarified: "The shadow of truth falls on the ideas (makes them particular—in enriched envisagement), and as such are taken up into memory" (77). Truth is a matter of realization, so it is definite fully realized actual entities that in their perishing cast a shadow of the truth of their achieved reality on the realm of ideas, on the realm of the totality of possibilities for realization, altering some of those possibilities by making them no longer merely generic but rather particular envisagements. That's how the Past influences the Present: by the shadow of prior achievements transforming pure possibilities into relevant ones by particularizing them. The particularization of a possibility narrows its scope, limiting it to a possibility that is possible only in the specific context of a newly emerging successor entity.

Almost all pure possibilities are impossible for an emerging entity, given the physical massive constraint imposed by the world's widespread and long-enduring stable environment. However, there are always a few possibilities about which that environment, as Whitehead puts it, will be patient. How the shadow functions is by tailoring those few possibilities to the entity's particular context, sharpening them into opportunities for realization. The particularization of a possibility gives it value for the emerging entity, a way by which to unify its myriad constraints and options. By valuing that particularized possibility and further particularizing it, or by disvaluing or even eliminating it, and similarly for all other real possibilities and impossibilities, the emergent thereby achieves realization as a fact. The final integration of fixed limitations and viable possibilities is the entity's work, but the shadow of things already fled away into the storm heightens the value of certain possibilities rather than others, suggesting ways by which that integration might best be achieved. Note that this means the Past is what makes novel possibilities relevant, not God. And it makes them relevant not by any purposive intent, not by a function of some transient final cause, but by the character of what it is. The shadow cast by perishing achievements conveys the possibility of fresh alternatives, often by conveying the impossibility of most of them.

Whitehead's second use of "shadow of truth" emphasizes its particularizing function: "The process of Realization is a process of *Garnering in*. You have 'The Shadow of Truth.' Therefore, the How is always a *particularized* How" (87) resulting in "a particularized value" (89). The shadow of truth is "how" the constraints and opportunities are garnered in, by which the results of prior realization are able to afford a transition to new realization. It is because of the shadow cast by the fading past that the transition is effected. A truth is always particular; it is what a fact is. The term "truth" can also be an abstraction, a useful way to generalize, to refer to multiple particular truths with respect to some common feature. Concretely, however, a truth is always a specific fact and its shadow is therefore always particular. What influences the emergence of a novel actual entity is not The Past, understood generically as the totality of things gone, ages long ago.

What influences its emergence is each of a number of particular achieved actual entities contiguous to it, those lovers fled away. Yet not those themselves, for they have perished ages long ago. Rather, the particular shadows they cast have confronted the nascent succeeding moments with what they had to accept, with what they could alter, and with the value of each altering. Past actual entities and enduring objects, and all that they have achieved, are what cannot be altered. The niches among these ineluctable facts are what point a way to some possible alterings in their successors. The shadow cast on the wall by settled fact reveals ragged edges that offer niches of opportunity for innovations to establish themselves, providing their nascent successors with the information they require to depart from a repetition of what has passed. And in turn, they in their own perishing will cast new particular shadows influencing how their successors' successors will emerge into an already different world.

The conditions a past actual entity's shadow imposes on each of its nascent immediate successors were shaped by the shadows its immediate predecessors imposed on it, and similarly for the predecessors of those predecessors, ad infinitum. Much like, at the macro level: as we influence our children, so our parents influenced us, and so they were influenced by their parents, and so on back generation after generation, each prior generation expanding the number of relevant ancestors but diminishing the importance of any one of them. Each moment perishes and is no more, but what it became in becoming that moment influences in some way its successors, the more time that passes the less the particular influence but the wider its scope.

It is not only an entity's vital presence that perishes, but also most of the content of that presence. When she was still living, my grandmother's actions had an immediate impact on her children, but she died years ago. Her shadow is all that remains, simply an aspect of what she was, her influence on me now only a nudge, a suggestion. Her shadow will grow more vague for my children and even more for my children's children, my grandmother's influence becoming increasingly indirect, an aspect of an aspect of an aspect. That young couple we once knew (or were) are still fondly recalled, but they themselves are gone forever, their importance for us already obscured by the swirling ravages of time.

As I briefly indicated earlier, this sequential transmission of influence is what Whitehead calls a "strain of control." My examples have been of thin sequences, lacking any similar parallel sequences, as though I were the only one my grandmother influenced, the only one remembering the young couple. Whenever my siblings and I recall something our grandmother did or said, however, the impact of her life increases. The impact of the young unnamed couple is considerable, thanks to Keats's poem. The impact of George Washington much greater, that of Jesus or Mohamed even more so. The impact of trillions of momentary achievements replicating themselves and the patterns of influence they have inherited over millennia and across vast spaces has such a powerful impact that it leaves no room for their successors to do more than pass on what they have received.

And yet bacteria mutate, species evolve, mountains push up and wear down, stars are born and disintegrate, and modes of cosmos are supplanted, due to the accumulation of opportune niches in the widespread intransigence. An event of any sort is a "*pattern* of aspects. And this pattern is nothing but the aspect in *this* event of the mutual determination of Events." An event "is an essential unity of a pattern of Aspects and these *include* 'Aspect of Control'—mutual determination of events" (168). "Science is the study of the point of view (side) of control, abstracting from the point of view of appearance" (471). It studies the strains of aspect inheritance that create the continuities, the stable patterns, we count on, "just that connection of Events on which our whole life is based" (168). Whitehead uses a number of times the same concrete example of a "school-boy catching a cricket-ball in an important game" (427) The boy sees the ball batted into the air, and runs toward the point where he predicts he will need to be in order to catch it. The ball he sees includes "data appearing as issuing from a strain of control," the "Perceptual object" (325), and the pattern of that data is a parabola that in his mind's eye guides him to the crucial location at the proper time.

"Activity . . . is what makes [the] process of realization possible," and therefore we should pay attention to "Entities discerned as setting the conditions satisfied by [the] concrete procession of reality itself." That is, we should look for "strains of self-conditioning process, . . . strain[s] of conditioning (of control)," which involve "an insistent localization of control" (31). I take "self-conditioning" to mean the strains conditioning the "concrete procession of reality itself" (31): the momentary facts, the actual entities, which come to be and perish. The evolution from flashes in the pan to massive strains of environmental stability, from trivialities to the flourishing of enduring entities and continuing diversity in such entities, is the work of those entities themselves, from the very simple to the very complex. The ontology of our cosmos is built up from a base of particular moments of achievement and the shadows they cast on their successors, without a need for any underlying primary ground or overarching primary control.

Whitehead's third reference to the shadow of truth widens the horizon of relevance from the procession of achievements in our particular cosmos to the procession of modes of cosmos. For the "Order of Nature is in a sense a *particular* entity; and defines *particular facts*" (144). It is that Order, that systematic framework for endurance and change, which is key to a cosmos, its "particular limitation in this particularity of being realized." It is the mode of a particular cosmos's realization, "having the processional, but transitional character which relates it to [a] *wider* community of modes" (144). The ordering framework for our mode of cosmos is the three dimensions of space and the single dimension of time. Whitehead speculates about what there might be in our cosmos that points beyond it to something else, something that might comprise the defining character of another mode of cosmos. He mentions "those data of Rationality which insistently refuse to put [them]selves under spatio-temporal guise (Arithmetic; Logic; Minds themselves)" (145). There is nothing contingent about the fact that 2+2=4, that if "p" is true and "q" is true then "p&q" is true, and that an idea exists independently of any time when or place where it is thought. Because Whitehead thinks they are not plausibly reducible to actualities defined by a physical location, he argues that they "are emergent entities that have their roots in a wider cosmos, and simply their aspects in [our] order of nature" (147).

Thus, not only can we theorize abstractly about modes of cosmos other than our own, with their distinctive orders of nature, but some of those "Potentialities for Order of Nature" (145) "have already on them the shadow of actuality of another cosmos" (147). What is strikingly different in what Whitehead is saying here from what he said about the evolution of modes of cosmos is that multiple modes of cosmos other than our own are said to actually now exist, and we are aware of them because the shadow of their actuality can be found in entities in our cosmos that are not actual, in the sense of not being particular achievements that come to be and perish. Whitehead also mentions, referencing Bergson's *Matter and Memory*, "the idea of Spirit" (144).

GROUNDLESS POWERS

The Past was posited by Whitehead as a mode of being so that past entities could have the ontological standing that seemed needed for them to have the impact they clearly have. They must *be* in some sense, even though they have perished as actual beings. But this Past, with its ever-changing content, then needs to be somewhere from which it can exert an influence. Whitehead's solution is to ground it in an Eternal receptacle, a reality that is not itself temporal but is able to sustain the things of the past, and to do so in a way that makes it possible for them to have an impact, to perish and yet to live forevermore. Such a Past is an Everlasting Past in contrast to an Ephemeral Present, a Past retained for ever and ever in the Eternal, whereas actual present achievements are momentary flashes, here and gone, their subsequent sequential nature a feature not of themselves but of the Past to which they are transported.

Unfortunately, the Past so understood undermines a clear-headed affirmation of the radical temporality of things, the fact that the world is composed solely of momentary achievements that perish and are no more, is thereby lost. It is replaced by a reality the endurance of which is not a contingent achievement but an ontological necessity, the way by which the contingent achievements of actual entities can be everlastingly preserved. In such an ontology, moments are not moments but elements of what is everlasting, and so become themselves everlasting. And eternity is not eternal because it is always changing, although not temporally but somehow timelessly. Whitehead's ontology of an everlasting past grounded in the Eternal, like his ontology in *Process and Reality* of it grounded in an eternal God who is the receptacle of all possibilities and yet also the everlasting agent of their relevance, is simply incoherent. And, once again, quite unnecessary.

There are no justifiable grounds metaphysically for insisting on a ground for a reality that is radically temporal. We should understand The Past as an abstraction, a useful bit of mythmaking that we ought not fallaciously think concrete. There is no actual past, it has no being. All facts, all things that are true, come to be and, realized, perish and are no more. But as each vanishes into the storm, its shadow is cast on newly concrescing facts in the form of particularized conditions influencing but not fully determining what they can realize. That influence is not solely on its immediate successors, for it in turn becomes, strongly or faintly, a feature of the shadows its successors cast on their successors. I have tried to use the notion of shadows of truth as a way to affirm Whitehead's account of how dynamic change can be a source of ordered permanence as long as its ragged edges leave room for adaptative adjustments and dramatic upheavals by the same temporal finite entities that were the agents of that order. To understand our cosmos metaphysically as through and through contingent, because composed in all its complexity and evolving stability of momentary events, is to do what I thought Whitehead said we should do: Take time seriously.

Whitehead eventually dispenses with The Eternal, replacing it in *Process and Reality* with God. God's Primordial Nature functions as the receptacle for pure possibilities, which he now calls eternal objects, and also as the agency needed to tailor those possibilities to the specific situational constraints confronting concrescing actual entities. These tailored possibilities comprise the options from which each actual entity selects its initial aim, by means of which it shapes the physical and conceptual content of its direct prehension of the predecessors comprising its past. God's Consequent Nature is the receptacle for the Past, for the achievements of past actualities, and also it is the agency that orders them valuationally so that they can be used to influence their successors over the long run. Hence, the Eternal is divided into two components: an Eternal aspect that houses all possibilities and an Everlasting aspect that houses all actualities. The Eternal aspect, rather than the Past, is the agency for shaping pure possibilities into initial-aim options; the Everlasting aspect is the agency for translating the achievements of the past into resources for devising better aims and effecting better ends. No such transcendental receptacle and agency is needed, however, if the shadows cast by perishing entities can provide the requisite relevant possibilities and firm necessities, each with their relative value, to account for the creative advance.

Appropriately, this chapter, as indeed this whole book, is no more than a silly sketch, a verbal diagram, a hypothesis spun about what I think Whitehead was arguing and why I think it metaphysically incoherent. I agree with Whitehead that diagrams and myths are especially useful modes of abstraction, because they force a reader beyond what they say or show, due to their unstable unification of systemic incompatibles. I illustrated Whitehead's claim with his phrase about "the shadow of truth," developing one of the possibilities I found lurking in its niches into the suggestion of a metaphysics that finds no need for the two ontological realities which in 1924/1925 he thought central: The Past and The Eternal.

By indicating how the coming to be and perishing of interdependent fact-events, so understood, provides a fully adequate basis for a mode of Whiteheadian process metaphysics, I have been spinning a story about not only our world but all there is and can ever be as intractably temporal. It is a story that finds strong roots in Whitehead's first-year lectures at Harvard, including the resources for purging his ideas of various nontemporal realities.

NOTE

1. This chapter is a slightly modified version of my article "Diagrams and Myths" in *Whitehead at Harvard, 1924/1925*, eds. Brian Henning and Joseph Petek. Edinburgh, UK: Edinburgh University Press, 2019: 283–306. All rights retained by author.

5

EROTIC POWER

Having looked at some of Whitehead's unpublished thoughts from a few years prior to *Process and Reality*, I would like now to turn to the first of the two books he published subsequent to it.[1] *Adventures of Ideas* makes only passing reference to the idea of God developed in *Process and Reality*. Whitehead's concerns with matters of ultimacy remain, however, but are in most cases differently expressed. I will explore these new ideas and will find in them resources for developing further my radically temporalist reframing of his metaphysics.

I will begin by exploring what Whitehead, creatively interpreting Plato, takes to be the notions fundamental to any adequate metaphysics, focusing on Psyche and Eros. This leads me to a critique of Whitehead's eagerness to reify—indeed, to deify—those two notions, after which I will offer an alternative interpretation in keeping with my earlier critiques. I will then turn to a consideration of four of the five notions Whitehead says are fundamental to any civilized mode of living. First, I will consider Truth, the agency which by relating Appearance to Reality grounds a stabilized social order. I will then turn to the importance of Beauty and Art as providing a way to foster and then exploit weaknesses in any stable system, opening pathways to possibilities not otherwise possible. Adventure then adds a moral dimension to the quest for novel possibilities. The fifth of the civilized notions, which Whitehead calls Peace, will be taken up in chapter 7.

BASIC NOTIONS

In the chapter on "Science and Philosophy" in *Adventures of Ideas*, Whitehead offers a "general characterization" of both those disciplines as composed of people "urged onward by the curiosity of the human spirit, permeated with criticism, and divorced from hereditary superstitions" (1967, 141). He then pauses to note that "the word 'curiosity' somewhat trivializes that inward motive," and so offers a richer definition: curiosity is "the craving of reason that the facts discriminated in experience be understood," that they be grasped, every one of them, as exemplifying some "principle which is capable of statement in abstraction from its particular exemplification" (141).

Whitehead is especially interested in Plato's attempt to do this by articulating the seven "basic notions connecting Science and Philosophy" (146). He argues that "all philosophy is in fact an endeavor to obtain a coherent system out of some modification of these notions" (275). Neither Plato nor Whitehead offer them as a dogmatic "final system" but as "the most likely tale." They are: "The Ideas, The Physical Elements, The Psyche, The Eros, The General Harmony, The Mathematical Relations, The Receptacle" (147, 275).

Ideas, considered by themselves, are inert: "static, frozen, and lifeless" (147). But when taken as possibilities for actualization, they are what make possible the creating, perpetuating, and altering of realities, of what together comprise the temporal flow of things, the creative advance comprising the origin and history of our planet, a history culminating for Whitehead in the emergence of civilized human existence. So the notion of Ideas immediately entails the notion of Physical Elements, the material facts that of themselves also would be static, frozen, and lifeless were they not infused with the Ideas that bring them to life, that give them relevance beyond their momentary existence.

Psyche, says Whitehead, is the agency by which this dynamic process occurs, "the agency whereby ideas obtain efficiency in the creative advance" (147). Psyche, like all the other basic notions, is a general notion, hence an abstraction, a collective noun for "finite souls of varying grades, including human souls" (147–48), which make "the determinations of compatibilities and incompatibilities" by which, from the motley of what at any moment is possible, a selection can be made "compatible for joint exemplification" (147). But Psyche's entertainment of Ideas is a matter of "mere knowledge, that is to say, of mere understanding" (148). Ideas can be efficacious tools in the creative advance only if the finite psyches that entertain them seek not simply their own "immediate realization" but also have what Whitehead calls an "urge towards the realization of ideal perfection" (275).

Hence Psyche is not enough: Eros is also required, Eros understood as the "inward ferment" of the soul, "an activity of subjective feeling, which is at once immediate enjoyment, and also an appetition which melts into action" (148). It is the soul stirring itself to "life and motion" (275) "in the enjoyment of its creative function, arising from its entertainment of ideas" (148). We can say that Psyche is the power to think, to plan, to scale means to ends, whereas Eros is the power to feel, to be curious about what could be, the drive by which "a new fact" is "woven out of the old and the new—a compound of reception and anticipation" which is "the end to which [Psyche's] indwelling Eros urges" it (275). And if so, then I take Whitehead as suggesting that Eros is the more primordial, Psyche the more distinctively human. Yet they are both equally powers of the soul, for they are both inherently teleonomic: activities directed, consciously or otherwise, toward an end. If either is omitted, "we should obtain a static world" (275). To entertain an idea, just as much as to feel an urge, is to sense a possibility and to be drawn toward it, lured by its potency into seeking its actualization. The difference is that Eros seeks to change the world for the better, Psyche to devise the most effective way to do so. Which makes them the agencies of, respectively, the Leibnizian and Aristotelean transcendentals.

Whitehead goes on to say that in *The Symposium* Plato articulates his "final conception" of Eros as involving "the urge towards ideal perfection" (148), the existential drive of each actual occasion toward concreteness. Not just any concreteness, however, but one possible for it to attain within the constraints of its finite capacities, a limited perfection always at best imperfectly achieved. Whitehead notes that Plato should have written a companion dialogue named *The Furies* that would have dwelt on "the horrors lurking within imperfect realization." Combining the two dialogues, we would have the notion of "an excellence, partly attained and partly missed" (148).

This excellence, so powerfully a lure orienting our choices, takes many special forms. It is expressed as "the beauty of a statue" or the "rightness of conduct," features belonging to "composite things" when their "many components have obtained in some sense their proper proportions," have achieved the fifth of Plato's seven basic notions, that of Harmony (148). The sixth basic notion, "exact Mathematical Relationships," find expression "in Geometry and in the numerical proportions of measurements." The fact that Mathematical Relationships also find expression in "beautiful composition" is what makes possible the "immense discovery" that "the qualitative elements in the world" are dependent on "mathematical relations" (149).

In this way, the achievements of the sciences and the arts, the work of Psyche and of Eros, can be harmonized. Psyche is the key to understanding a world Eros motivates us to love; reason and feeling find common ground in a world the order, goodness, and beauty of which are united, its many facts comprising one cosmos—the many also a one. Something else is still required, however, to actualize that cosmos: The Receptacle, the notion of a "community of the world, which is the matrix for all begetting"—what Plato calls "the foster-mother of all becoming"—because its essence is "retention of connectedness." It is "the necessary community within which the course of history is set" (150), "the essential unity of the Universe conceived as an actuality" (275). It makes possible the continuity of achievements, the enduring actualities that turn a flux of coming to be and perishing into a dynamically meaningful world. It is the continual exemplification of the Hobbesian transcendental. Whitehead notes that "the space-time of modern mathematical physics, conceived in abstraction from the particular mathematical formulae which applies to the happenings in it, is almost exactly Plato's Receptacle" (150). And it is also "in abstraction from all the particular historical facts." Which is to say, says Plato according to Whitehead, the Receptacle is "bare of all forms" (150). It is a reality "in abstraction from the 'life and action' in which all actualities must partake" (275).

I take Whitehead to be finding in Plato's basic notions, and especially the powers of Psyche and Eros, resonances with his principle of Creativity. It is a ferment-toward that melts into concrete activity, a vectoring dynamic exhibited by each and every actual entity, but in no sense an actuality above and beyond them. The passional and rational powers of finite agents give material realities and possibilities life, and so make the creative advance of the world possible, a process by which differences are harmonized, the perfections of beauty and mathematical relations approximated in realizations constantly needing to be achieved anew.

ELUDING REIFICATIONS

If we are to take Plato's seven basic notions as a toolbox for creating a viable metaphysical theory, it is crucial that they be understood as abstract generalizations not specific realities. To do otherwise turns the tools in that toolbox into monkey wrenches, which when used in the consideration of Whitehead's metaphysics wreak havoc with its coherence. Nonetheless, Whitehead does exactly this with three of the tools, treating them not as abstractions but as concrete agents. It is ironic that Whitehead should so obviously succumb to the fallacy of misplaced concreteness, not once but thrice:

[1] Whitehead, like Plato before him, identifies The Receptacle as a specific reality. Its essence is "retention of connectedness" and therefore it serves as the "foster-mother" for every act of creation. It is the "unity of the Universe conceived as an actuality" because it unifies all things. It is the agency that holds together the manifold outpouring of actual entities, of all that has become concrete fact. It "imposes a common relationship on all that happens" (1967, 150), and yet it is itself devoid of form, an agent but not an entity.

[2] Whitehead also applauds Plato for taking the notion of Psyche to be not only an abstract generalization referring to finite souls but also to be a real existent. Plato's Psyche, says Plato with Whitehead's approval, is the "Supreme Craftsman, on whom depends that degree of orderliness which the world exhibits." It is "a basic Psyche whose active grasp of ideas conditions impartially the whole process of the Universe" (147).

[3] Whitehead, but not Plato, makes this same move with Eros when he asserts the existence not merely of the urges of finite souls toward perfection but also the real existence of that abstract generalization, described by him as the "supreme Eros" which functions as "the determinant of the struggle" going on "within the past for objective existence beyond itself" by "incarnating itself as

the first phase of the individual subjective aim in [every] new process of actuality" (198).

So a foundational reality, a super-agency, a combination of Psyche, Eros, and The Receptacle, is said to be needed as the condition for the effective use of a finite soul's teleonomic powers. Whitehead claims that a cosmic agency is required to link together into a single matrix whatever finite harmonies have been and might be wrought: a new rendition, as it were, of the notion of a Receptacle along the lines of The Eternal discussed in the previous chapter. Whitehead also thinks a cosmic primordial order of all things is needed, and therefore a Psyche that is the primordial agency crafting a starter content for that matrix, and thereby providing a dynamically stable enduring structure within which finite souls with their erotic urges and masterful psychics can function effectively: a new rendition of God's Primordial Nature. Whitehead believes furthermore that a continuing Erotic omnipresence is also required, shaping whatever finite harmonic ends might be attempted, an ongoing cosmic tinkerer, needed lest the finite agents wreak havoc with the creative advance, lest they undo whatever existing order there be and send themselves careening toward a chaos from which there could be no return: a new rendition of God's Consequent Nature.

However, Whitehead's three oxymoronic agencies are not a propaedeutic against metaphysical chaos but are themselves a source of it. Abstractions cannot be agents: by treating them as though they were, Whitehead's renders his metaphysics incoherent. So I suggest, first, that we jettison, as unneeded, the notion of a primordial stabilizing order of finite things not itself made by finite things. Second, I suggest that we jettison, as intrusive meddling, the notion of a nonfinite omnipresent guide. And third, I suggest we interpret the Receptacle as concrete and dynamic instead of formless and changeless, as a matrix of living finite powers rather than yet one more of the Eleatic Stranger's "everlasting fixtures."

We can take the Receptacle as the ongoing totality of acts, as composed of the lives of organisms acting on or reacting to other organisms, fashioning a continuous ever-changing webwork of finite agents affecting and being affected, continually exemplifying the Hobbesian transcendental. The Receptacle so interpreted is an organism's ambient, its specific situation, the relevant context within which it acts. An organism's ambient induces its impulse toward change, either threatening it by actions that press against its conditions for survival, or opening it to opportunities for sustenance and shelter, or both. Each creature has its own ambient, always thickly overlapping with the ambients of other nearby creatures. The conflicts among each organism's own incipient impulses, and between its consummatory efforts and those of other organisms, is what comprises the matrix of all becoming. Agential actual entities are what make the matrix that makes them what they are. The creative advance of life is thus a richly variegated interplay of particular and regional teleonomic agencies. There are ambients grounding every action, but no ultimate ground; goals galore, but no single overarching goal; endless values achieved, but no everlasting retention of those values.

On four occasions in *Adventures of Ideas*, other than the one I have just mentioned, Whitehead seems to identify Eros with the God of *Process and Reality*. The first is just a suggestion: Whitehead wonders if "the animal body and the external regions are not attuned together," and asks whether "nature does not contain within itself a tendency to be in tune, an Eros urging toward perfection" (251). Perhaps Eros is a cosmological agency, accounting for a tendency in things toward the harmonization of diverse elements of an inherited past, a drive—exhibited everywhere through this cosmic epoch—toward the fashioning of order from disorder, attunement from cacophony. I have critiqued this notion in chapter 1.

The second mention of Eros occurs when Whitehead is describing the origination of ideas. He says that "the mental pole has derived its objective content alike by abstraction from the physical pole and by the immanence of the basic Eros which endows with agency all ideal possibilities" (210). Some possibilities are derived by an actual entity from its physical prehensions, whereas other possibilities—the ideal ones, those not previous realized—are provided by the immanence of God, an agency that endows each actual entity with the novel possibilities and with the evaluation of their relevance. This double immanence is how every nascent actual entity is able to carry out its erotic task of fashioning itself from the many elements of its inheritance. To turn Eros into an agency, however, rather than understanding it as an abstract generalization referring to the multiple particular creative agential powers exercised by multiple agents that are each particular concrescing actual entities, is to deprive actual entities of their inherent power—of their essence. Eros, not they themselves, is said to be the source of their agency. They are benefactors but not originators of the power to create. To reify Eros in this way, to turn a basic notion into an active agency, is to commit a fallacy of misplaced concreteness. I have critiqued this notion in chapter 3.

Both these first two references sound like basic tasks of God's Primordial Nature. A paragraph earlier than the second reference, however, Whitehead gives a different account of things. He describes the phase of conceptual prehension as "a ferment of qualitative valuation," explaining that "these qualitative feelings are either derived directly from qualities illustrated in the primary phase [of a concrescence] or are indirectly derived by their relevance to them. These conceptual feelings pass into novel relations to each other, felt with a novel emphasis on subjective form" (210). This account does not identify the derivation of qualitative novel feelings as coming directly from God, however. It denies that novel possibilities are found in any of the conceptual feelings derived directly from an actual entity's initial physical feelings. Rather, they are derived from those derived conceptual feelings because of their relevance to them and presumably therefore their relevance to the underlying physical feelings. This is exactly what a conceptual reversion is (Categoreal Obligation v). A novel idea is arrived at by shifting from an inherited idea to an idea similar to it, where the criterion for similarity is relevance. Relevance is a general notion, of course, an abstraction covering everything from functional relevance—a slightly different aim or a slightly different way to achieve an aim—to qualitative relevance—a slightly different shade of blue. And relevance includes the subjective form of such feelings, how they are valued as having a slightly better use than the possibilities they replace in the integration being sought. These judgments of relevance are what concrescence is all about. At the same time he locates these powers in Eros, Whitehead makes claims that support the insistence that it is always and only an agential actual entity that "endows with agency all ideal possibilities" and is able to turn them into possible specific features of a goal or of a means for its attainment (210).

On a third occasion, Whitehead makes the same reification mistake in his discussion of qualities as qualifications of subjective form. These qualifications occur, he says, through conformal feelings, qualitative valuations, and "the valuations involved in the Primordial Nature of

God, here also termed the Eros of the Universe" (253). This claim makes explicit the identification of Eros with God but gives no new reasons for why such a universal agency is possible, much less required. So my response to the previous reification mistakes applies here as well.

The index to *Adventures of Ideas* has an entry on the "Primordial Nature of God," citing page 281, but the phrase doesn't occur anywhere on that page. Presumably, the citation should be to page 253, which I've just discussed and which is the only time that phrase is used in the book. What Whitehead has to say page 281, however, is interestingly related to my reification critique, so let me consider it. Whitehead is explicating the process that constitutes the existence of an occasion of experience. In the "primary phase," the phase where he claims God alone can introduce any novel possibilities, Whitehead says that "the past," which is the "Reality from which the new occasion springs," is "energizing" its "diverse individual occasions," thereby "initiating the process" that will result in a new actual entity. This process is "urged onward" by the operation of the entity's mental pole, which provides "conceptual subject-matter for synthesis with the Reality." What emerges is a "transformed Reality," the initial inherited Reality "after synthesis with the conceptual valuations" (281). No God is involved in this account; the Reality referred to is the past. There are only actual entities in this account, powers which are able to transform their varying inherited pasts into new unique present actualities.

A fourth occasion where Whitehead merges God and Eros is when discussing how "history can only be understood by seeing it as the theatre of diverse groups of idealists respectively urging ideals incompatible for conjoint realization" (276–77), and the "evil" therefore intrinsic to their "attempted conjunction" (277). Whitehead notes as an aside that this issue of supposedly "intrinsic incompatibility" has "an important bearing upon our conception of the nature of God." There are ideals it is impossible for God to realize in one synthesizing totality: "We must conceive the Divine Eros as the active entertainment of all ideals, with the urge to their finite realization, each in its due season. Thus, a process must be inherent in God's nature, whereby his infinity is acquiring realization" (277). Whitehead then drops this line of thought—"it is unnecessary to pursue theology further"—and returns to his general discussion of how incompatible ideals can be conceptually entertained as a phase in the process by which some ideals are realized in physical fact. However, that last sentence is interesting because it treats Eros as God, with respect to his Consequent Nature rather than his Primordial Nature.

Nonetheless, this brief theological reflection is at odds with the rest of the book. In a chapter on philosophic method, Whitehead makes a point about the inadequacy of the specific words we use when engaged in philosophical generalization. As an example, he takes as a "working hypothesis" (235) the notion that "the ultimate realities are the events in their process of origination," in their passage from "ideal disjunctive diversity" into "concrete togetherness" (236). This is more or less a restatement of *Process and Reality*'s Category of the Ultimate, of Creativity understood as a generalization of particular processes of concrescence. Whitehead then rejects the doctrine of an "external Creator, eliciting this final togetherness out of nothing." He opts instead for the doctrine "that it is a metaphysical principle belonging to the nature of things, that there is nothing in the Universe other than instances of this passage and components of these instances" (236).

Whitehead wonders what terms might best be used to explicate this latter doctrine. Creativity nicely captures the notion that "every event is a process issuing in novelty," but it also suggests an immanent Creator, which unfortunately has about it "an air of paradox, or of pantheism" (236). The notion of concrescence is a better way to underscore the idea of concrete togetherness as the result of a process of growing together, but it "fails to suggest the creative novelty involved" (236). So in his typical way, Whitehead ends up with a set of ten different terms, which mutually "correct each other": "Together," "creativity," "concrescence," "prehension," "feeling," "subjective form," "data," "actuality," "becoming," and "process" (236–37). Notably missing is the word "God" or any of its synonyms.

So, to summarize: Whitehead in *Adventures of Ideas* often affirms as nonfinite actual agents what are better understood as abstract generalizations about finite actual agents. My negative claim is that doing so is to reify abstractions, which is to commit the fallacy of misplaced concreteness. My positive claim is that Whitehead also explicates, in alternative ways that involve no reification, the issues he addressed by appealing to reified entities. I recommend the alternative explications as the more adequate and coherent approach.

TRUTH

In Part IV of *Adventures of Ideas*, Whitehead elaborates the five qualities of mind that he says define a civilized mode of existence: Truth, Beauty, Adventure, Art, and Peace. I will deal in this section with the first of these, associating it with the notion of Psyche. To do so, I need to add to the five two additional notions that Whitehead also considers: Reality and Appearance.

Physical Elements and Ideas are the two "inert" basic notions in Plato's list of the seven needed for an adequate metaphysics. Reality is similar to Physical Elements, both notions referring to matters-of-fact that are physical in the sense of physically prehendable by actual entities or available for human sense perception. "Reality is just itself" (1967, 244), a general term for any and all facts. An Idea is similar to that of an Appearance, both referring to objects of a conceptual not physical prehension, possibilities not facts, indeterminate not determinate. It too is just itself, although itself is vague, its features and relationships not yet fully specified.

The things expressed by these notions that are inert, that are just what they are, need an agency able to relate them. For civilized beings it is Truth, which "is the conformation of Appearance to Reality" (241). Truth is neither the fact nor the idea of this conformity, but rather its creator. In its simplest forms, Truth connects an idea and a fact, thereby exhibiting their likeness: the idea is shown to be a conceptual representation of the material fact. The idea of this cat being on that mat is true because there really is this actual cat located on that actual mat. The physical reality and what it appears to me to be are alike, but not identical. One is a state of my mind and the other a feature of something external to my mind: the concept of a physical object and the physical object itself.

A more complex Truth connects two or more matters-of-fact with a single idea, exhibiting the facts as identical to each other because the same idea is like each of them. Each fact is a unique individual, so in order to treat them as identical some of the features that make them unique must be ignored (242). This creature and that creature may seem to be completely unrelated, but if "their common natures may include a common factor" (241) it would permit using an examination of one to disclose some factor belonging to the other. These different entities might share an identical "partial pattern," a pattern "abstracted from the original" of each, in such a way as to omit elements that "involve the differences which belong to their diverse individualities." They can therefore be treated as identical although they are only similar because they are seen as "united in a truth-relation when they severally participate in the same pattern" (242). One creature is a male with orange fur, the other a female with grey fur, but we ignore gender and color to focus on their shared genetic heritage, and take them as both being cats. The idea linking different facts can be, as with the cats, a category defined by objective features such as color pattern, physical shape, gender, or species. Or they can be linked by subjective features such as the definer's preference for female cats or a bias toward cats which look like a cat the definer once owned.

Taking similar things as identical is a commonplace of experience, "an intuition of a limited identity of pattern" taken as self-evident. We assume it to be obvious that "what is appropriate to one is appropriate to the other" (242). I may not know what species each of them is, but I know for sure they are both cats. What appears to be the case is often not really the case, however. Our sense of Truth is to accept a vividly clear and distinct Appearance as the mirror image of a Reality and to take two such similar Appearances as identical instances of the same Reality. However, because neither truth-relation is an identity but is rather a similarity interpreted as an identity, an abstraction that ignores differences, it is easy for us to confuse what seems to be the case with what actually is the case.

Moreover, establishing a precisely accurate mirroring or a perfect identity is not necessarily what we want. Sometimes ignoring their actual differences reveals a pattern among matters-of-fact, or among ideas, that we find more important. It makes no difference to us by whom, when, and how the sweater was made that we are about to purchase, because we assume all sweaters of that design and size are more or less the same. We want that kind of sweater; which one specifically is irrelevant. Ignoring a difference or even a lot of differences can make a very significant difference. Whitehead's example is Newton, who would likely not have worked out the laws of gravitation had he been aware of the small errors his use of Kepler's laws was introducing into his analysis. "The Truth," says Whitehead, "must be seasonable" (243).

One of the "conspicuous examples of the truth-relation in human experience" is that mode of truth involving propositions. A proposition is an "abstract possibility of an assigned nexus illustrating an assigned pattern" (243). It is "a notion about actualities, a suggestion, a theory, a supposition of things" (244). The proposition could be an idea about the nature of a physical object seen in the distance or glimpsed fleetingly in passing. We suspect that the person we see at a distance is John; as we get closer, this possibility will be shown to be true or will prove to be false. Or the proposition could be a prediction, an idea about what will become the case at a future time and place if certain conditions are met. We project that there will be an eclipse of the moon visible from where we are standing tomorrow night at 2 a.m.; we will find out whether this possibility is truly realized or not by being in that place at that time and observing what happens.

A proposition could also be a hope, a vague unspecified belief that if we carry out some plan on its behalf we will be promoted to a more prestigious and higher paying job, or we will help achieve some small neighborhood improvement, or help usher in a better order of the ages. In this kind of truth-relation, we need to do something for the possibility to be actualized, for there to become a Reality that is the Truth of the Appearance. Whether or not this will happen depends on how successful we are in what we do, how relevant that action will turn out to be for bringing about what we hope will occur.

A proposition, especially one of the third kind, needs to be more than the assertion of a possibility, however. Because its being true involves agency, it needs also to be "an incitement to believe, or to doubt, or to enjoy or to obey." That is, to make the point in Whitehead's technical vocabulary, the assertion of a proposition always "endeavours to fix the subjective form which clothes the feeling of the proposition as a datum" (243). A proposition is a proposal to act, and every action has, in addition to the end it seeks, the way in which that end is pursued, the how of it, the means by which it is achieved or fails to be achieved. For every verb there is an accompanying adverb, for every action the manner of enacting it. We speak cautiously about the identity of the man toward whom we are walking; authoritatively, about the time and place of the eclipse, passionately, about the importance of the collective action to be undertaken. A proposition, that is, needs an "emotional lure" so that we will find it "interesting" enough to actualize what it has proposed (244).

In saying this, Whitehead does not mean it in a superficial sense. The possibility is clothed in an alluring subjective form in order to give it importance, not momentary attractiveness. When our interest in a proposition is because we think it important, crucial in some way to our traditional beliefs or fervent hopes, we are usually more willing to take it as true. And the more important the proposition, the more willing. Cardinal Bellarmine refuses even to look through Galileo's telescope at the moons of Jupiter, so deep is his theologically based belief in heavenly objects as purely immaterial realities rather than as material entities like the Earth with a capacity for having attending moons. So likewise, the crowds of those who enthusiastically affirm as true whatever their political leader tells them is true do so because of the leader's style, his or her way of making an idea seem important, the choice of words or the timing of gestures, the well-chosen location for the speech.

Plato's combined notions of Psyche and Eros can thus be understood as similar to the general notion of agents of Truth. Psyche refers to the capacity of agents, from actual entities to human beings, to organize their experience by identifying or inventing a possibility by virtue of which divergent features of that experience can be reconciled sufficiently to achieve an outcome. How we experience Reality is by fashioning it into an Appearance we find at least interesting but preferably important. Eros refers to the capacity of agents to do this by "simplification" of the complexity of the Reality, by a "process of emphasis and combination," lifting a few enduring objects into the foreground and endowing them with a "wealth of emotional significance" while consigning the "mass of undistinguished occasions" to an undifferentiated background "providing the environment with its vague emotional tone" (281). We deem these Appearances Truthful if they have emphasized "connections and qualities of connections" actually present in the underlying Reality, False if they have "introduced qualities which have no counterpart in Reality" (281). Achieving an outcome important to the agent is the motive for this process of simplification, and if that can be done only by settling for an Appearance with deficiencies in connective qualities and even some unconnected qualities, we often find that acceptable. The judgments of Psyche are always most effective when clothed in the passions of Eros.

Another of Whitehead's examples of the truth-relation is sense perception, which differs from propositions in that the Appearance, the data perceived, are "derived from bodily activities" which are "precipitated upon the regions of the contemporary world" as so obviously the truth about those regions that a "note of mere suggested possibility is eliminated" (245). The Appearance is clothed in the strongest of emotional lures not by us but by the Reality we are perceiving; it is not proposed, as with propositions, but demanded. It is difficult for us to believe that our sense data of the stars we see so plainly in the sky on a dark night are not the Reality of that sky at the time we are looking up at it (247). The reason why we trust our senses is because the sense data of what we take to be clearly and distinctly presented have subjective forms of "qualifications of affective tone" that are so intimate, so intense, that they are "objectively perceived as qualifications of regions" (245). We take them as "the blunt truth that we require" for our practical concerns (250). Seeing is believing; if we can kick it, it must be real; the smell of garlic is unmistakable. We can hardly avoid experiencing "a green woodland in spring" except as full of joyous possibility, young love, and new beginnings, because we experience it with an affective tone derived from "the delicate shades of the green" new leaves. And as we know, to take a quite different example, "a red-irritation is prevalent among nerve-racked people and among bulls" (246).

Yet another mode of truth-relation is 'symbolic truth,' which is a "relation of Appearance to Reality" where a perception of an Appearance leads to the perception of a Reality, "such that the subjective forms of the two prehensions are conformal," even though there is "no direct causal relation" between them (248). The word 'cat' neither looks like nor sounds like the feline animal it invokes. The linkage is arbitrary, the result of the "adventitious consequences" comprising, in this case, the history of the English language (248). Whitehead calls special attention to situations in which "the conveyance of objective meaning is at a minimum, while the conveyance of suitable subjective form is at its height" (249). For example, Appearances such as the music used in ceremonial events convey "strong sentiment," whether "patriotic, martial, or religious," by "providing the emotion which the votaries dumbly feel ought to be attached to the apprehension of national life, or of the clash of nations, or of the activities of God" (249). The music changes an otherwise "dim objective reality into a clear Appearance" (249) by transforming the vibrant subjective form of the musical sounds into the powerfully affirmative subjective form of the cultural Reality. The soldiers march in steps synchronized by the 4-4 beat of tunes which in their loudly persistent major-key harmonies confirm for the watching citizens as well as the marching soldiers their loyalty to God and Country—and not incidentally, to the nation's current leaders. This "linkage of an idea to an apparatus of expression" is as old as human societies: the ceremony is experienced as expressing the idea and the idea as interpreting the ceremony (250). The importance of certain matters turns Psyche into the servant of Eros. Or perhaps it would be more accurate to say that Eros can make certain matters extremely important, to which Psyche must thereafter conform.

There is one feature of this analysis of Truth that I want to emphasize. Whitehead's account of the modes of truth-relation is about the contingencies of individual agencies. Sometimes we take Appearances as referring to features of the realized actualities comprising our ambient, features we highlight for some purpose. And sometimes we take Appearances as referring to future possibilities that by our actions we would hope to actualize. In both these modalities, we require "the blunt truth," a sense of "the conformal correspondence of clear and distinct Appearance to Reality" (250). We assert the importance of the Appearance for the direct access it provides to the importance of the Reality.

"Appearances are finally controlled by the functionings of the animal body," and those functionings and the "happenings within the contemporary regions are both derived from a common past, relevant to both." Hence, Whitehead argues, "the animal body and the external regions," agent and ambient, can be said to be "attuned together, so that under normal circumstances, the appearances conform to natures within the regions" (251). From highly stylized ceremonial events that are explicitly designed to interpret important cultural ideas, to features of natural processes repeated day after day, year after year, and unconsciously felt as familiar intimations of intimately personal memories, finite agents shape and are shaped by experiences they take to be blunt truths about themselves and their world—truths they take as self-evident commonsensical certainties not subject to the intrusive efforts of finite agencies and the disintegrating effects of temporal duration. We take the Truth as blunt because of our confidence in the conformal correspondence between what we are experiencing and what is in fact the case. Our confidence is a belief, however, not a necessity. We can be wrong. The Reality may not be as we have interpreted it, or it may be true today but not tomorrow. There are no necessary truths, always only the contingent interpretations of finite agents.

In tune with this propensity to claim certainty for our beliefs, however, Whitehead poses a question I mentioned in the previous section of this chapter as alluding to a reification of Eros: "we have to ask whether nature does not contain within itself a tendency to be in tune, an Eros urging towards perfection" (251). Whitehead answers the question in the affirmative. The perfection he has in mind here is that of Truth as attaining an identity of Appearance and Reality, a final merging of what we perceive and understand and strive to achieve with what is in fact the case in our context. The urge we feel, Whitehead argues, is caused by an Eros which prods us toward that perfection, a power not compelling us but rather urging us, indeed urging all nature, toward identity with a reality that transcends us.

Were I also to answer Whitehead's question positively, I would be denying his account of the truth-relation we have been examining in this section. I would be denying that truth relations are contingent acts of finite agents, interpretations that are unavoidably partial and so never perfect. I would be reifying Psyche and Eros, and thereby denying radical contingency. Instead, therefore, I have been answering Whitehead's question in the negative, attempting to defend his process metaphysics against his yearning for something more. However, Whitehead says that "this question cannot be discussed without passing beyond the narrow grounds of the truth-relation" (251), so I will defer further comment until we examine the wider grounds provided by a consideration of Beauty, the other of the two "great regulative properties in virtue of which Appearance justifies itself to the immediate decision of the experient subject" (241).

BEAUTY AND ART

I have been interpreting Psyche as an abstract generalization for the effort of finite agents to bring their experience into accord with the relevant facts, to come as close as they can to overcoming any differences between that of which they are aware and that which is in fact the case. Psyche is thus a label for the harmonizing activities of entities, their effort to bring what their senses tell them into conformity with what is actually occurring, to secure what is truly the case so as better to attain their ends. Hence it can also be thought of as a portmanteau for rational agencies in the broad sense of agencies attempting to clarify whatever is vague, organize whatever is disparate, and alter wherever can be altered to achieve a coherent understanding sufficient enough to contribute to an ongoing attempt to live a viable life.

However, Psyche is never enough because its aim is in accord with the Aristotelean transcendental: to succeed in achieving a viable outcome, no matter what the cost. When viability is taken to mean stability, the relationally safe conformation of the present and future to the past, when every action is either in defense of the status quo or an attempt to recover it, that cost can eventually lead to decline. In a radically temporal world, the pressure of constant changes overruns the capacity for neutralizing them. Eros is needed to augment Psyche's aim by an urge toward the better, by the willingness to break with stability in the hope the Leibnizian transcendental affirms as fundamental, indeed as key to the success of the very stability it questions.

Eros is the general notion for agencies aiming to accomplish change, for entities whose energies are directed toward an outcome felt to be an improvement on its inheritance. The aim is not at perfection, as we have just seen Whitehead thinks it is, but at "the mutual adaptation of the several factors in an occasion of experience" in such a way that "the objective contents of the various prehensions [of those factors] do not inhibit each other" and thereby "raise the intensities of conformal feeling in the primitive component feelings" (1967, 252). The civilized expression of this approach is Beauty. Adaptation implies an agency with a twofold aim. On the one hand, it is an urge toward an "absence of mutual inhibition," an effort to enlarge the scope of elements included in the achieved end, to increase its massiveness. On the other hand, it is an urge toward "new contrasts of objective content with objective content" (252), an effort to retain as far as possible new differing dissident features of those elements, to make them mutually compatible not by eliminating their individual differences but by integrating them into a more complex whole, by intensifying rather than simplifying.

The weaving of massiveness and intensity is a familiar Whiteheadian notion, of course, explicated in *Process and Reality* by classifying the satisfactions of actual entities in terms of the ways in which their creations reconcile "triviality," "vagueness," "narrowness," and "width" (1978, 111–12), a reconciliation most effectively wrought through the use of "contrasts" (228–29) in order to achieve "balance" (278–79). "All aesthetic experience is feeling arising out of the realization of contrast under identity" (280).

In *Adventures of Ideas*, this notion of contrast under identity is discussed in terms of how Beauty involves Harmony but attains its highest expressions when Harmony is reconciled with Discord (1967, 261–64). Art involves "the claim for separate individuality advanced by component factors" (264), even as they are woven into the Harmony of a unified final composition. Whitehead offers the Cathedral at Chartres as his paradigm: details of its architecture, such as the statues along its facades, all with their own "vigorous characters," yet tightly integrated into the aesthetic experiencing of the cathedral as a whole, so that the whole is not merely a "pattern of qualitative beauty" but "a beautiful system of objects," its components rendered systemically compatible without loss of their contrasting differences (264). "Strength of experience, in massiveness and in intensity, depends upon the substratum of detail being composed of significant individuals" (263).

A work of art can achieve considerable value, of course, at a far remove from this paradigm, flirting with the extremes of maximal massiveness and minimal intensity or minimal massiveness and maximal intensity. A Brancusi bird daringly eliminates detail and difference in order to intensity unity, as does a Schubert lieder or a Japanese haiku. Obversely, in a Miró painting clashing disparate elements brashly destabilize but do not destroy the integrity of the whole, and this same journey to the edge of chaos characterizes a Mahler symphony or a sprawling novel such as *Don Quixote*. Aesthetic excellence, however, usually lies around a Chartres-like golden mean: as much massiveness as possible combined with as much intensity as possible. There is no formula, however, for achieving such optima of value. Creating great art is an art.

It is an obvious but controversial move to extend these considerations of value in the fine arts to encompass ethical values as well. The traditional claim is that the sort of activities to which ethical judgments apply are a *praxis* rather than a *poiesis*, doing rather than making. Art is said to be the fashioning of tangible objects, making things of beauty that can be seen, heard, or touched. Moral actions, in contrast, whether private or public, are said to be behaviors in which nothing is made. We promise to honor and obey, we vote for a candidate in the election, we argue about the merits of a political decision—in all such activities, something is done but no artifact results. This distinction vanishes, however, in a perspective where events are made, where we engage in no metaphorical attributions by saying people make choices, construct arguments, rework their purposes, and build character.

Pointing out not merely a similarity between artistic and ethical forms of *poiesis*, but making the more general claim that any creation of an Appearance is a work of Art, gives us a hint of why Art is never simply for its own sake, why Eros is an urge toward the beauty of the better. Art is the weaving of massiveness and intensity into a specific Reality, the work of art, which is also an Appearance disclosing a possibility for altering that Reality for the better. Art is a "purposive adaptation of Appearance to Reality" (267), for the achievement of Truthful Beauty. In the specific sense of the aesthetic objects created by human artists, works of art—images, sounds, or activities crafted by a creative combination of imaginative insight, manual dexterity, and astute judgment—are the kind of Appearances Whitehead is emphasizing as crucial to civilized experience, crucial due to the profundity of their importance. "Thus civilization in its aim at fineness of feeling should so arrange its social relations, and the relations of its members to their natural environment, as to evoke into the experiences of its members Appearances dominated by the harmonies of forceful enduring things" (282).

These artful Appearances can be evocative even when largely fanciful, even when they depart significantly from the Reality of which they are simplified expressions. Even when they are false. For, as Whitehead famously puts it: "It is more important that a proposition be interesting than that it be true" (244). Although, he immediately adds: "But of course a true proposition is more apt to be interesting than a false one. Also action in accordance with the emotional lure of a proposition is more apt to be successful if the proposition be true" (244).

Whitehead later explains why: "The importance of the Truthful relation of Appearance to Reality" lies in the power of truth to summon "from the recesses of Reality" what falsehood cannot: "the magic by which a beauty beyond the power of speech to express can be called into being, as if by the wand of an enchanter" (283). A great work of art is a novel creation. Its evocative power lies in an Appearance that is not a mere replication of the Reality to which it refers but a transformation of that Reality. It means bringing fresh possibilities into play, creating ideas that are literally false in order to disclose truths about the objective world to which we have been blind or which we have overlooked in our standard ways of perceiving it and thinking about it. Art as expressed in the Beauty of artistic creations is false to the explicit system of things, to the reality delimited by the careful prose of scientific and commonsense discourse, in order to reveal the Truth of a fuller Reality that discourse has obscured.

Conscious human awareness, expressed exquisitely in the scientific formulations of how best to understand the world, seeks clarity and distinctness in its abstractions, giving these Appearances an enhanced importance "relatively to that of the initial Reality," which "lies dimly in the background with its details hardly to be distinguished in consciousness" (270). Focused on what is vividly clear, rational thinking tends to dismiss this vague background as unimportant precisely because only dimly grasped. But it is "these dim elements," which are in fact "massive, and important," that "provide for art that final background of tone apart from which its effects fade." So the Truth that Art expresses is more concrete than the abstract Truths of reason, but less visible and so not easily if ever fully grasped. "The type of Truth which human art seeks lies in the eliciting of this background to haunt the object presented for clear consciousness" (270).

ADVENTURE

Whitehead describes Adventure as "the search for new perfections" (1967, 258), which would seem to be what we've just seen to be the task of Art. The difference, he argues, is that Art is the "adaptation of immediate Appearance for immediate Beauty," insistent in its inventiveness on results that have "some immediate harvest" (269). In this sense, "the merit of Art in its service to civilization" is that it "exhibits for consciousness a finite fragment of human effort achieving its own perfection within its own limits," a "fragment of nature with the mark in it of a finite creative effort." A work of art is a unique finite creation emergent from "the vague infinity of its background," the fact of its achievement heightening our "sense of humanity" (270). Whitehead says that sunsets are "glorious"—we might say awesome—because they remind us of how insignificant we seem in contrast to the universe we inhabit. We need Art to spur us on toward those civilized undertakings that "are nothing other than the unremitting aim at the major perfections of harmony," undertakings able "to evoke into consciousness the finite perfections which lie ready for human achievement" (271).

In contrast to Art, Adventure seeks to realize ends "whose justification lies in aim at the distant ideal," at the attainment of possible goods that lie "in depths and distances below and beyond appearance" (268). These are possibilities that are glorious because they remind us of what we might be able to accomplish if we tried. The "inevitable anticipation" of a future ideal "adds to the present a qualitative element which profoundly affects its whole qualitative harmony" (269), a disruptive, unsettling sense of immanent change that we have the power to shape. However, "The effect of the present on the future is the business of morals" (269), and we cannot aim to realize a moral ideal, "except from the standpoint of a well-assimilated system of customs" (269), which will be altered if our adventurous ideal were to be accomplished. A dilemma emerges: what the advocates of change see as good, the defenders of the status quo will see as bad. Whitehead is critical of the defenders. "In human society the champions of morality are on the whole the fierce opponents of new ideals. Mankind has been afflicted with low-toned moralists, objecting to expulsion from some Garden of Eden" (269). Or, to put it more strongly: "the defense of morals is the battle-cry which best rallies stupidity against change" (268). We have seen earlier in this chapter the power that Art has to clothe beliefs and practices in emotional garments that serve the interests of the defenders of the established social order, creating an "orthodoxy" that "suppresses adventure" (277).

Morality is far too often associated with static stability once a civilization has reached its culmination, but "the culmination can maintain itself" only if "fresh experimentation within the type is possible." When the stock of minor improvements has been exhausted, "staleness then sets in," the "imaginative force" of fresh ideas and their "vivid appreciation" tail off (277). Decadence sets in, followed by decay. "There remains the show of civilization, without any of its realities" (278). Whitehead offers us a different sense of morality, one that finds its Truth in Art and its expression in Adventure. "One incidental service of art to society lies in its adventurousness" (269). Having denied Art a moral role, insisting instead that its aim ought to be solely on the present, Whitehead applauds its moral role. "It is a tribute to the strength of the sheer craving for freshness, that change, whose justification lies in aim at the distant ideal, should be promoted by Art which is the adaptation of immediate Appearance for immediate Beauty" (269). This seeming about-face is due to the ambiguity in the meaning of morality. On the one hand, it refers to the effort to preserve established good, to prevent the loss of values achieved and stabilized with great difficulty. On the other hand, morality refers to the effort to achieve a better good, and to destabilize the status quo in order to make room for it. The former role of morality is self-destructive; the latter, of fundamental importance for Whitehead: "A race preserves its vigor so long as it harbours a real contrast between what has been and what may be, and so long as it is nerved by the vigour of adventure beyond the safeties of the past. Without adventure civilization is in full decay" (279).

The greatest works of art fashion an Appearance that refers us to a Reality beyond "the dictionary meaning of words" (267), sending us "a message from the Unseen," disclosing something of the mystery of things, unloosing "depths of feeling from behind the frontier where precision of consciousness fails" (271). This role of Art is to unsettle our established ways of seeing, thinking, and doing by puncturing the systemic envelope that defines and sustains them. We are blind to what lies outside the world of meaning that envelopes us until an imaginative work of art pulls us beyond that world's confines, confronts us with aspects of a reality too diverse in scope and rich in qualities to all fit into any one coherent and consistent systemic whole. Art exposes us to what from the perspective of our established ways seem to be unbelievable facts, irrational methods, and incomprehensible possibilities, and suggests how a new system might be devised that would retain the old foundations but by shaking them up, transforming them by nurturing them with the milk of those previously unknown—freshly fashioned, reasonably construed, viably available—novelties.

Our power as human agents is our ability to fashion imperfect social worlds and to live within them as best we can. Our finite acts of invention are primarily focused on possibilities that can solve the immediate problems of our own finite present, taking into account what we presume to be our relevant future and constrained by what we think is our own inherited finite past, in the hope of being able to live well. Whitehead is saying that this power of ours finds its highest expression, however, its civilized apotheosis, in the ability to create those Appearances we call great works of Art and, in opening ourselves to them, to gain access to aspects of our inheritance that have been excluded from our explicitly ordered systems of meaning, aspects that are nonetheless there in their implied background.

For a civilization to survive, "Adventure is essential, namely the search for new perfections" (258). This is only possible when "the vigor of the race has then pushed forward into the adventure of imagination, so as to anticipate the physical adventures of exploration. The world dreams of things to come, and then in due season arouses itself to their realization" (278–79). Adventure is enlargement, expressing the Hobbesian transcendental that reconciles immediate and future satisfactions. For if an inheritance of social stability, of well-grounded customs, is required for novel aspirations to have any significant scope and intensity, so likewise the quest for something "beautiful beyond the hope of antecedent imagination" (266), something true beyond "the stale presuppositions of verbal thought" (267), is that without which individual, societal, and cosmic stability cannot be sustained.

Obviously, it is often the case that Adventure is conducted within limits: it calculates a reasonably attainable end and then attains it. These are the "ripples of change" by which a society "of a given type preserves its freshness." But "given the vigour of adventure," eventually the "leap of imagination reaches beyond the safe limits" of the established order, indeed "beyond the safe limits of learned rules of taste. It then produces the dislocations and confusions marking the advent of new ideals for civilized effort" (279). This is the distinction I developed in chapter 3 between reformative and transformative purposes. Sometimes what works is tinkering and adjusting, accommodating and modulating. At other times, what works requires a disconcerting break with the old, a refusal or revolt, an exodus. The deeper broader reality that Art discloses is a freshening breeze stirring in the leaves, hinting at an impending change. Adventure accepts its challenge to seek after the novel possibilities of which it hints. By drawing on these depths, we finite creatures are able to transcend our finite limits, to venture tentatively toward a new but largely unknown situation lying somewhere just beyond the horizon. "Adventures are to the adventurous" (279).

FINITE AUTONOMY

In accord with the admonition of the *Sophist*, I have tried to avoid taking Whitehead's parade of capitalized terms as entities capable of agency, of having the power to make a difference. They are abstract generalizations, linguistic shortcuts for describing the effects of actual entities, whether they be momentary or enduring, inorganic or organic. Hence when Whitehead says that spontaneity "belongs to the essence of each actual occasion" as it seeks "freshness, zest, and the extra keenness of intensity" in its accomplishments" (1967, 258), I understand the spontaneity to be that of a particular entity. When Whitehead lists the metaphysical principles descriptive of "the adventure of ideas, and the adventure of practice conforming itself to ideals" (259), I take those principles as referring to entities since they specify that all actualization is finite, that it requires exclusion of alternative possibilities, and that the mental function in finite processes of actualization is how "subjective forms conformal to relevant alternatives excluded from the completeness of physical realization" are introduced as vehicles for achieving actualizations. The possibilities introduced by finite entities are not only "previously excluded" ones, but also ones differing from a familiarly reiterated "finite group of possibilities," ideals "of another type of perfection" (259).

This "bolder adventure" beyond possibilities to be found in an entity's stable inheritance is needed because of the "basic disharmony" of that inheritance (259). The strategy of reconciling two contrasting, seemingly incompatible, systems by retaining them both in the full richness of their particularity, so as to be able to break out beyond the given, is "by spontaneity of the occasion so directing its mental functions as to introduce a third system of prehensions, relevant to both the inharmonious systems" (260). The spontaneity of imagining the possibility of that third system, as well as the spontaneity of implementing it, are solely the occasion's.

In talking about Art, Whitehead says that the "final autonomy" of the process of synthesizing a finished work of art is "not settled" by any sort of "regulative principles" supplied by antecedent fact. Rather, it is "derived from the novel unity which is imposed on them by the novel creature in process of constitution" (255). Thus "the immediate occasion from the spontaneity of its own essence must supply the missing determination for the synthesis of subjective form." The resources for the synthesis are provided "by the spontaneity of the novel individual occasions as in their season they come into being" (255). Both the novel possibilities and their use in regulating the inherited data into an ordered unity are the particular occasions' expressions of the spontaneity that is their essence.

Whitehead succumbs to the reification his use of abstract generalizations encourages, when he transforms the erotic agencies of the multitude of concrescing actual occasions, each in its own season, into the "Eros of the Universe" (253). Which he says is "an Eros urging toward perfection" (251). Which, since Eros is the Primordial Nature of God (253), means that "the teleology of the Universe is directed to the production of Beauty" (265). And therefore, the perfection found in Art can also be found in "the slow outcome of nature," which is "due to some wide universal purpose" (268).

However, if we reject Whitehead's reifications, we have ample grounds for the claim that the emergence of relevant novel possibilities, and through them the formation of progressive tendencies in the cosmos, is due solely to the finite agencies of actual and enduring occasions. For, "All realization is finite, and there is no perfection which is the infinitude of all perfections" (257). There can be no achievement of perfection in a world where all things are finite, so there can be no universal agency directing the slow outcomes of nature toward some purposed end. Whitehead's intuition of an intrinsic suitability in the nature of things need not be explained by invoking a God able to provide it. It is an intuition, I would argue, of shadowy but accessible possibilities lying at depths of experience beyond prosaic articulation. These obscure possibilities are made by Art into propositional Appearances, becoming resources for the transformation of current Reality into something better, releasing our energizing power to fashion new realities in which what was once poetic and inchoate is made prosaic and pragmatically effective. The ground of this intrinsic suitability is not a primordial agent but the nature of things, and the agency by which it is made relevant to present exigencies is not a primordial divinity but simply we humans. Or rather, to generalize, the agents of creative innovation are we finite creatures, great or small, enduring or momentary, who in our various ways comprise Creativity, who all have as our essence the capacity to grasp the intrinsic suitability a given situation harbors and then to shape the intensity of its relevance and the expansiveness of its scope in accord with our individual and collective preferential adaptations.

The erotic Adventure that leads us to novel possibilities never before imagined, and to the creation of new worlds that give them meaning, is how civilized order is able to sustain itself and how simpler forms of order can give rise to more complex ones. The Adventure lies in the fact that the novelties are disruptive because by definition we do not at first know what to do with them. The lure of their beauty, however, and the lure of the beauty of their possibly refreshing, possibly transforming integration with the old familiar ways, motivate our search for a path along which we might venture in an attempt to turn them into the truth of a new and more adequate world. As Frodo says, we will take the ring although we do not know the way. Our story can never be written in advance of how that way is found, and if it is found whether it leads to victory or defeat—or leads, as is more likely the case, to partial success and partial failure. Ours is a story to be recorded only afterward as a part of the meaning of the new order that has resulted.

A necessary condition for our story to have any success, albeit partial and only for a brief time, is that our ideals be in some sense attuned to the way things actually are, that our dreams be realizable. It is crucial that a dream "has not built itself up by the inclusion of elements that are foreign to the reality from which it springs," that it is "a generalization and an adaptation of emphasis; but not an importation of qualities and relations without any corresponding exemplification in the reality" (293). The past is our resource for improving the future: our oughts need always to be a function of our is. We change our circumstances not by rejecting the past and starting over afresh, but by reshaping what we have. In order to overcome the inadequacies of our situation, its discords cannot merely be "dismissed into irrelevance"; a way must be found instead to "rescue discords from loss" (294). If the good we want is pie in the sky, our efforts will yield nothing tangible. If the pie we want is a pie able to feed our actual needs, it must be an actuality made from antecedent actualities, made new in part but not in whole. Our ideals must hug close the reality we would make over into something better. Adventurous Beauty must be a Truthful Beauty.

NOTE

1. This chapter includes some material from my article "Another Footnote to Plato" in *Conceiving an Alternative: Philosophical Resources for an Ecological Civilization*, eds. Demian Wheeler and David Conner. Anoka, MN: Process Century Press, 2019: 15–27. Used with permission, all rights reserved.

6

METAPHORIC POWER

Modes of Thought is Whitehead's last extended metaphysical essay.[1] It abandons the claim that possibilities are eternal objects, which permits abandoning the idea of a God whose primordial nature, and eventually whose consequent nature as well, is required for those possibilities ever to be relevant to an ever-changing temporal world. Instead, we are given a sketch of that world as thoroughly contingent, a world in which actualities are all finite components of finite dynamic systems. In earlier chapters, I have attempted to elicit from Whitehead's metaphysics this core of ideas, arguing that notions of realities that are eternal or everlasting are not compatible with it and should be discarded. I do not know Whitehead's intentions, whether he was abandoning such notions or simply not mentioning them. Whatever his motivation for doing so, I think *Modes of Thought* gives us just that core in a convincing form.

I will use this chapter to display the radically temporalist ontology of that book, focusing on its key ideas about how existence and meaning—fact and value—are intertwined forms of finitude. They are how our understandings and our practices give rise to contingently situated achievements, to interpretive standpoints fashioned and sustained in the midst of endemic instability. I will develop my interpretive understanding of *Modes of Thought* in four parts, which I identify by four gerunds: mattering, interpreting, rationalizing, and civilizing.

MATTERING

Whitehead begins *Modes of Thought* by calling attention to "some ultimate notions" that are "presupposed in the directed activities of mankind," notions that he says "occur naturally in daily life" as "general characterizations of our experience" (1968, 1). Whitehead insists that "there are no definitions of such notions" because there are no "factors more far-reaching than themselves," nothing more fundamental in terms of which they can be explained. Rather, "each must be displayed as necessary to the various meanings of groups of notions, of equal depth with itself" (1). The "habit of mind" that entertains these "notions of large, adequate generality" is "the very essence of civilization" (3). They are presupposed in our social structures, our cultural expressions, and our scientific understandings. We take them for granted; they go without saying.

Whitehead does not offer an inventory of these ultimate notions, nor does he associate them with those developed in *Adventures of Ideas*. Whatever notions there might be, they cannot be organized into some sort of hierarchy or other formal structure, because they are the conditions for "the work of systematization," features of the broader reality that allows us to "avoid the narrownesses inherent in all finite systems." Since "philosophy can exclude nothing," it should therefore not start with systemization. "Its primary stage can be termed *assemblage*" (2). From the amorphous realm of ultimate notions, Whitehead selects a single one, "the notion of importance, the sense of importance, the presupposition of importance," as the one on which he will focus. He immediately contrasts it with another ultimate notion, "matter-of-fact," which is "the basis of importance" in the sense that "importance is important because of the inescapable character of matter-of-fact" (4).

A matter-of-fact is a particular thing: a this-here-now, as distinct from all the other things that are but which are not here or not now, which are at another place or another time. There are a lot of thises and thats, an inexhaustible multiplicity of them, each one uniquely itself. Walking along a seashore, my eye is caught by a flash of light in the sand, reflected off a pebble. I reach down and pick it up. I hold that pebble in my hand, not the pebble that was next to it, nor any of the myriad others scattered along the beach. Its graceful shape and striking color distinguish it from the other pebbles, but it also differs from each of them by being the only pebble in my hand. In contrast to a matter-of-fact, importance is a value—a generalization or idea or feeling—that gives matters-of-fact some kind of unity. It brings them together meaningfully, disclosing a whole of which they are components. "We concentrate by reason of a sense of importance. And when we concentrate, we attend to matter-of-fact." There is no such thing as meaningless facts or meanings independent of facts. "The two notions are antithetical, and require each other" (4).

The paradigm of conscious experience, claims Whitehead, is the linking of these two ultimate notions, the "fusion of a large generality with an insistent particularity" in a judgment that "This is important" (4). The particular matter-of-fact is not taken as a bare indifferent thing but as something of value because of its inherent quality and because of the wider significance it evokes. However, that judgment of value is not based on any "detailed analysis of such quality," but is rather an imprecise general claim like "That is difficult" or "This is lovely" (4).

When emphasizing the inherent qualities, "the individuality of the details" of a thing's importance, we often speak of its intrinsic *"interest"* and therefore our interest in it. When emphasizing the wider implications, up to and including "the unity of the Universe," which this interest intimates, we speak of its *"importance"* (8). Whitehead treats the two terms as synonymous, as emphasizing different facets of the same paradigmatic judgment that a particular matter-of-fact is significant. "Our enjoyment of actuality is a realization of worth, good or bad. It is a value experience. Its basic expression is—Have a care, here is something that matters!" (116). The coloring of most of these pebbles is strikingly different, so I think it worth putting a couple of them in my pocket until I can visit my geologist friend who I suspect can tell me of what they are made, whether their oddity is of any significance.

Importance can thus be understood as the patterned webwork of interrelations by which the myriad possible components of a matter-of-fact are integrated, how one fact is made of them. Meaningful facts are always specifically organized systems of particular components. These components are not aggregated into a whole but become part of the whole by how they function within it. The elements of a meaningful system interact with each other and with elements beyond the whole in ways that sustain its factual unity, that keep it functioning, that maintain the effective coordination it has achieved. A system that isn't functioning effectively is on its way to being no system at all. And reciprocally, a fact that isn't a component of factual systems other than itself is an all-but meaningless surd, a momentary blip of insignificance.

Things are their importance; to be is to be meaningful. Nothing is important as such, however, but always in some way. Judgments about the importance of facts come in a variety of "types" or "grades" or "species" or "senses" (6, 7, 11, 26). Whitehead's lists vary, but in each case the kind of judgment correlates to a fundamental kind of human endeavor. Judgments that "this is right" correlate with morality; that "this is sacred," with religion; that "this is beautiful," with the arts; that "this is valid," with logic; that "this is true," with practical activity and, when combined with logic, the sciences. The fact of a thing's existence is not prior to and distinct from its attractive or repulsive qualities. The thing is its mattering. The spontaneity of our curiosity, our wanting to toy with a murky thought, pick up a sparkly pebble, or help an injured animal, is because we experience them as mattering. And because we care about them, we take the time to figure out what they are and what we should do with them or for them or because of them.

The relation between the one and the many is a familiar problematic for philosophy because of the traditional insistence that it be understood in terms of hierarchies in which the many components of a system are inferior to the one that is their unification. At each level of the hierarchy the many different components, each themselves unifications of lower-level components, find their completion in a higher-level unity, and so on until a one that has no peer is reached. The ground of such a traditional hierarchy is essential difference. In the Great Chain of Being, for instance, the one at any level is less limited, less material, and less contingent than the many subserving it, with an infinite, immaterial, and necessary being located at the apex. Whitehead's approach is not hierarchical, however, but functional. What gives components functionality and therefore gives a matter-of-fact its importance—its meaning—is an orientation: an aim, an end-in-view. Values are particular achievements, made by virtue of particular aims: like that poem or this casserole, those skyscrapers or these trains arriving right on schedule.

What is crucial about an aim is that it is a principle of exclusion and inclusion. It is both a reason for selecting from a wealth of alternative components those able to comprise a system, and also a reason for assigning each of the components a specific role or roles in the process by which the system fulfills its constituting aim. An environing inheritance of facts and potentialities is boundless, indefinite in its scope even if never infinite. However, only a few of these facts and possibilities can usefully serve the furtherance of a given aim, although what components are brought into play, and how they play their parts, will have a lot to do eventually with what the aim becomes, how it is specified. No integrative process can ever unify the totality of the many facts and the many possibilities for their unification that are available. It must omit, subordinate, abstract, and sequence them if it is to succeed in its purpose. Without the aim, there would only be the chaotic flux of particulars, each a momentarily important flash in the pan. And without an effective aim there would be trivial aggregation but not the emergence of meaningful order. An aim is contextual: it is the key to how limited situational resources can be fashioned into a finite result. Whatever actually is—an important fact, a thing that matters—is thus unavoidably a contingent and parochial achievement.

System-making is necessarily a narrowing process. "We always think within limitations" (15), and always act within them. We cannot be fully adequate to experience if we are to make sense of it. Some things will need to be emphasized, foregrounded, valorized, while others are ignored, diminished, denied. Distinctions need to be made, a "clear division among genera," and more specifically a "clear division among species," and so forth and so on (15). Procrustes is the mentor of intelligibility and effectiveness, forcing Proteus's boundless bounty into a finite bounded whole—bending, stuffing, distorting, and lopping off as needed, in order to make things fit properly. As soon as "you push your observations beyond the presuppositions on which they rest," the divisions lose their clarity. "All classification depends on the current character of importance" (15). Our systems are fragile accomplishments; Procrustes is always haunted by the wider vaguer Protean reality that he limits.

Sometimes our aims are clear and highly specified, the process of actualizing them routine; other times the aims emerge slowly and the process moves unpredictably by frustrating reversals and surprising breakthroughs to a finished product. But along that whole spectrum, it is having an aim that makes the deployment of a meaningful system possible. We think the resulting system significant because unique, a new fact wrought from unlimited resources that we had to find an effective way to limit so that it could exist. Our aim makes possible a unification of many things into a new thing that we believe worth actualizing, that we think important: morally important, logically important, artistically important, or religiously important.

Making, sustaining, and enhancing a particular system matters to us because we believe it to be right, or true, or beautiful, or what God wills. We are then prone to take our kind of importance "as exhausting the whole meaning of importance" (11). Furthermore, describing importance in terms of an identifiable list of species leads far too easily to treating those species as together providing an absolute grasp of the meaning of everything there is, was, and can ever become. However, "importance is a generic notion" that "stretches beyond any finite group of species." Each species is a finite perspective, and there are "perspectives of the universe to which morality is irrelevant, to which logic is irrelevant, to which religion is irrelevant, to which art is irrelevant" (11–12).

For any species of importance to claim ultimacy is to trivialize it "The generic aim of process is the attainment of importance, in that species and to that extent which in that instance is possible" (12). Developing systemizations of experience is how we transform brute fact into resources for the pursuit and effective realization of meaningful ends. The ends are finite, the meanings motivating their pursuit and the means devised for achieving them are finite, and likewise the values thereby created: this finite good, those finite truths, that finite beauty. "The ultimate aim infused into the process of nature" (12), is the endlessly emerging and perishing variegated aims of organisms that together comprise the creative advance of this world, its predecessor worlds and its successor worlds, worlds without end.

Having begun with the aim-defined character of meaningful human experience, its ontological generalization to the character of all entities brings us immediately into the familiar terrain of concrescence as the primary characterization of actual entities. The technique by which new facts come into existence is the same as the technique of effective thought and action: developing available resources into a functional system. The emergence of a unique organized whole, a spatiotemporal actuality, involves shaping an inheritance of factual and potential influences, of physical and conceptual prehensions, under the guidance of an evolving aim, by virtue of selective exclusion of possible features of that inheritance, so as to integrate what is not excluded into a new fact that matters. The possibilities provided by the cognitive prehensions derived from its physical prehensions constitutes the emergence of a nascent entity's initial aim by means of a simplifying perspective on its inheritance, making possible the becoming of a new actual entity. Individual actual entities, human individuals, and groups of either, fashion their own aims and methods from the world of their inheritance, the particular systemic ambience that made them possible. For none of these kinds of entity is God needed to provide their initial aims or secure the importance of their accomplishments.

"This is important" is thus an ontological description of the cosmos. Coming to be is an agential activity with the power to fashion a matter-of-fact which is a functionally integrated system of component elements. That element are themselves systems, but also features of agents whose aims give rise to other systems, just as such systems are in turn elements in the process of fashioning of yet other systems. It follows that there are no ultimate systems and agents more fundamental or more ultimate than finite contingent systems and agents with limited aims and limited powers of accomplishing them. Nor is there any system or agent not a subordinate element of other systems and their creators. Matters-of-fact and their varied kinds and grades of importance are bounded actualities, dependent on other actualities for the possibilities from which they are made and with which they make successors.

So this is my first claim about *Modes of Thought* having a radically temporalist metaphysics. Whitehead thinks that inquiry and action are functionally integrative finite processes, and that we are able to understand things and accomplish things more effectively if we take our inquiries and our courses of action to be the deployment of functionally effective specific aims, rather than taking them in more traditional ways as having to do with the pursuit of timeless or everlasting truths grounded in universal or transcendental conditions and explicated in necessarily hierarchical structures. Whitehead's functionalism is ontological as well as epistemological because he claims that why systemic functionality makes conscious experience meaningful is because it is what makes facts actual. Our ideas work best when they work like how the world works.

INTERPRETING

Meaningful conscious experiences are judgments of factual importance that involve the development of systems oriented with respect to aims specified in the specifying of the systems. Thus another way of thinking about meaningful experiences is to say that they are perspectives. "One characterization of importance is that it is that aspect of feeling whereby a perspective is imposed upon the universe of things felt" (1968, 11). Those things, those facts, are not independent atoms brought together by an imposed external system. No matter-of-fact is ever simply itself. A fact "essentially involves is own connection with the universe of other things." They are all creatures formed through their connectiveness, the connections functions of their aims resulting in "the perspective of the universe for that entity" (66). They *are* their perspective. The "connectedness [that] is of the essence of all things of all types" (9) is a perspectival feeling. What feeling provides is relevance to an interest, a "gradation of importance" that "reduces the universe to its perspective for fact" (10), simplifies it, makes it accessible for the pursuit of some unifying end. This reduction, however, means eliminating alternatives, both those immediately present and those that these immediate choices thereby render impossible. If I decide to spend an afternoon on the beach looking for shiny pebbles, I can't spend that evening at a friend's home a thousand miles away.

When I look at an object, an apple for instance, I stand at a particular location and orient my eyes so that they focus on its presence. This direct line of sight defines a vision cone that widens the further it extends, so that the apple as focal point is surrounded by a context of other objects: other apples, the bowl containing them, the table on which the bowel rests, the window farther back, the trees in the yard seen through the window. If the object is close at hand, as when two people glower at each other nose to nose, arguing over who gets the apple that one of them has picked up but that the other also wants, it dominates that context, filling the perceptual area with its bulk. If the object is far away, as when I glimpse a hawk soaring far off beyond the background trees, the context dominates and the focal object may be no more than a tiny speck. A focal object may be obscured by things that interfere with the light rays reflected from it, reducing my information about it, as on a foggy day. Or the interference may alter my perception of the object's features, as when a straight stick in water looks bent or my sun-glasses give it a reddish hue.

What I see is also influenced by what I take to be the content of its intangible context. In addition to the crockery, and trees, there are also the concepts and memories I bring to my viewing of the apple: apples I've enjoyed on prior days, the claim that eating apples contributes to good health, the visual memory of an apple grove visited long ago. A perspective is a standpoint from which things are viewed, a specific location that excludes things. When I look at an object, I cannot see what is behind me nor what is behind the object. When it is the focus of my attention, I am insufficiently aware of what is going on at the edges of my visual field; I presume the background in order to attend to the foreground. To see is to be blind to what although seeable is not being seen, although I can include some of the things that my perspective excludes simply by altering my position, by looking in a different direction or stepping to one side, or by pushing aside some partially occluding object. The concepts that help me characterize the object at which I'm looking, the remembrances of prior experiences similar or contrasting to this one, my anticipation of what might follow this viewing: these also can alter my perspective and so mark it as incomplete, as neither all-encompassing nor permanent.

In this and other ways, I omit in order to find meaningful what is retained, and I omit and retain what I do because of the purpose that has led me to having that particular experience or that guides my response if it is an unexpected experience. I never just look. To perceive is to have a standpoint, to orient the content of my experience toward an objective, to organize it in a functionally effective way around an emerging aim—to systematize it by reference to a purpose.

As in our consideration of mattering, here also the key features of human standpoints can be generalized to characterize all entities. Each matter-of-fact "essentially involves its own connection with the universe of other things," and this connection is "the perspective of the universe for that entity," either "in the way of accomplishment or in the way of potentiality" (66). A multitude of possible connections, of "alternative potentialities," is reduced by "the elimination of alternatives" to those relevant to the "realization involved in that present occasion, and the reduction of alternatives as to the future" to the single connection that is that perspective (67). To be an actual entity is to be an interpretation of an inheritance composed of the accomplishments and potentialities of other entities, an interpretation making them relevant to that actual entity's own accomplishment and its potential for those of subsequent entities. An actual entity is important because in its own special way it integrates past and future into a present perspectival interpretation "In the absence of perspective there is triviality" (84).

I am usually quick to acknowledge the perspectival character of my personal standpoint, although I usually think it objective in the sense that anyone else standing in the same place and looking in the same direction would see the same things I am seeing. I am likely to be reluctant, however, to say that my standpoint, in being perspectival, is therefore interpretive, that it is impossible for two people to see the same thing, that every standpoint is unique. This reluctance is because we typically are concerned only with a focal object, not the details of its context, certainly not with the countless background elements too trivial even to be thought of as details. We both see the same elephant in the room and think that suffices to say we have the same view of things. When the perspective is familial or ethnic, tribal or national, we think of ourselves as sharing a worldview with all our blood brothers and sisters, with all our fellow descendants or fellow patriots.

The danger is that we come to think our scientific or religious perspective so encompassing as to be not a point of view at all, not an interpretive standpoint, but the world as it really is. In simplifying our ambient experience, it is easy to "abstract from our experience the brute particularity of happening here, and now, amid this environment," to eliminate whatever has "essential reference to the passage of events" (67–68). We are left with "the eternal realm of forms. In this imagined realm there is no passage, no loss, no gain. It is complete in itself. It is self-containing. It is therefore the realm of the 'completely real'" (68). The "human imagination" in general and philosophy more specifically are "haunted" by these twin notions of "timeless forms" and their "perfection," which combine into a "vision" of "self-sustaining and complete reality" (68, 69). Whitehead impugns such notions as "naïve" or "idiotic" because "in the house of forms, there are many mansions," imperfect forms each of which "in its very nature refers to some sort of [specific] realization beyond themselves" (69). The notion of forms is a synecdoche for possibilities, which by definition refer to more than themselves: to the range of particular actualities that could be their realization, to the contextual conditions and agential powers that might be instrumental, passively or actively, in securing a realization. Every possibility "refers to life and motion. It refers to inclusion and exclusion. It refers to hope, fear, and intention, . . . it refers to appetition. It refers to the development of actuality" (69).

Importance is necessarily a function of a mode of thought, a judgment of worth limited to the perspective that mode imposes, and to the historical and cultural context interpreting it. What the Hellenic Greeks or Tang Dynasty Chinese took to be the conditions for an object's beauty or a person's morality are not ours. We cannot understand those ancient cultures without taking seriously the distinctive ways in which they gave life to the various modes of importance and how they weighed their relative significance. And we cannot understand ourselves without appreciating our own unique cultural interpretations and weightings, and how they are different and how similar to Hellenic and Tang realizations of importance. It is important for us, whether or not it was for either or both of them, to respect these differences, even as we respect also the historical or potential relevance of their judgments of worth to our current ones.

The key to the success of those who make systems is that they limit their concern to some finite and therefore manageable arena. "The whole of science is based upon neglected modes of relevance, which nevertheless dominate the social group entertaining those scientific modes of thought" (74). Progress in knowledge varies among the modes of importance within any culture as well as among cultures. In all these dimensions, both "the discovery of the intricacies of composition which that systems admits" and "the discovery of the limitations of the system in its omission," need constantly to occur (74). System-making interpreters of experience need to set boundaries to their subject matter—and take the matters-of-fact comprising that subject matter as similarly bounded. When they cease to acknowledge those limits, they are likely to treat their bounded content as all the content there is. They presume, and rightly so, that facts always come in finite units organized into finite systems. Since it is possible, at least in principle, to know completely any finite fact or system of finite facts, those who have achieved such knowledge tend to be certain about it. And if they think that what they know is all that can be known, they tend to be absolutely certain. Their knowledge knows no bounds.

Dogmatic certainty about the unambiguous meaning and absolute authority of any claim that "this is important" is a distortion, presuming clarity and imposing closure on what is unavoidably open-textured, invincibly vague around its edges. There is always something not clear and thus ambiguous lurking on the other side of every boundary. Nothing of importance is ever finally settled. Questions need constantly to be asked. A perspective is an interpretation, a finite limited way of approaching the world. Although I can always choose my perspective, I cannot choose not to have a perspective. The only kind of conscious experience possible for me is from a standpoint that is necessarily interpretative.

Thought and action, the making of knowledge and of physical or cultural objects, is a process of limitation, of system building. The ideal would seem therefore to be the construction of a closed system: a theoretical standpoint that is both logically consistent and factually adequate, a way of life that is both a consistent expression of one's character and an adequate fulfillment of one's potential. Despite all his well-known criticisms of closed systems, Whitehead celebrates those adept as making and using them. He says of scholars and experts of all sorts that they are "the main support of civilized thought" (173). Indeed, he defines moral "greatness" as the ability to attain the maximal harmony available in any given situation, to achieve the best possible integration of scope and intensity, to actualize the "perfection of importance for that occasion" (14). The expert's mastery of a finite system permits clarity in the grasp of the details of the system's nature and functions. Clarity enables penetration to what is essential, and when combined with "delicate accuracy of expression" (173) results in publicly verified transmittable knowledge, cost-effective machinery, well-founded stable institutions, and socially responsible citizens.

The fatal flaw in closed systems, of course, is the certainty that their perfection seems to justify. Experts know for sure what the text says, how the machine was designed to function, what the organization's rules are. Within the bounds of their expertise, they are masters of a system. The problem is when their success obscures an appreciation of the fact that their mastery is limited to that system, that systemic adequacy does not mean completeness. A finite certainty about a finite system can be justified. Certainty that leaps beyond that limit, however, that knows no bounds, that because of its limited perfection claims absolute certainty about absolutely everything, is, as Whitehead puts it in his understated way, "the Fallacy of the Perfect Dictionary" (173)—which fallacy is a version of the fallacy of misplaced concreteness, the failure to realize that systems are functions of matters-of-fact and are therefore standpoints fashioned for particular ends. For systems to be consistent, they must be inadequate. They are therefore transient expediencies, valuable in some contexts, in certain times and certain places, but not in others.

Interpretive theories and parochial ways of life need to recognize their limits. Fortunately, the very character of concrete realization is suffused with traces of what has been omitted, with intimations of past results and potentialities that have been neglected or explicitly denied, that have been marginalized and obscured by the success of the currently effective interpretation. The well-tended garden of the familiar rests solidly on the foundation of its supposedly self-evident, because constantly reaffirmed, adequacy. But it cannot fully hide the presence of the untended wilderness that lies just beyond its carefully ordered perimeter, its seeds and tendrils finding their insidiously quiet ways into the garden.

So my second claim about Whitehead offering in *Modes of Thought* a radically temporalist metaphysics is that he thinks functionally integrated processes are interpretive standpoints, that we ourselves and what we know are limited—finite and contingent—accomplishments. What saves us from overconfidence in the success of these accomplishments is the ontological fact of the beyond of every boundary we can fashion. "There is always a vague beyond, waiting for penetration in respect to its detail" (6).

RATIONALIZING

Matter-of-fact and importance are polar opposites reconciled in "this matters" judgments. I have explained these judgments in terms of aims that guide a process of emphasis and exclusion, through which a multitude of unique constituents becomes a functional unity. The process might be called concrescence, its power the creativity of actual entities. In *Modes of Thought*, however, using a term appropriate to conscious experience, Whitehead calls that power rationalization. But how does it work? How does it bring disparate things together, interpreting their differences as features of a meaningful unity? In the previous chapter, we saw how rationalization of the interplay of unity and plurality, sameness and difference, was explicated in terms of Appearance and Reality, especially the functions of propositions and symbolic form in generalizing Truth. Here Whitehead takes a different tack: "The procedure of rationalism," he says, "is the discussion of analogy" (1968, 98). When we think effectively, when we rationalize experience, we are thinking metaphorically.

We seek perfection, but it comes in two flavors. The ideal of a complete unification of things, the amalgamation of everything whatsoever into the perfect harmony of an ultimate totality, is one mode of perfecting the world as we find it. But the ideal of a unique fully self-sufficient individual, independent of anything extraneous, not needing anything else to complete itself, is equally a mode of perfection we extol. These two sorts of perfection are unreachable, however: no individual is absolutely unique, no totality absolutely encompassing. For every matter-of-fact there are other matters-of-fact that are similar to it in some way and to some extent, compromising its uniqueness. For every encompassing system there are other totalities that have a similar form or genetic structure or function, compromising its universality.

Metaphors and analogies are how we rationalize the polarities that result from literal thinking: by marking the partial identities to be found amid the diversity of things and the partial diversities to be found amid their identity. "Analogies survive amid diversity" (98), helping us realize that our love is like a red red rose; that in certain faraway places the sun comes up like thunder; that, as a good approximation, we should imagine the atom as a miniature solar system; that it helps people understand our theological vision if we note how obvious it is that the night has a thousand eyes and the day but one.

We give a particular object a proper name, but when we find another object that has a similar shape or color or way of functioning, we bring them together by applying the description of the one to the other. We refer to the process of making furrows in the soil as plowing, and so when we notice how the prow of a ship cuts through the waves, we indicate the likeness by saying that the ship plows the ocean. A simile or an analogy indicates the likeness; a metaphor transforms the likeness into an identity.

Since a matter-of-fact is a reality fashioned from components derived from other facts, its unity is systemic, a uniquely specific integration of uniquely specific elements. Hence the importance of a matter-of-fact is the quality of its unifying metaphors, of the creative insight, or action explicating it, that make of its constituent divergencies a concretely unified system. We can also think of a system as a schema, however, as an abstract pattern of possible relationships. The notion of a schema is how we generalize our particular experiences. A judgment that two things are the same is a claim that their features are similar enough to be treated as actualizations of the same schema, as systemic clones. The specific system actualized in one fact can be taken as actualized in other facts as well, if we focus on a schema derived from their relational features and ignore the differing entities' situational detailings of how these features actually function in each particular case. We ignore or downplay the distinguishing dissimilarities of two or more facts in order to affirm their distinguishing similarities. We interpret them as the same, because their schemas are.

Insofar as the metaphor is fresh, the identity is appreciated as interesting and perhaps insightful but not literal. It is taken as a rhetorical device for pointing out important similarities. I know that the windmill there on that hill doesn't really have arms, but its blades have a shape similar to that of my arms. I call this item of furniture an armchair because, although it has no feature that looks anything like my arms, it is designed to do what arms do: to hold something, to support me when I'm sitting in it. After constant use, however, the rhetorical identity asserted by the metaphor comes to be taken as a literal identity; it becomes a dead metaphor. We think of the windmill and the armchair as really having arms, and so the meaning of the word 'arm' is expanded: its definition becomes ambiguous. The ambiguity can be generic when the different meanings are systematic, as when the various kinds of primate upper appendages are all called arms. Or the meanings can be completely unrelated, as in the case of homonyms such as the reign of a king and the rain that in Spain falls mainly on the plain, although often homonyms with seemingly unrelated meanings turn out to have a single etymological ancestor.

The practical importance of metaphors is that by their means we can expand the reach of our interpretive standpoints. By rationalizing incompatible differences, by finding that things which seem radically disparate are not, our understanding of the scope and character of the meaningful world is enhanced. By taking a systemic relationship that in one situation is concretely familiar, schematizing it, and then applying the schema to another situation, we are able to treat the new as though it were the old, as though they shared an identical pattern of relatedness. We take the new to be functioning with respect to that pattern in the same way the old did. With our arms we can reach out and grasp an object, taking control of it, bringing it close in order to examine it. So we say that the police officer is an arm of the law, that she is able to reach out on behalf of the community to grasp a person, bringing him into custody so that we can determine whether to treat him as a law-abiding citizen or as a law-breaker.

In Whitehead's metaphysics, microfacts such as actual entities, mesofacts such as conscious human experiences, and macrofacts such as our cosmos are rationalized in this way. All the different kinds of things, and kinds of kinds, are integrated metaphorically. They are each taken as interpretively realized standpoints achieved by a selective ordering of includable elements, and the metaphysics that integrates them that way is also taken as itself an interpretatively realized standpoint selectively ordering them all. This exuberant metaphorical extension of matter-of-fact importance to all things great and small invites us to shift our understanding, and thereby how we ought to act, to a radically temporal standpoint. We see why every particular entity, and every community of entities and every effective theory about entities and communities, is of necessity contingent. For each, in its own distinctive way, is an important thing, but its unavoidable neglect of some of the elements available to it implies the presence of viable alternatives—different standpoints, different ways of being something that matters—that could have been realized but were not, or that might not yet be realized but will be, or that are opportunities irretrievably lost.

Actualized entities, enduring objects, human persons, social institutions, cultures: they are all partial and contingent ways of being; they are all successful rationalizations. The polarity of identity and difference, the one and the many, cannot be overcome, although it can be rationalized. And precisely because rationalizations are metaphorical interpretations, they are able constantly to change in order to survive as functional wholes, by emphasizing different schemata of identity and difference, ones more adequate to changing circumstance. When every matter-of-fact is a meaningful rationalization, there can be no definitive mode of existence, no certain truth, no trustworthy guarantee of the best way to live a fulfilling life or bring about a just society. Regulative principles can be devised for creating, sustaining, and even enhancing meaningful achievements, but there can be no fundamental constitutive principles determining the essential character of truth or goodness or beauty, nor determining the necessary means by which to arrive at its definitive realization. We live solely by means of temporary scaffolds of our own making and mending.

The ability to rationalize differences among things by finding the ways in which they are also the same means recognizing that nothing is purely different nor purely the same. They differ or are similar in varying degrees and manners. Each fact is unique but can be interpreted as an interchangeable instance of a class of facts. Each system is composed of many different components but can be interpreted as a single entity. These interpretations are not arbitrary. As Whitehead notes, when we are able to find significant commonalities among an aggregate of divergent particulars, or disruptive incompatibilities among the elements of a functioning whole, "we necessarily introduce the notion of 'potentiality'" (99). In this way, we grow increasingly aware that "all our knowledge consists in conceiving possible adjustments" in the relation between "the potentiality of the facts" for the "forms" and of those forms for the facts (99). Metaphorical thinking works because of the potentiality inherent in the many matters-of-fact for fitting into many different uniquely fashioned systems, and the potentiality inherent in a single system for giving shape to many differing particular matters-of-fact. As Whitehead insisted by his reference in *Adventures of Ideas* to Plato's *Sophist*, this inherent potentiality of things is their power and hence their ontological reality.

The schemas functioning as creators of compatibility are not static. They are what Whitehead calls "forms of process" or "serial forms" (99). The "fundamental intuition which lies at the basis of all thought" is fourfold: that there is an "essential passage from experience of individual fact to the conception of character [form]," that this form is stable "amidst the succession of facts," that this stability provides a "partial identity of successive facts in a given route of succession," and that there is thus a "potentiality of the facts for maintaining such partial identity amid such succession" (99). The organizing patterns never fit perfectly; they provide the multiplicity of particulars with a stabilizing but not permanent character. They are approximate forms, useful in the context for which they are fashioned but not necessarily in a different context. They are temporary scaffolds not timeless templates.

"A fortunate use of abstractions is of the essence of upward evolution" (123). We think rationally, are conscious in a rational way, when we abstract from the matters-of-fact that fill our concrete experience, taking their insistent vivid particularities as instances of something general: an interpretive pattern, an organizing rule, a guiding orientation. We find an analogy that binds things together: the gigantic planet Jupiter and the much smaller Mars have orbits similar to a mathematical ellipse. Then we explore the possibility that this analogy might apply to other planets as well, such as strangely-ringed Saturn or distant Pluto with its distinctively tilted orbit. We can even extend our analogy to planetary moons and to the electrons swirling around atoms, to planets orbiting other suns, to the movement of whole galaxies, and, if we are bold enough, to vague unknowns we conjure as maybe somewhere somehow existing beyond our spatial and temporal horizons but as nonetheless also bound by the same pattern or rule or purpose: the federated planets of the Galactic Empire in a galaxy far far away, or those orbiting suns in alternative universes parallel to our own.

We don't arbitrarily impose our interpretations on things, but rather exploit to our advantage the potential they have for supporting how we take them. More than one interpretation can be a legitimate way of rationalizing our experience of some factual importance. Wittgenstein's duck-rabbit is the drawing of either a duck or a rabbit depending on what elements of its lines are emphasized. It's a duck that could also be taken as a rabbit, or a rabbit that could also be thought of as a duck. But it cannot be interpreted simultaneously as both duck and rabbit. Nor is there any warrant whatsoever for taking the drawing as that of an elephant.

A rationalized experience is thus an objective experience. It is just not a definitive one, since shifting purposes and contexts can often lead to other interpretations. As William James puts it, there is no interpretive *"édition de luxe"* of the world, "eternally complete" and the objective measure of our various limited subjective ways of taking it (1981, 116). The world is completed by our interpretations, some of which work better than others and are therefore more objective with respect to a relevant context and purpose. None is intrinsically better.

Decisions we make about what similarities and differences are important are justified by how well they function objectively: whether they effectively guide us toward the realization of our personal and communal aims. These aims cannot be static, however, if they are to serve us well. So metaphors need to be robust enough not only to serve our immediate purposes in a particular situation but also to stimulate our imagination in the exploration of other somewhat different aims, ones that may turn out better suited to changing contexts: more adaptable, more useful over the long run. As our way of doing things changes, as we alter our purpose or shift our context, as sharp-edged new facts are discovered that shred the fabric of our theory, we need to reexamine the metaphors upon which we have been relying, the scaffold we have been using to construct our perspective. It may be time for a new scaffold, a metaphorical sally more promising for our purposes, seemingly better suited to our needs. The new scaffold may not hold, of course, but new and newly relevant matters-of-fact make old scaffolds uncouth and so urge us, indeed compel us, to venture novel ones.

Matters-of-fact are intimately related and derive their importance from the enduring character they have in common. But that character is only partial, enduring only for a limited time across a limited space. If we recognize that the commonality is metaphorical not literal, if we are habitually on the lookout for the disanalogies even as we explore the analogies, then our practice will be to set the accomplishments of the given world against a background of possible other worlds. In searching always for a better fit between facts and theories, we will be ready to abandon our theories, deconstruct our interpretive standpoints, call our stories into question. This seeming negation is actually a recovery, however, an enrichment of our abstractive frameworks by recourse to the concrete resources from which they were constructed. Sometimes what our new wine needs is old wine skins, perhaps to fill with the new wine but perhaps instead to stimulate the fashioning of a new kind of wine container.

Novel alternatives may actually turn out to be worse rather than better, as we have acknowledged, but where mere repetition is stultifying and hence dangerous, reasonable innovations even when they fail are worth having been tried. Rationalization relativizes ideals, but by doing so exhibits the creative power it provides for the formulation of new and better ideals. Rationalization is how we escape the familiar but blinding vistas of closed systems into the adaptive potency of the flexible vistas open systems provide.

So my third claim about the radically temporalist character of Whitehead's metaphysics in *Modes of Thought* is that he understands reason not as a fixed faculty of the mind but as a useful way of being conscious. He sees it as a method for devising fresh interpretive standpoints, ones able to resolve theoretical and practical problems that have resulted from the clash of divergent purposes and the incommensurable truths and values they entail. Our knowledge is necessarily inadequate because our perspectives are limited and the facts they interpret unstable. But inadequate doesn't mean ignorant, nor does limited mean erroneous. Approximations are the best we can manage, and they suffice if we use them as opportunities for furthering our purposes, for enhancing the effective range and subtlety of our ability to predict and control the conditions of our well-being. A radical temporalist settles for warranted assertions of what is true or good or beautiful, finding it sufficient that the truths are fruitful, the actions optimal, and the satisfactions generous.

Whitehead does not idolize change but acknowledges its dominion, and then seeks to explore the ways by which we can adapt to its necessities by harnessing its possibilities. Perhaps it would be good were there a God who guides and comforts us, but as finite creatures living amid other finite creatures, we can manage well enough on our own. We have the power to make our way in such a way that temporal possibilities become dynamically functional elements of our individual and communal ends, and of the interpretive systems by which these ends are expressed.

CIVILIZING

At the end of *Modes of Thought*, Whitehead famously says that "philosophy is akin to poetry" (1968, 174; also vii and 50); or as he puts it midway through the book: "philosophy is analogous to imaginative art" (117). Philosophy and poetry are in some ways the same, for "truth is to be sought in the presuppositions of language rather than in its express statements" (vii), and each in its own way, "suggests meaning beyond its mere statements" (117), makes "reference to form beyond the direct meaning of words" (174). Their activities are analogous because they both are good at thinking metaphorically. They both abuse language, rationalizing experience by using metaphors to break through conventional boundaries of what is worth knowing or doing, of what is intelligible or practical. They are the masters of open-system thinking, seeking in their differing ways "to express that ultimate good sense which we term civilization" (vii, 174).

Poetry invests particular facts with overtones of their general significance. It uses precise meanings to convey the "fundamental emotional importance of our naïve general intuitions" (5). Whitehead mentions Coleridge's objection to tourists who gaze at "an awe-inspiring spectacle" like a red sunset over calm water and exclaim fervently "How pretty!" The cliché is stupefyingly vague; it "lets down the whole vividness of the scene." Yet we shouldn't be too critical of those tourists, for the primary function of words is to "indicate useful particularities," to refer to concrete specifics such as the color of that daffodil, the roar of those rapids, this rising of the crescent moon. It is no easy task to employ them instead "to evoke a sense of that general character on which all importance depends." This is what poetry does—it uses particular words in ways that "evoke a vivid feeling of what lies beyond words" (5).

Sunsets are about the end of things. They are "pretty" not just because of the play of changing color tones but because when the sun sets the day's work is at last concluded and we can rest. A day's ending also hints at a life's ending, and poets often make precisely that connection metaphorically. As Tennyson does in his poem "Crossing the Bar," when "sunset and evening star" make "one clear call" to him: that death is like deciding to "put out to sea" as dusk begins to darken the known world.

> Twilight and evening bell,
> And after that the dark!

He assures us, however, that we should have "no sadness of farewell" when he departs this life,

> For tho' from out our bourne of Time and Place
> The flood may bear me far,

> I hope to see my Pilot face to face
> When I have crossed the bar.

Sunset and evening bell initiate a journey under divine guidance to which he looks forward hopefully.

In the poem "Ulysses," however, Tennyson replaces that connection with its opposite, turning sunset into an image of new adventure in this life. Old age with its sense of approaching death which "closes all" is not yet a time of closure but an opportunity for at least one more achievement:

> The lights begin to twinkle from the rocks:
> The long day wanes: the slow moon climbs: the deep
> Moans round with many voices. Come, my friends,
> 'Tis not too late to seek a newer world.

The words all refer to particulars: the moon rises; today's fading light glimmers over there on the rocks; those ocean waves, one after the other, lap against them. This dusk is not for resting, for it is marked by restless processes: twinkling, waning, climbing, moaning. They do not call us to rest but to action, not to find eternal peace in another world but to seize right now the chance to remake our world in some newer better way. Tennyson's metaphors work powerfully because they are so fresh, not only because they evoke the importance of creative action but because they do so in contrast to a contrary importance, that of life's inevitable end. In "Crossing the Bar" Tennyson uses familiar metaphors to make an important but unsurprising point about hope: hope for a meaningful life beyond one's death. "Ulysses" is also about hope, but here the metaphors break free of their clichéd use to make a surprising point: hope for a meaningful life even now toward the end of life, for new resolve rather than resignation.

Metaphysical philosophy uses metaphor in a way the inverse of poetry, says Whitehead. It invests conventional generalities with overtones of vivid particularity. It takes an everyday word that expresses the obvious in vague generalities, and gives it a precise but novel meaning. Metaphysics speaks of such things as 'formal causes' and 'the categorical imperative,' 'ultimate truth' and 'the end of time,' but by investing those words with expanded and therefore disconcertingly unfamiliar meanings, we must "shake ourselves free" from our "acquire[d] learning." We are forced to "grasp the topic in the rough," and only then take seriously the need to "smooth it out and shape it" (6). Philosophic neologisms avoid the tourist's trivialization of language by jarring us out of our taken-for-granted sense of what vague but familiar generalities mean, helping us recognize that "the obvious embodies the permanent importance of variable detail" (5), of startling details obscured by the vagueness to which we have become accustomed. Troubled, we attend to the novel generality, and by means of its expanded content grasp concretely the functional importance it expresses.

When William James says that truth is what works (1981, 98), he speaks metaphorically. The conventional meaning of "work" is vague, and confusingly ambiguous in its vagueness. Persons are said to work when they labor at a task, any task, expending time and energy to complete it. Their work lies in the effort they make, whether the job gets done or comes to naught. Machines of any sort, however, work only if they run as they are supposed to, if they function as they were designed to function: with optimal efficiency and simplicity. If the machine runs erratically and can no longer be counted on, we say it isn't working, like a watch that doesn't keep time. In a third sense of work, the plan is said to work if it succeeds, not merely if an effort is made to carry it out and not merely if things run smoothly. It works only if the labor and the functionality achieve the intended result, no matter how excessive the labor required or how convoluted the process.

The usual interpretation of James's definition by its critics is that he means any idea—any possibility, any aim—is true if it satisfies our desires, if it gets us where we want to go. It is pragmatic in the pejorative sense of the end justifying the means. Whatever it takes, just get it done. James's metaphor allows that interpretation, of course, because if he means that truths are similar to plans then the sufficient condition of their working is that their importance be a systemic structure that satisfies end-justifying criteria.

The metaphor invites other similarities between truth and work, however, and James is quite explicit that he intends work to mean a specific kind of functional effectiveness: a system that works is one that runs without a hitch and by doing so achieves a goal. Yet not just any efficiency and not just any aim, but ones that are sustainable and can be enhanced. So James's truths preserve old truths, take account of current situational facts, and continue doing so for a reasonable length of time. The pragmatism at work here is sophisticated not crass, far-sighted and wide-visioned in its opportunism, at once conservative and progressive. In a word, civilized.

James takes a vague general concept, that of work, and gives it a new meaning: persons, machines, and plans work. But so, in a specific sense, do truths. This novel meaning for truth is jarring because it associates truth with practical processes and seems to neglect the notions of correspondence or coherence with which it is usually associated. James finds a schema in ideas, processes, and objects that we interpret as examples of work, and applies an enhanced version of the schema to truthful concepts. The metaphor extends a familiar concept, expanding its reference from a well-established range of facts to facts usually thought too different to be relevant.

In doing so, it opens our thinking to a wider range of possible similarities and differences concerning both what counts as work and what counts as truth. For instance, people who work grow tired because of their efforts, effective machines eventually break down, and our best laid plans gang aft agley. So if we think of truths as ideas and practices that work, then we should expect even the best of them to break down eventually. They are limited devices of limited importance. And like any other device, truths need to be serviced: readjusted, repaired, renovated—and eventually replaced with truths better suited to the situations for which they are needed.

James's metaphor carries us a long way from truths that are propositional copies of empirical realities, or are themselves, everlasting or eternal realities. In doing so, he introduces an exciting vivid relevance to those familiar ghostly generalities. The relativism and contingency of things and of our knowledge of them are thereby rescued from incipient nihilism by being shown to be objective features of things. We are able to see subjective limitation not as a brick-walled cul-de-sac but as a porous boundary, as having gates in its walls, as a moment of achievement pointing ever beyond itself.

Metaphysics and poetry use language to break through the boundaries that language has imposed over the centuries of its use on our sense of what facts are important and why. They rationalize experience by creating the tools through which we are able to expand the depth and scope of the meaningful world, to repair its inadequacies by disclosing new kinds of fact and fresh ways of interpreting how these new kinds and the familiar kinds are related. Metaphysics and poetry offer the tools for developing the habit of thinking rationally, which is to say metaphorically, for transforming matters-of-fact and importances into a vibrantly inquisitive dialogue between separately inadequate but interactively creative realities.

Whitehead opens and closes *Modes of Thought* by saying of poetry and philosophy that they seek "to express the ultimate good sense we term civilization" (1968, vii, 174). The assertion is normative not descriptive, of course. Not all poets manage to invest particular works with general meaning, and some don't even seek to do so, perhaps insisting that meanings are only particular. And not all metaphysical philosophers think metaphorically or even show an interest in particulars, perhaps because they do not think concepts are abstractive generalizations and so believe that metaphysical airplanes need not depart from or return to the concrete particulars of common experience.

The best metaphysicians and the great poets, however, seek to foster civilized values in what they do because they think metaphorically, and therefore think it important to help us recognize the inadequacy of any of our conceptual or institutional frameworks, to realize that the frameworks are inadequate because the facts they interpret are themselves inadequate actualizations of prior possibilities. If the closure required for the making of new fact from the many things available as its constitutive elements can never be complete, then closures to succeed must have more than filters able to strain out incompatibilities and so permit unification. These filters must also allow osmotic processes that lead from the achieved enclosure into subsequent arenas redolent with possibilities for attempting further closures.

We should realize that systems must be adaptive, that they need to be flexible enough to adjust to problems they were not originally designed to solve, that how their components function can be altered or different components substituted for ones no longer functional. A civilization flourishes when its stabilizing features are dynamic, when they work not merely by returning conditions to a state of equilibrium but more importantly by permitting or encouraging an exquisitely moderate disequilibrium in which novel patterns of thought and action can be explored without immediately threatening the wider social order. Adaptive systems are able not only to tolerate but actually to encourage the development of a multiplicity of contrasting schemas of importance that test constantly the viability of the boundaries of established order, poking holes in them and then finding ways to turn those holes into progressive features of the ongoing social whole. The way this occurs is by treating some established identities as different and some established differences as the same, by devising new standpoints that recast the accepted conditions for what is meaningful. And how to inquire in this creative manner is by thinking and acting with the help of metaphors.

So my fourth claim about Whitehead as a radically temporalist metaphysician is that he thinks both poets and philosophers have a crucial role to play in sustaining the viability of civilized modes of thought and practice by helping to prevent the success of currently effective ideas and institutions from blocking the emergence of successors with differing perspectives, ones that may be more adaptively suited to altered conditions. They may quite well not turn out to be more adaptively suited, of course. They may unsettle things without improving them; they may contribute to the emergence of less adaptive attitudes and institutions. But the risk of failure is the price that must always be paid for enhancing the quality of individual and collective life. Philosophers and poets are effective practitioners of their differing but complementary disciplines when they are adept at inventing metaphors, at thinking in the open-ended manner suited to an open-ended world. They stand at the cutting edge of civilization, purveying in their halting approximate ways that ultimate good sense without which civilized modes of existence can neither flourish nor long endure.

NOTES

1. This chapter is a revised version of my article "Ultimate Good Sense" in *Thinking with Whitehead and the American Pragmatists: Experience and Reality*, eds. Brian G. Henning, William T. Myers, and Joseph D. John. Lanham, MD: Lexington Books, 2015: 25–40. Used with permission, all rights reserved.

7

THE SOLEMNITY OF THE WORLD

This final chapter is about finalities: the ultimate meaning of the temporal process, of the endless emergence and perishing of finite things.[1] I begin with the two notions of ultimate meaning found in Whitehead's last two books: the notion of Peace in *Adventures of Ideas*, and the notion of Totality in *Modes of Thought*. I explicate both notions as being about the sense finite things have of belonging to an ever-emerging, ever creating, ever perishing ultimate community composed of predecessors, contemporaries, and possible successors. I follow this with a consideration of the explicit antithesis of this view: that this ultimate community is an everlasting ontological reality, the transformative work of an ontological agency, the consequent nature of God. I conclude by a return to Whitehead's notion of Peace, focusing on his discussion of Tragic Beauty as a way to summarize the metaphysical hypothesis I have been developing throughout this book.

PEACE

In chapter 5, we considered four of what Whitehead in *Adventures of Ideas* calls the "essential qualities, whose joint realization in social life constitutes civilization": Truth, Beauty, Art, and Adventure. But "something is still lacking," he says, without which the pursuit of a civilized way of life "can be ruthless, hard, cruel" (1967, 284). What is missing, the fifth essential quality, is the sense of Peace.

Whitehead hesitates about what word he should use to name this sense (284–85). He turns for help to the Platonic list of basic notions discussed at the beginning of chapter 5. However, he finds in "'Harmony' only hints," a "sort of atmosphere," of what he means, and 'Eros' "somewhat at variance." "Ideas" and "Mathematical Relations" are rejected because of their "absence of 'life and motion.'" The remaining of the seven notions—"Psyche," "Receptacle," "Physical Elements"—are passed over in silence, presumably as obviously inappropriate. So he turns to other possibilities but finds them also inadequate: "Tenderness" and "Love" emphasize the rejection of "restless egotism," but they are otherwise "too narrow," at best specializations of what he wants; "Impersonality" is simply "too dead."

Whitehead settles for 'Peace,' immediately hastening to insist that Peace is "not the negative conception of anaesthesia" but a "positive feeling which crowns the 'life and motion' of the soul." Nor is it "a hope for the future," nor "an interest in present details" (285). It is not a focus on importance or a focus on matter-of-fact, but rather on their integration. Not in the sense of a task, however, a goal to be sought in the hope of achieving it. "The experience of Peace is largely beyond the control of purpose. It comes as a gift" (285), the result of that "first-hand experience" the "necessity" of which Hume said is "inexorable" (287).

Whitehead's first attempt at a definition of Peace describes it as "a quality of mind steady in its reliance that fine action is treasured in the nature of things" (274). He doesn't elaborate, but after his meandering search for a suitable word, offers a second definition: Peace is "a surpassing of personality," a "broadening of feeling due to the emergence of some deep metaphysical insight" the first effect of which is "the removal of the stress of acquisitive feeling arising from the soul's preoccupation with itself" (285).

Peace is a sense of the importance of all those matters-of-fact that are ignored by our tendency to focus attention on things directly concerned with our interests. It enlarges our concerns from self to world, from only me to all of us. It is "a grasp of infinitude, an appeal beyond boundaries," whereby "interest has been transferred to coördinations wider than personality" (285). This broadening and deepening of the scope of what matters is the result of "a trust in the efficacy of Beauty," in its "self-justification," which nurtures in us "a sense that fineness of achievement is as it were a key unlocking treasures that the narrow nature of things would keep remote" (285). It enlarges our sense of the nature of things from something hostile or indifferent to our interests to something that treasures them insofar as those interests have themselves been expanded, maturing into a concern with fine action. That's why Beauty is so key, for it is a matter of possibilities for fineness both in ideals sought and in values achieved. A trust in its efficacy, says Whitehead, "introduces faith, when reason fails to reveal the details" (285).

Peace may come as a gift, but for it to be experienced firsthand, which it must be for us to receive it, we need to experience the fineness of purpose bit by bit, the surpassing of an emphasis on personality slowly occurring, until it culminates in "the love of mankind as such" (286). Whitehead organizes a sketch of this process into steps of growth extending from Youth to Maturity. "Youth is distinguished for its wholehearted absorption in personal enjoyments and personal discomforts" (287), both the joys and the sorrows brief but intense, each quickly following on the other. The "short-sightedness of youth matches the scantiness of its experience," the lack of awareness of implications worth remembering so that the next time to avoid or to again seek out. Youth is not simply self-absorbed, however, because it is "peculiarly susceptible to appeals for beauty of conduct" (287), losing itself in the "ardour" of its "devotion" to Beauty in some specific form, to "ideal aims that lie beyond any personal satisfaction" (288).

This awareness of ideals worth one's loyalty can turn back on itself, however, into "the egotistic desire for fame," for feeling that "each act of [one's own] experience is a central reality, claiming all things as its own" (288). The "craving to stand conspicuous in this scheme of things" softens into "the love of particular individual things," one's commitments passing beyond oneself, "but with explicit, definite limitation to particular realities" such as family members and friends. Eventually the focus is a person with whom one falls in love, for whose benefit one is passionately concerned, feeling that success in caring for the loved one is akin to "what would happen if right could triumph in a beautiful world, with discord routed" (289).

A shift in the object of one's devotion from an individual to a society, to the willingness to sacrifice one's own gratification, indeed one's life, for the group, is to become a patriot, to "aim at a social perfection" to which one contributes by one's actions while alive and by one's example after dying. Patriotism is the "conformation of purpose to ideal beyond personal limitations," an ideal "with which the wise man can face his fate, master of his soul" (291). As the society expands to which one gives oneself, contributing to the fulfilling of one person or group is felt as also contributing to the fulfillment of others beyond that group. One's concerns move to wider and wider societies and to societies of societies, until it culminates in "a high-grade type of order" and a fully mature individual. One arrives at a situation where self and society "coalesce," each recognized as the necessary condition for the other: "The essence of Peace is that the individual whose strength of experience is founded upon this ultimate intuition, thereby is extending the influence of the source of all order" (292).

What Whitehead means by a sense of Peace is, to say the least, complicated; in many ways understanding it is to embody it, and that's the task of a lifetime. A necessary condition for having a sense of Peace, however, and a way therefore to understand its core of meaning, can be found in Whitehead's answer to the question of "whether there exists any factor in the Universe constituting a general drive towards the confirmation of Appearance to Reality," a drive which is "a factor in each occasion persuading its aim at such truth as is proper to the special appearance in question" (293). It is not enough that we have ideals that reach beyond our personal needs and interests and that we recognize our ideals as intrinsically worth actualizing. We need also to recognize that we are not alone in our struggle to actualize them, that we are part of "an Adventure in the Universe as One," an adventure embracing all particular drives toward various conformations of various Appearances to Reality, but which "as an actual fact stands beyond any one of them" (295).

Our ideals and undertakings are not isolated even though they are contextually grounded and so necessarily parochial. Although our aims and efforts are about matters or our immediate concern, about ourselves and those we love, they belong at the same time to a vast community of others with their differing immediate concerns, their own distinctive aims and efforts. We are, all of us, to some extent, therefore, and with various degrees of self-awareness, struggling to actualize what we think is the best future possible not only for ourselves and our family but also for our neighbors and our nation, for humankind and for all creation.

Whether we recognize it or not, we are part of an adventure that goes on everywhere and has gone on seemingly forever, an adventure in the universe that includes all its constituents, they and we alike seeking to make possibilities into actualities, to transcend the given facts toward the creation of new facts. Peace is the sense that these many adventures comprise one grand adventure. We will honor our forefathers and mothers and will hope to be honored by our grandchildren when we understand ourselves as joining with them in the never-ending effort to actualize possible goods that constitute the creative advance of the universe. We will honor our biological ancestors stretching back along the many-branched bush of evolution to the origins of life, and we will hope to be honored by future life-forms beyond our imagining when we understand ourselves as indebted to them for their achievements and knowing we will pay that debt by how our actions shape the course of future evolution. We honor the universe and all the cosmoses that long ago and now and long after give it particular expression by understanding that we are a part of its unbounded process. Peace is the sense of ourselves as active participants in this community.

TOTALITY

Although a reference to it is not included in the index, the notion of 'Totality' is fundamental to understanding Whitehead's argument in *Modes of Thought* that "at the base of our existence is the sense of 'worth,'" which is "the sense of existence for its own sake, of existence which is its own justification, of existence with its own character" (1968, 109).

As he does typically, Whitehead dismisses specific details grasped clearly and distinctly as an acceptable candidate for comprising that base. Clarity "results from an effort of concentration and elimination," from "an ever-shifting process of abstracting shifting quality from a massive process of essential existence." Hence our "clear consciousness of qualitative detail" is "superficial" and "flickering," and also "never sustained" (108). It is crucial that we not "forget the background" from which we abstract, the many things eliminated that leave the few things or the single thing on which we concentrate. We must not ignore the "fullness of existence" that we sense as "vaguely haunting" what we clearly know, for without it "the result is triviality" (108). The details are how we "add definition" to our concerns; they "introduce powers of judgment," by which we are able to organize the details into meaningful hierarchies. But all these efforts are "interpretive and not originative. What is original is the vague totality" (109).

The most "primitive stage of discrimination" is a "vague grasp of reality" as divisible "into a threefold scheme, namely, 'The Whole,' 'That Other,' and 'This-My-Self'" (110). Or put in a slightly different way: "there is the totality of actual fact; there is the externality of many facts; there is the internality of this experiencing which lies within the totality" (116). No one of these three aspects is more significant than the other two. I sense my own intrinsic importance, my here-and-now factuality as a unique person with my unique story of achievements and failures, striving as best I can to live as well as possible. I'm also aware of other matters-of-fact, ones of which I am presently aware, but also those previously encountered, or remembered, or heard about, or imagined as possible: friends and enemies, animal vegetable mineral, each with its own intrinsic importance. And I'm aware of myself and these others comprising a whole world stretching indefinitely in all directions, modes, and manners, a boundless totality of intrinsically important finite achievements. "We are, each of us, one among others; and all of us are embraced in the unity of the whole" (110).

What Whitehead calls the "existential essence" of a thing (116) is the sheer fact of its existence. Particular facts have value because to exist is to have been made, to have been brought into existence; it is to be a possibility actualized, an aim fulfilled, a many become one. Insofar as a thing is aware of its essence, no matter how dimly, no matter how lightly touched by consciousness, it is aware of itself as valuable. "Our enjoyment of [our own] actuality is a realization of worth, good or bad. It is a value experience": an experience of ourselves as being "something that matters!" (116). "My importance is my emotional worth now," and "actuality is the self-enjoyment of [that] importance" (117). Whitehead then yokes this sense of intrinsic importance with our "sense of power." Power is the "compulsion of composition" and "the essence of power is the drive toward aesthetic worth for its own sake." "There is no other fact" than this, he insists: "composition attaining worth for itself," an exercise of the power of things so as to fashion existential value (119).

A judgment of factual importance always involves, at first, reference to the unique importance actualized, to this fact as the effective system it is, to each of us as aware of our individual importance. Our sense of importance also involves, perhaps only dimly, reference to the thises and thats we are not, to the other important facts that surround us, influencing us and being influenced by us. Yet persistently and unavoidably, the judgment that we are important also involves reference to Totality, to a recognition of all else: not only facts and systems of facts relevant to our existence but also all that is beyond this and that, self and other, but is nonetheless there. We sense all other entities intertwined with our present individual actuality, and the same for all other actualities, each with the others enjoying the totality we share, "the unity of the universe" (118) that we are and that encompasses us. These other entities are "the many factors which form the historic environment" for the composition of immediate worth. Plus one further factor: "our sense of the value, for its own sake, of the totality of historic fact in respect to its essential unity" (119). Our sense of worth includes an awareness of the worth of the components of the given world that influence our own creative efforts, and an awareness of these components as comprising a totality of things, a "unity in the universe, enjoying value and (by its immanence) sharing value" (120). Totality includes a sense of other individuals with their differing actualities, including those the actuality of which is only possible, and at the same time a sense of myself and all those other selves as a boundless ongoing interdependent whole.

Our sense of this unbounded Totality kindles our awareness that each particular thing is a limited thing, an accomplishment among accomplishments amid a vast horizonless and depthless expanse of what our immediate interests have momentarily excluded, all of them particular resources potentially available for the actualization of possibilities alternative to the ones with which we are currently concerned. We exist within a finite ambient that has made us and that we can use to make our successors; we exist within wider and wider ambients that have made our ambient and its resources possible; we exist within a Totality of which we and our ambients are all finite, limited, and fundamentally important parts.

Note carefully that the Totality of things is not a thing; it does not organize everything into some great absolute all-encompassing unity. It is not God or some other transcendent agency. It is more than any agent and any unity that agent might achieve, more than all the agents and unities that have been and are and could yet be. Whitehead refers to a sense of the "full solemnity of the world" (78) as arising "from the sense of positive achievement within the finite, combined with the sense of modes of infinitude stretching beyond each finite fact" (78). My recognition of an ultimate indefinite environment, an ambient implied in the experience of any definite thing, in any interpretive standpoint, a Totality inviting perspectives but not one itself, evokes my solemn sense of its grandeur. It also evokes my solemn awareness of the "necessary relevance" of my finite fleeting here-and-now self, of this that I have made of my life, to what lies "beyond [my] own limitations" (79).

This sense of my relevance beyond my finite matter-of-fact self is my proper "perspective of the universe" (79), a perspective that is felt as necessary, for "mere matter-of-fact refuses to be deprived of its relevance to potentialities beyond its own actuality of realization" (83). My perspective, when it includes an appreciation, however dim, however far short of specific knowledge, of the perspectives of all other matters-of-fact, is the sense of Totality. Totality is therefore not a reality other than myself. It is my importance, that of what I am that reaches beyond me, and that reaches beyond every other matter-of-fact, because it is our common creation. We stand solemnly before the awe-inspiring realization that there is no absolute order or perspective, no absolutely encompassing whole, no bounded totality. Our closed systems are boats precariously underway on a stormy sea, and there is no harbor except what the boats themselves provide. As William James puts it: "All 'homes' are in finite experience; finite experience as such is homeless. Nothing outside of the flux secures the issue of it" (1981, 117).

Solemnity in the face of a boundless "more" that escapes the confines of any meaningful fact is the resource we need to function effectively. It teaches us that all important things are limited perspectives. "All forms of realization express some aspect of finitude," express themselves as this or that, as those of us and these others. Realization "expresses exclusion; and exclusion means finitude" (1968, 78). This recognition of inescapable finitude encourages us to find in even the worst of situations opportunities for meliorative thought and action. Limitation is the engine of both human and cosmic betterment. Our sense of who we are, of what we have achieved, is unavoidably "incomplete and partial," presupposing relation to some given undefined ambient, "imposing a perspective and awaiting exploration" (43), thereby evoking a "sense of vast alternatives, magnificent or hateful, lurking in the background, and awaiting to overwhelm our safe little traditions" (45). Because "any knowledge of the finite always involves a reference to infinitude" (44), any sense of completion also involves sensing "dimly the unexplored relationships with things beyond" (48).

Hence although "system is essential to rational thought," nonetheless "the closed system is the death of living understanding" (83). Appreciating the beauty of a particular fact or a system of facts, a sunset or an explanation of sunsets, can be an exquisite experience, sometimes even a sublime one. Yet only when a system is appreciated as both an achievement and a failure, as a bright light revealing something about the world, but revealing its penumbra of shadows as well and the dark umbra beyond the shadows, only then does the world's solemnity dawn on us. Only then does our life become an endless adventure essential to who we are, an adventure we receive as a priceless inheritance, pursue for a brief moment, and then bequeath to our successors. And as Tennyson reminded us a few pages ago: it's never too late for us to explore those unexplored things.

Whitehead's references here are explicitly aesthetic, for it is in this context that he comments on the "flower in some isolated glade of a primeval forest." Its beauty is not only because of the subtlety of composition it exhibits but also because it is "a grand fact in the universe" (120). Our sense of its value includes a "sense of the value of the details for the totality." We appreciate the way in which its genetic heritage and its cellular development have contributed to the elegance of its "total effect" (120). And we also appreciate how the details of its total effect contribute to the total effect that is the present universe. "The sense of being one actuality in a world of actualities—is the gift of aesthetic significance" (120–21). For ourselves, as for the flower, our sense of our own intrinsic importance, our aesthetic significance, is as though we were among the statues along the cathedral walls at Chartres, aware of ourselves as actualities each with our own detailed integrity, who are also contributing that integrity to the total effect which is the cathedral as a whole.

Whitehead refers to this sense of the aesthetic totality of which we are a contributing factor as "the intuition of holiness, the intuition of the sacred, which is at the foundation of all religion" (120). The value of the totality is the value of its details, a value not reducible to the details but vacuous without them. To sense how precious each particular thing is, and how it is so intrinsically valuable to how precious every other particular thing is, is to sense how precious the Totality is, how interdependent the fragile finite makings of the world. This world, the grand fact that is the Totality of grand facts, is sacred because beyond price, holy because intrinsically precious. It is the world of particulars in communion, endlessly creating value and created by it. Hence the Totality is never completed, never an achieved totality, for the universe, unlike the Cathedral of Chartres, is necessarily open-ended. There is no single cosmic satisfaction, no universal determinate outcome to the multiplicity of concrescences. The one that the many become is always one more among a multitude of other ones, distinct from them that have also become. Their ultimate everlasting unity—whether hierarchical or temporal, under the aegis of a single organizing first principle or an eschatological endpoint—is but a dream.

The intuition of the sacred, as Whitehead uses it here, is not a reference to God in the sense developed in *Process and Reality*, but to "deity" in the sense Samuel Alexander develops it in his book *Space, Time, and Deity*. "Deity," says Whitehead, explicating Alexander's vocabulary, is "the lure of the ideal which is the potentiality beyond immediate fact" (1968, 101). "Time" refers to "the transitions of process," to "experiences of origination from a past and of determination toward a future." "Space" refers to "the halt for attainment" and "the experiences of joint association," of "interwoven existence," that constitute "the complexity of immediate realization" (101–3). Deity is how space and time are linked. The multitude of particular past achievements and the transition toward new particular achievements are linked in our experience by a sense of "worth beyond ourselves" (102), by our experience "of ideals entertained, of ideals aimed at, of ideals achieved, of ideals defaced" (103). To experience "the deity of the universe" is to experience ideals and the "intertwining of success and failure" by creatures in their effort to realize those ideals. Our intuition of deity is how we go about "measuring ourselves in respect to what we are not." It is how "amid futility and frustration" we are able to envision "other ideals involving novel forms of order" (103), and so are able to act transformatively, able to seek ways to make a particular intrinsic good from the limited resources available, and, unsatisfied, to reach toward a better making.

Whitehead associates the intuition of holiness with "Descartes' notion of perfection." It is "that power in history which implants into the form of process, belonging to each historic epoch, the character of a drive toward some ideal, to be realized within that period" (120). Deity conveys this same sense of perfection, of holiness: a generalization of the drive of finite entities to seek the actualization of parochial ideals, a drive toward finite perfections that is never fully realized, an ideal that is "beyond realization, and yet it moulds the form of what is realized" (120). Totality is our sense right now that what we are accomplishing right now we are not accomplishing alone. We stand on the shoulders of our predecessors, whose efforts to realize certain possibilities have made this standing possible. What we now aim to do will result in the place where our successors will stand as they seek to make their own dreams concrete. In other words, our sense of Totality is the sense that our compulsive powers of composition are also everywhere else manifest—are now manifest, have been manifest from times past beyond reckoning, and will be manifest henceforth until the end of a time that has no end. Our sense of our intrinsic importance, of the fact of ourselves as something that matters, lies in the creative power of that doing, a power that is ours but not uniquely ours, a power we share with all creation.

Thus a sense of Totality is akin to a sense of Peace; both are recognitions of the profound meaning of our brief existence, the solemnity of its radically temporal significance. We are passing moments in an all-encompassing open-ended process, passages in a story without a specifiable beginning or end, members emerging and perishing of a community composed of all such entities, creating by means of our interdependence a world of priceless things, of contingent actualities, realities that need not have been made but were and are and will yet be made.

THE OPEN SEA

I began this book with a critique of Whitehead's notion of God with respect both to a related set of metaphysical functions he calls the Primordial Nature and to a different set of metaphysical functions he calls the Consequent Nature. I would like to pause for a moment before concluding my account of Whitehead's notion of ultimate meaning to consider an argument on behalf of the Consequent Nature which, although frequently mentioned, has not been the focus of my earlier critiques. I have been critical of Whitehead's argument that values achieved by the concrescings of actual entities cannot be simply transient. He insisted that for there to be a cosmos, stability is required, continuity over time, and that this requires an everlasting entity able to retain past value achievement as relevant features of the creative advance. Whitehead's notion of the Eternal, critiqued in chapter 4, is an earlier version of that argument, focusing on the ontology of transient entities requiring a ground for their activities. Here, I want to discuss a related but different argument of Whitehead's, one that is epistemological, centering on enduring objects such as human beings who are aware of their achievements. The argument is twofold: were it the case that we thought the values we create have no everlasting relevance, our creative efforts would be meaningless; we can be absolutely certain, therefore, that those values are indeed of everlasting worth.

Whitehead approaches his argument in *Process and Reality* for God having a consequent nature by asserting two premises. The first is that "the ultimate evil in the temporal world lies deeper than any specific evil. It lies in the fact that the past fades, that time is a 'perpetual perishing'" (1978, 340). This is so because "objectification involves elimination"; things in their becoming and their enduring are "mutually obstructive" (340). Concrescence is a process of selection, eliminating some actual and possible elements of its inherited past in order to include others. The creative advance in inherently destructive as a condition of its being creative. Many things, with all their intrinsic value, must be sacrificed so that new things can emerge. "So long as the temporal world is conceived as a self-sufficient completion of the creative act, . . . the best that we can say of the turmoil is 'For so he giveth his beloved—sleep'" (342). Whitehead questions, however, "whether metaphysical principles impose the belief that it is the whole truth" that this is the best that can be said (342). "There is no reason, of any ultimate metaphysical generality, why this should be the whole story" (340). No matter how "far our gaze penetrates, there are always heights beyond which block our vision" (342). "Why should there not be novelty without loss"? (340).

Accordingly, Whitehead's second premise is that we need to take seriously the "vague insistence" by which our "physical feelings are haunted" of "another order, where there is no unrest, no travail [correcting the text's 'travel'], no shipwreck: 'There shall be no more sea.'" Why can it not be that "the process of the temporal world passes into the formation of other actualities, bound together in an order in which novelty does not mean loss" (340)? That would be possible were "the perfection of God's subjective aim, derived from the completeness of his primordial nature" (345), to issue in a complementary perfection, a consequent nature by which the values the world creates in each moment's "unison of immediacy" are retained without loss. Which is to say: are made "everlasting" (346).

The key notion is that of perfection, a quite different one from what has just been discussed: the transformation of a finite mortal creature into elements of a reality neither limited nor perishable, devoid of the endemic conflict resulting from irreconcilable differences. God in his consequent nature "prehends every actuality for what it can be in such a perfected system—its sufferings, its sorrows, its failures, its triumphs, its immediacies of joy—woven by rightness of feeling into the harmony of the universal feeling, which is always immediate, always many, always one, always with novel advance, moving onward and never perishing" (346). The transformation is redemptive. It "loses nothing that can be saved," including even "what in the temporal world is mere wreckage" (346).

Whitehead thus offers a metaphysical interpretation "of that vision upon which the finer religions are built—the 'many' absorbed everlastingly in the final unity" (347). Mortal flesh is offered a "sense of worth beyond itself," which is "immediately enjoyed as an overpowering element in individual self-attainment." In this way "the immediacy of sorrow and pain is transformed into an element of triumph. This is the notion of redemption through suffering which haunts the world" (350). All the opposites found in "the nature of things" are harmonized in God's dynamic perfection. Not the fleetingly momentary work of a self's temporal creation, but that work perfected, become ever after a part of the divine life. "This incredible fact—that cannot be, yet is" (350)—justifies our "insistent craving that zest for existence be refreshed by the ever-present unfading importance of our immediate actions, which perish and yet live forevermore" (351). Whitehead finds "no reason" why this should not be true, and since it "haunts the world" and is a "vision" fundamental to all "finer religions," even though it seems "incredible" he cautiously affirms it.

Two of Whitehead's most influential successors, whose importance lies in their development of his ideas in fruitfully new ways, are not so tentative. For them, there is ultimately no sea: our lives, lived uncertainly amid the tumultuous waves of temporal oceans, will always find secure harbor on the solid ground of an everlasting reality. They insist on the centrality of God's Consequent Nature providing that security, assuring us the possibility of living meaningful lives.

David Griffin argues that "the religious longing for immortality" (2001, 197) is not merely an expression of our vulnerability, a terrifying recognition of our transience and a desire to overcome it. The source lies deeper than that. Our longing expresses one of our basic human "hard-core commonsense beliefs": that "somehow what we do matters in the long run" (380). "Among our deepest desires is the desire for our actions to make a permanent contribution to the universe." Moreover, since "our most fundamental emotional-purposive responses to reality generally reflect the actual nature of reality" (198), there must exist a reality that provides that very permanence we need. "The reason why we are not satisfied with the conception of ourselves as purely transient phenomena of the universe, even if our lives be otherwise immensely enjoyable, is that we have a direct prehension of the consequent nature of God." Our "longing for immortality is itself a product of a veridical perception" of that reality (197). We long for immortality because we are able to have a first-hand absolutely veridical perception of its reality. Not by an act of faith but by direct prehension, we know that we are saved.

Charles Hartshorne takes this argument a step further, claiming that "all importance, all value, hence all meaning, is relative to possible contributions to the one Life whose adequate perceivings alone can render immortal the character of an event" (1984, 154). The linkage is unequivocal: value of any sort is dependent on its attaining permanence. The worth of any event, any action, any person's life, is determined by its contribution to the divine life. Absent that contribution, it has no value whatever. "What does our being definite matter if the universe has no way to retain the definiteness?" (1983, 360).

In an essay on "Time, Death, and Everlasting Life," included in *The Logic of Perfection*, Hartshorne uses the metaphor of a book to explain his contention. Our lives, like books, are finite. Our life begins on the first page with our birth and our death writes the last page, after which the book is irrevocably closed. What ends does not therefore perish, however. "Death is not ultimate destruction but simply termination, finitude" (1962, 251). As a book, once completed, is thereafter available for others to learn from, so also for us: "once an individual is there to refer to, he continues to be there even after death, as object of reference, as a life which really has been lived" (247). The direct relevance of our achievements to other persons or groups, to our nation or to the human race, to this planet or this cosmic epoch, is only a transient relevance, for governments and organic species and planets and even cosmic epochs will eventually perish. Therefore "our adequate immortality can only be God's omniscience of us" (252). We are prehended by God as what we are, the whole finite book of us loved "in our present reality for the sake of that reality," and in being so loved we know that this reality of ours "will never be destroyed" (261). We perish, but God's appreciation of us does not, "so that we function as a theme for literally endless variations in the use God makes of us as objects of His awareness to be synthesized with ever additional objects" (262). Or, shifting metaphors, Hartshorne suggests that "we mold the picture which forever will hang in the divine mansion. God will make as much out of the picture in beholding it as can be made. . . . The true immortality is everlasting fame before God" (259).

For both Griffin and Hartshorne, to deny the existence of God entails denying that there is any value to the universe, since only God can provide the everlastingness that the transient achievements of transient creatures need for anything whatever to have significance. For if there is no ultimate importance, then there can be no objective importances, only ones that are functions of a person's subjective desires and choices, which are as transient as their source and so eventually will be devoid of their significance—that is, will have become meaningless.

Hence Griffin argues that it is a "nihilistic answer" to respond "no" to the question "whether our struggles really [make] any ultimate difference," since it is only by making a difference that an action or a life has value, and making a difference for God is the only way that action or life makes a difference worth making. Thus "it belongs to the very idea of God to be the ultimate ground of the meaning of life" (2001, 232). Hartshorne likewise finds atheism nihilistic. He argues that a reality which cannot "preserve *forever* the value we have achieved" is one which "cannot guarantee any value difference in ultimate outcome between wise or conscientious and rash or wicked choices" (1984, 53). To deny ultimate significance is to deny God, and to deny God is to deny the ground for objective value and hence the possibility of nonarbitrary moral judgment. Griffin agrees: "Those who have encouraged atheism in the name of morality have been engaged in an ultimately self-defeating enterprise" (2001, 303).

Hartshorne goes further. Since a denial of ultimate importance is an atheistic claim, and since our deeply rooted belief that our lives have an ultimate significance is grounded in a dim but universal sense of God's reality, such a denial cannot be a genuine belief. "I have yet to be convinced that human beings can really demonstrate their belief in an absolute renunciation of everlasting (however modest) significance for having lived as they in fact have" (1983, 360). The assertion that "the eventual significance of these lives may one day reach zero" is "sayable in words, but what is the mode of living that expresses believing it?" There is simply no possibility for someone to act on the basis of such a belief. "One may say that the practical conclusion is, nothing matters. But this is mere words; while we live, we show that for us something does matter" (360). It is simply not possible to think that something matters and not believe that it matters forevermore.

Griffin then adds the *coup de grace* in the form of a Darwinian-like argument against the denial that our achievements have permanent significance. The universe has evolved creatures with a capacity for "intrinsic value," including the capacity to ask if there are any ultimate values. If it were true, however, that whatever those creatures achieve is only of transient value, "the resulting disappointment can empty our 'transient enjoyment' of most of its enjoyment, a result that would mean that the evolutionary process has brought about a self-defeating result" (2001, 231). Heaven forefend this should be so!

When push comes to shove, all three metaphysicians appeal to intuition. Whitehead, in introducing the notion of the consequent nature of God, admits "there is nothing here in the nature of proof." He says his views are simply an "elucidation of somewhat exceptional elements in our conscious experience—those elements which may roughly be classed together as religious and moral intuitions" (1978, 343). Griffin, more emphatically, refers to his own intuition as one of the "hard-core commonsense notions . . . inevitably presupposed in practice by all human beings" (2001, 5). Hence to assert as true any notion contradicting that intuition would be "irrational," indeed "metaphysical lunacy" (30). Hartshorne finds the denial of value as ultimately so irrational that he argues that those who hold such a view cannot really believe it because "apart from my (direct or indirect) contribution to God I am indeed literally nothing of any value whatsoever" (1983, 217), and no one can go on living believing that of themselves.

I am tempted to reject these intuitions in the only way appropriate when someone makes an absolutist claim for their intuition: by appeal to my own counter-intuition, my sense of the radically temporal contingency of all things. To do so is in accord with William James's remark that "the history of philosophy is to a great extent that of a certain clash of human temperaments" (1981, 8). My intuition is as hard-core as Griffin's, my sense of value as firm as Hartshorne's, its truth as haunting for me as its denial is for Whitehead. I was born on a bleak wintery day on the borders of the vast windswept plains of North Dakota in the midst of the Great Depression. What I learned with my mother's milk was that good things are born or made only with difficulty and that even the best of them perish all too soon. Yet my parents and others around me found no fault with this way of the world. They taught me to celebrate the good things when they came, and when they were gone to rejoice that once, uniquely and fortunately, they had been.

As a result, my deepest intuition is the sense that all things perish—not some things, not a lot of things, but absolutely all things, from flashes of lightning to cosmic epochs, from passing fancies to metaphysical principles. And to believe that this is so is not evidence of foolishness or nihilism. It is not a cause for despair but for rejoicing. For it is good that we are finite creators of finite goods; perishable achievements are the most precious values because they need not have happened, but yet did. Such a claim appears to me self-evident, a hard-core commonsensical notion if there ever was one. Its obverse, therefore, seems a misguided yearning to be plucked out of the creative advance of the world, and to be set down in that new heaven and new earth where there is no longer adventure but endless rest, no longer creative labor but endless quietude, no longer the shipwreck of our hopes but a life in which there is no longer any need for hope—a flight away from our storm-tossed lives into a place where there is no more sea.

I am astounded by Whiteheadians who have this yearning. What excited me about process thought is what I took to be its affirmation of temporality, its insistence on the primacy of becoming. If Whitehead was correct, if objects are made of events, if events are themselves made from an inherited residue of prior objects and events, and if nothing has ontological status that is not a feature of an event or events, then all things are fundamentally occurrences. Endurance is an abstract feature of sequences of events, the notion of endless endurance an unwarranted extrapolation from that abstraction. The only possible locus of value is temporal events, to which all other values are reducible or upon which they are dependent. Hence the notion of an everlasting reality is simply oxymoronic, as is also the notion of an eternal reality.

Intuitions may seem hard-core: inevitable, rational, and verified by direct experience. I have offered a counter-intuition with equal insistence on the depth of its roots and breadth of its self-evidence. I would suggest, however, that this clash of hard-core intuitions is foolish. Intuitions are actually soft-core, notoriously biased expressions of a personal or cultural context. Appealing to commonsense as grounding for an intuition is more than likely merely dressing up yesterday's familiar local practices in the regalia of absolutism. I will therefore attempt in what follows to supply metaphysical reasons in support of my soft-core intuition—although, of course, I've been doing just that throughout this book.

The problem with celebrating the value of everlasting relevance as fundamental is that doing so undermines the intrinsic value of temporal achievements by shifting their worth from the achievements as such to the utility of their transformed value as everlasting. In *Process and Reality*, Whitehead speaks of the transient creations of actual entities and enduring agencies as "multiple unifications of the universe, which are free creations of actualities arising out of decided situations"—a "discordant multiplicity of actual things, requiring each other and neglecting each other, utilizing and discarding, perishing and yet claiming life as obstinate matters of fact" (1978, 349). That's the world as I find it, and I neither find nor hope that there is more that can truthfully be said.

"At the base of our existence," Whitehead argues in *Modes of Thought*, "is the sense of 'worth.'. . . It is the sense of existence for its own sake, of existence which is its own justification, of existence with its own character" (1968, 109). No process thinker, of course, and certainly not Whitehead, nor Hartshorne and Griffin, would deny the intrinsic worth of processes of making values. At issue is how best to understand what the proper relationship is between intrinsic and extrinsic worth—between the value of what is here and now fashioned, the uniqueness of achievement appreciated for its own sake, and its significance, that achievement appreciated for its enduring worth. I am claiming that intrinsic worth is neither augmented nor diminished by its eventual significance, and that to insist otherwise is to undermine the value of intrinsic values, and thereby to undermine the value of the transient world where alone these values—and their significance—are made.

In talking about intrinsic value, my language, as Whitehead's, is aesthetic. The making of a space-time quantum, an enduring object, or a cosmic epoch is like the making of a work of art. It is a *poiesis*, the construction of a single whole from a range of contributing elements, the ordering of a congeries, the evolving of a system. The contributing elements may be determinate or indeterminate, concrete particulars or abstract possibilities, but both the how and what of their unity is initially indeterminate: a task to be carried out, a labor to be accomplished. The keystone of Whitehead's philosophy of organicism, I have been arguing, is the denial that anything can be imperishable, serving as the perfect uncreated timeless foundation for what is created or as the perfect non-iterated everlasting unity of what is created. To be actual in any sense is to have been imperfectly made. All existent entities are creatures, all creatures are created, and everything created, everything that comes to be, also perishes.

The intrinsic value of the result of these creative efforts is a function of how well the object made satisfies two conflicting criteria for success, one having to do with the scope of elements included, the other with the intensity of their integration. Scope is a measure not just of quantity, a summation of the number of elements included in an integration, but also a measure of their variety, the ways in which they differ from each other. Intensity measures the extent to which these elements are brought together into a single whole, their disparities harmonized. The wider and more varied the scope of elements, the more difficult the task of integrating them and the more intense the result of doing so. Intensity is achieved in complex situations by modifying the character of the elements available for integration, adjusting their individual uniquenesses and their distinctive differences in order to attain some kind of well-ordered interrelatedness. But the conflict between scope and intensity is endemic, so the reconciliation achieved is necessarily partial, unstable, always in need of repair, renovation, transformation. Perfection is an idle dream, whereas improvement is a reasonable aim, its achievement a real but not assured possibility.

The crocus pushes through the frozen ground, a streak of tender green and a splash of yellow. Its existential value is the presence it achieves, and the longer it can endure the more value it thereby produces, value persisting because iterated with appropriate modulations. The expected duration may be shortened, however, the crocus eaten by a hungry squirrel, picked by an inquisitive human, caught by an early freeze. When these things happen, the value lost is quite extensive, to be sure, but the value that was briefly achieved is no less a value. The loss of the crocus's presence is tragic but the presence it had is not. It has a worth precious beyond all price: that presence which need not have been but nonetheless is, coming to be when and where it has, for this time and not another, whether perishing prematurely or not.

The Vermeer painting, *Girl with a Pearl Earring*, is a creation of such exquisite value that we will travel great distances to see it firsthand. We enjoy its presence, as did Vermeer when he painted it and perhaps as did the young girl who posed for him. Were we never to go see it, the possible values we experience would be thereby diminished. If the painting were destroyed tomorrow, our failure to have seen it would be an irretrievable loss, one shared by many other unfortunates. If Vermeer had destroyed the painting immediately upon completing it, the loss would be the whole world's loss. But the intrinsic worth of the painting would remain what it was when Vermeer at last put down his brush and dismissed the girl. A creation's intrinsic value is not diminished when its significant value ends.

I would push my argument further by claiming not only that intrinsic values do not need to be preserved in order to be valuable, but that, on the contrary, an achievement is valuable precisely because it perishes, and the greater the value of its accomplishment the greater the likelihood of its perishing. The greater the value, the more distinctive the accomplishment of which that value is a feature. However, precisely because of its greater degree of uniqueness—and hence its greater complexity and intensity—its value is more difficult to sustain, much less to enhance, than is a less complex value, a less distinctive achievement. Survival, as Whitehead reminds us, is something at which inanimate objects excel. Organisms are fragile because they achieve their determinateness at the expense of their surroundings; they are at greater risk because they are of greater value. This direct correlation of value and vulnerability means that the most precious things in the universe are not those things that endure for long periods of time or even forevermore, but those things that perish. The price they pay for the excellence they achieve is that their value cannot but be fragile and so its complexly integrated unity will soon, all too soon, break down.

I'm perplexed by the claim that for an undertaking to be good it must succeed. Such a stridently utilitarian sense of value is misplaced; it has no way to combat arguments and practices claiming that the end justifies the means, that if it succeeds then the end is good, that might makes right. Both claims resolve a false dilemma by subordinating means to ends or ends to means, privileging one of two equally necessary aspects of value creation. Ends and means are separately meaningless and the prioritizing of one over the other subverts the genuine value that only both can create. It is crucial to recognize that ends and means, however initially framed, are shaped and reshaped in the process of any creative pursuit. The reconciliation of scope and intensity in a concrete situation requires both ideals proposed as goals and means devised for their actualization, proposals capable of being shaped by the devices for their realization and devices able to be redirected by proposals about how best to succeed. The efforts of both are needed collaboratively to provide matters-of-fact with their full importance, which should be at once intrinsic and significant.

I therefore resist the argument that if we recognize our efforts are going to be in vain that's reason enough to abandon them, that the failure of an enterprise renders it worthless. I would also resist the argument that if we recognize our ideals to be prejudices wrapped in a cloak of pragmatic effectiveness, that its reason enough to declare the enterprise worthless.

There are ends worth seeking whether or not they are attained; there are means worth utilizing whether or not the end is justified. Because it is difficult to tell specifically, in the context of an actual making of something, what ends are really worth seeking and what means really best for doing so. It is nobler to have tried to reach some seemingly attractive goal by some seemingly prudent route and to have failed in doing so, than never to have tried. How else to know if the goal was really attractive or the strategy really effective, or both? Indeed, I should think this attitude is what process thinking is all about: Giving primacy to the doing, to the adventurous projects of finite limited creatures attempting to make new viable moments, the intrinsic and significant worth of each actively at stake.

My counter to those who insist on the metaphysical necessity of a power able to rescue the things of this world from their seemingly endless perishing is that the ultimate meaning of life is to be found solely in the finite power of finite entities to create things of value. Our lives are meaningful because they are filled with accomplishments we experience as intrinsically valuable, satisfactions that shimmer with the truth they bring into being, and with the beauty and the goodness they thereby made manifest. They are likewise meaningful because they are filled with failures: Goals that continued to seem good but that we could not manage to achieve, goals that proved not good at all, perhaps even evil, and did so only because in fact we achieved them. In a contingent universe composed of finite agents, values are never self-evident and our judgments about them never certain. Our accomplishments, and our failure as well, involve venturing beyond established securities, out into the open sea of ideal and practical possibilities, without any ultimate assurance that our aims and out methods, in whatever ways they are mutually shaped, can—or should—succeed.

TRAGIC BEAUTY

The strongest argument against the notion of a God whose consequent nature redeems the achievements of transient entities by transforming them into its everlasting reality is the notion of Tragic Beauty, which is crucial to an understanding of Peace.

Our sense of Peace is the sense of our participation in a Totality of endeavors stretching back and forward, upward and downward, beyond the outer edge of all possibilities, sustaining our zest for creative adventure. We realize we are not alone in what we do but are part of a vast community of similar adventurers, living and dead, known and unknown, remembered and long forgotten. However, our acceptance of the final Truth to which Adventure leads requires a further realization: that of Tragic Beauty.

The pursuit of ideals is not only a high-risk adventure in which we are all the time suffering setbacks and needing to refashion our plans and rethink our purposes. We must also recognize that it is an effort doomed to failure. We must acknowledge "the tragic issues which are essential in the nature of things" (1967, 286). Youth is the stage of "Life as yet untouched by tragedy" (287). Tragedy is the recognition, as youth gives way to maturity, that "Decay, Transition, Loss, Displacement belong to the essence of the Creative Advance" (286). Thus it is that "at the heart of the nature of things, there are always the dream of youth and the harvest of tragedy" (296). This trajectory from dream to harvest, says Whitehead, is a fact about the world, always a fact, not occasionally or unfortunately but essentially a fact. A fact located not at the periphery but at the core of the cosmos, at the heart of the very nature of things. Our aim should always be toward the better, even though our journey will always run afoul of problems we are unable to resolve. The resulting failure is tragic because success was not impossible. Our strengths offer a possibility of fulfilling our aim, but our limitations hinder or undercut, befoul or destroy, our attempt to do so. Always the fecund dream, the transcendent aim; always also the fracturing evil, the tragic harvest.

What is true for our achievements is true for all other achievements as well. Whether meager or cornucopic, they are not only intrinsically valuable but also have instrumental value as resources for subsequent creative efforts. And these resources include not only previous achievements but just as importantly the ideals those achievements failed in part or whole to actualize, ideals which are not lost but in having become integral to those efforts have also become available for its successors, including us, to actualize. In recognizing that our efforts fall short, and will be fleeting even should they succeed, we admit the inescapable tragedy not only of achieving things but also of having ideals.

Failed ideals are still ideals, however. "Each tragedy is the disclosure of an ideal:—What might have been, and was not: What can be. The tragedy was not in vain." We should see "the tragedy as a living agent persuading the world to aim at fineness beyond the faded level of surrounding fact" (286). Note that for Whitehead the "living agent" disclosing an unrealized ideal as still capable of realization is tragedy. The novel possibilities we take as adumbrating ends worth seeking, as goals orienting our actions, motivating what we do, are not manna from heaven, not divine gifts from beyond or from within history, from God's primordial or consequent nature. They are, rather, the flotsam and jetsam remaining after the sinking of our achievements and the destruction of all those dreams of ours they had been nurturing.

The tragedy of our failures—the hope dashed, the gaping fissure opened, the opportunity misused or disdained, the cowardly compromise or self-serving injustice accepted—can be the catalyst by which hope is salvaged from the surrounding wreckage and used in an attempt to fashion some finer fact. The tragedy of Tragic Beauty is that we failed to get the job done. The possibility could have become a reality, but we fell short in our attempt to make it happen. The beauty of Tragic Beauty is that it is also Truthful, that it was a reasonable goal and so remains, despite the failure, a viable possibility.

We experience a tragic loss, but we discover in this experience a possibility that redeems the loss. That other ship didn't make it through the rock-bound strait, but the passage is navigable and so we decide to give it a try ourselves. Those political leaders and their armies thought they had made the world safe for democracy, but although the fledgling democracies have stumbled into chaos and fled into tyranny, democracy is still the better way and we should take up their cause anew, chastened by their naivety but encouraged by their dream. And so it always is: the dream ending in tragic failure but the dream still potent, our decision to carry on motivated by a conviction that those who died for it should not have died in vain.

"The Reality which the Adventure transmutes into its Unity of Appearance," the tragic fact that harbors a cause we embrace as worth our allegiance, is "the final Beauty with which the Universe achieves its justification" (295). The world as we find it is a meaningful world because, although each ideal is either lost in the attempt to incarnate it in the world, or if incarnated lost far too soon thereafter, versions of that ideal always remain available for some renewed attempt. Peace, which is Tragic Beauty appreciated, believed in, and acted on, is the way by which "Beauty has always within it the renewal derived from the Advance of the Temporal World" (295). Peace infusing the strivings of all the world's creatures "is the immanence of the Great Fact" uniting the exuberant dreams of Youth and the chastised hopes of Maturity with "this final Beauty which constitutes the zest of self-forgetful transcendence belonging to Civilization at its height" (295–96).

Whitehead says that Peace "calms destructive turbulence and completes civilization" (285). Our attempts to perfect reality, to achieve goals to which we are firmly committed, can sometimes intensify when thwarted. A failed idea can be simply a marginal improvement we will have to do without, or a slight decline in our quality of life we will have to accommodate. We may simply try again by repeating what didn't work out as we had hoped, or by modifying our aims or methods slightly, or by turning our attention elsewhere. Failure is often more fundamental, however: an unresolved problem that spirals into a crisis and then a catastrophe, a threat to the continued existence of the things that give our life meaning, a direct threat to that life itself. So we redouble our efforts and grow more frantic when they also prove inadequate. Desperate times call for desperate measures, and so the finer qualities of civilized behavior give way to the short-sighted aims and extremist actions of an attempt to save ourselves at whatever price.

A sense of Peace rescues us from such a downward spiral by keeping our focus on the worth of the ideals by which we have been guiding our actions rather than on their success or failure. We can weather the storm by remaining calm, sustained by our sense of fellowship with all those others who like us have been caught by the threatening waves and looming rocks endemic to this world and, whether weathering the storm or destroyed by it, have remained faithful to their ideals. "Amid the passing of so much beauty, so much heroism, so much daring, Peace is then the intuition of permanence" (286), and "the individual whose strength of experience is founded upon this ultimate intuition, thereby is extending the influence of the source of all order" (292), which is the drive to make and preserve what matters. Peace is the conviction that Beauty, although necessarily Tragic, is also Truthful, and so despite inevitable failure justifies our zestful persistence in Adventures by means of Art's boundary-transgressing inventiveness toward novel reworkings of Reality.

Whitehead's point is captured practically in Robert Browning's claim in his poem "Andrea del Sarto" that "a man's reach should exceed his grasp, / Or what's a heaven for?" (1984, 97–98). Heaven is a star by which we navigate the open sea, not an ultimate destination. There are always ports of call with their momentary satisfactions, each a pragmatic goal that tests our skill and judgment to secure, but soon we are on our way elsewhere. If we must be assured safe passage to a final resting place before we will be willing to embark, then either we will never journey anywhere significant or we will assure our destruction by deluding ourselves into thinking that the sea poses no threat, or that our boat and its helmsman have no flaws, or that we or at least our achievements will be rescued by some transcendent power, made in some way or another everlastingly relevant. But these are fanciful dreams, illusory hopes.

We should always be reaching for something barely glimpsed at the edge of the visible horizon, even though as we set out in its direction it always recedes, eluding our grasp. Our efforts are not in vain, however, if their importance lies in the worth of our effort. That our successes will be at best partial and transient should detract in no way from the worth of our undertaking them. The temporary harbors we reach on our journey and the expertise by which we negotiate the treacherous obstacles to reaching them are achievable goods sometimes achieved, and sometimes extremely significant in what they accomplish. The good which our accomplishments best serve, however, the more fundamental good, is the journeying itself, the recognition that it is more important to be embarked on a worthwhile venture across the open sea than to arrive safely at our hoped-for destination.

Our appeal is not to an infinitude lying beyond the transitory, an Eternal Receptacle or an Eternal and Everlasting God, but to the finite efficacy of Beauty. Which when we trust it, teaches us that what we have the power to do is what others had the power to do, and still others will also have the power to do: to create what matters, with the help of others and on their behalf. We realize that we are not alone, that our inadequacies are conditions of our humanity, and that what is true of humans is true of all things: that their value lies in what they are, and that what they are is a gift from what has preceded them, offered for them to remake as a gift for what follows after them, for these others then to shape as best they can.

Whitehead says, in summarizing his argument, that "the secret of the union of Zest with Peace" is our power to appreciate the fact that the suffering of tragedy "attains its end in a Harmony of Harmonies" (296). Peace is our capacity to realize that the only Harmony of Harmonies, the only ultimate perfection, is an ideal—an ideal not of some final achieved perfection, however, for there can be none, but an ideal of the endlessly recurrent drive toward the particular perfections that give our finite lives their meaning.

"At the heart of the nature of things, there are always the dream of youth and the harvest of tragedy" (296). At the heart of things. Comprising the world's essence, its very nature. Not just the dream, nor only the harvest, but both. Always. Always ideals of what should matter, embraced and pursued. Always with results that fall short. Always lessons learned, hopes chastised. The sense of Peace is "the immediate experience of this Final Fact, with its union of Youth and Tragedy" (296). All those dreams, all those partial failures, including my dreams and my partial failures, united in one ongoing temporal process stretching indefinitely in all modes and dimensions. My life finds its meaning not only in this finite, fragile, actual, important matter-of-fact that is myself here and now; not only in all the other actualities, in all the thises and thats which have ever been and ever will be; not only in the intrinsic value of each of us; not only in the infinitude of those values. Where our lives find meaning is in the Totality comprising our union, in the Great Reality that is the world ever-changingly what it becomes. Through our sense of the Tragic Beauty at the beating heart of the world, which is the intuition of Peace, "the World receives its persuasion towards such perfections as are possible for its diverse individual occasions" (296).

Whitehead offers no vision of an ultimate end. There is no eschatological goal eventually to be realized, no Kingdom of God in history, no salvation of all created value in an everlasting region beyond the reach of the restless sea, beyond the comings to be and the perishings of temporal things. What exists is our journey out from safe harbor into that sea, with the endless struggle it requires for achieving finite goods even though they fall far short of the possibilities for good that could have been achieved. And yet these finite goods always also hold out those unrealized possibilities, and possibilities beyond our imagining, as reasons for renewing the struggle, for continuing our journey. Solemnly, adventurously, the shore soon no longer visible, we once more set sail, outward into the boundless sea.

NOTE

1. This chapter's section "The Open Sea" makes extensive us of portions of my article "Ultimate Value" in *Process Studies* 33 (2004): 284–302. Used with permission, all rights reserved. This chapter also includes some material from my article "The Solemnity of the World" in *The Routledge Handbook of Religious Naturalism*, eds. Donald A. Crosby and Jerome A. Stone. New York: Routledge, 2018: 129–39. Copyright © 2018 Routledge. Reproduced with permission of Routledge through PLSclear, all rights reserved.

BIBLIOGRAPHY

Alexander, Samuel. *Space, Time, and Deity*, 2 volumes. London: Macmillan and Co., 1927.
Aristotle. *Metaphysics*. In *The Basic Works of Aristotle*, ed. Richard McKeon, tr. W.D. Ross. New York: Random House, 1941.
Bergson, Henri. *Matter and Memory*, tr. Nancy Margaret Paul and W. Scott Palmer. London: Macmillan and Co., 1911.
Bogaard, Paul A., and Jason Bell, eds. *The Harvard Lectures of Alfred North Whitehead, [vol. I] 1924/1925: Philosophical Presuppositions of Science*. Edinburgh, UK: Edinburgh University Press, 2017.
Bradley, James. "Transcendentalism and Speculative Realism in Whitehead." *Process Studies* 23 (1994): 155–91.
———. "Act, Event, Series: Metaphysics, Mathematics, and Whitehead." *Journal of Speculative Philosophy* 10 (1996): 233–48.
Browning, Robert, "Andrea del Sarto." In *Robert Browning: Selected Poems*, 115–22. New York: Penguin, 1989.
Dewey, John. "Whitehead's Philosophy." *Philosophical Review* 46.2 (1937): 170–77.
Ford, Lewis. "Allan's Atheism." *Process Studies* 39 (2008): 307–18.
Griffin, David Ray. *Reenchantment without Supernaturalism: A Process Philosophy of Religion*. Ithaca, NY: Cornell University Press, 2001.
Hartshorne, Charles. *The Logic of Perfection and Other Essays in Neoclassical Metaphysics*. LaSalle, IL: Open Court Publishing Co., 1962.
———. *Insights and Oversights of Great Thinkers: An Evaluation of Western Philosophy*. Albany: State University of New York Press, 1983.
———. *Creativity in American Philosophy*. Albany: State University of New York Press, 1984.
James, William. *Pragmatism*. Indianapolis: Hackett Publishing Company, 1981.
Keats, John. "The Eve of St. Agnes." In *The Complete Poetry and Selected Prose of John Keats*, 255-66. New York: Modern Library, 1951.
Plato. *Meno*. In *Plato: Complete Works*, tr. G.M.A. Grube. Indianapolis: Hackett Publishing Company, 1997a.
———. *Sophist*. In *The Dialogues of Plato, volume 1*, tr. Benjamin Jowett. Oxford, UK: Oxford University Press, 1892.
———. *Symposium*. In *Plato: Complete Works*, tr. Alexander Nehamas and Paul Woodruff. Indianapolis: Hackett Publishing Company, 1997b.
Tennyson, Alfred. "Ulysses." In *Selected Poetry of Tennyson*. New York: Modern Library, 1951a.

———. "Crossing the Bar." In *Selected Poetry of Tennyson*. New York: Modern Library, 1951b.
Vermeer, Johannes. *Girl with a Pearl Earring*. The Hague, Netherlands: Mauritshuis Art Museum.
Whitehead, Alfred North. *Adventures of Ideas*. New York: Free Press, 1967.
———. *Modes of Thought*. New York: Free Press, 1968.
———. *Process and Reality*. Corrected Edition, eds. David Ray Griffin and Donald W. Sherburne. New York: Free Press, 1978.

INDEX

Adventure : concept of, 109, 119, 129–132, 135, 163, 166, 185, 186–187; actuality of, x–xi, 43, 71, 100, 133, 158, 167, 171, 180, 185
aims: ideal, 165–166, 184; of finite actual entities, 39, 44–45, 48, 76, 86–87, 107, 140–145, 149, 155; physical purposes, 64–67, 69, 71, 77; provided by God, 22, 55, 56–63, 64, 96, 107
Alexander, Samuel, 172–173
ambient, 61, 66, 114, 124, 146, 169–170
analogy. *See* method of inquiry: metaphoric
Appearance, 119–121, 123, 125, 128–129, 131, 134–135, 143, 166
Aristotle, 56, 59
Art : concept of, 70–71, 109, 119, 127–131, 133–134, 163, 187; actuality of, 71, 87, 88, 127–132, 133, 140, 142, 156, 181
atheism, 178

basic notions, metaphysical, 110–114, 164; Eros, 109–117, 122–126, 128, 134, 164; Harmony, 111, 127; Ideas, 110, 112, 119; Mathematical Relations, 111–112; Physical Elements 110, 119; Psyche, 109–114, 119, 122–123, 125–126, 164; Receptacle, 112–114
Battle of Waterloo, 49–50

Beauty: concept of, 113, 119, 125, 126–127, 128, 129, 130, 134, 135, 163, 164–165, 184–185, 186, 188, 189; actuality of, 50, 56, 59, 69, 71, 88, 111–112, 127, 127–129, 135, 139, 140, 142, 147, 152, 156, 171, 184, 186, 187

Bergson, Henri, 105
boundlessness. *See* nature: its open-endedness
Bradley, James, 33
Browning, Robert, 188

Categoreal Obligations, 32–33, 33–34, 37, 37–38, 39, 40, 51, 52, 65, 68, 77; Conceptual Valuation, 34–37, 38, 42–43, 45, 65, 66, 80, 117; Freedom and Determination, 33; Subjective Unity, 33, 38; Subjective Harmony, 33, 38; Objective Identity, 33, 38; Objective Diversity, 33, 38; Subjective Intensity, 39–40; Conceptual Reversion, 42–43, 45, 66, 116; Transmutation, 44–51, 75, 80. *See also* Transcendentals; Categoreal Scheme, 26, 30, 33, 51, 53; categories of existence, 12; categories of explanation, 15; category of the ultimate. *See* Creativity ; categoreal obligations
Chartres Cathedral, 127, 171–172

193

Civilized society, qualities of, 119–135. *See also* Adventure; Art; Beauty; Peace; Truth

cosmos. *See* nature: order(s) of

Creativity: concept of, 10, 18, 30–33, 33, 37, 38, 38–39, 39, 47, 51, 52, 64, 65, 66, 69, 77, 112, 118, 134; actuality of, 18, 20, 26, 30, 31, 65, 68, 118, 149, 157

Darwinian processes, 9, 178

defining characteristic. *See* enduring objects

Deity. *See* Alexander, Samuel

Descartes, René, 25, 29, 173

Dewey, John, 29–30

diagrams. *See* method of inquiry: scientific

Duns Scotus, John, 33

enduring objects, 6, 7, 14, 17, 18, 19, 32, 43, 47, 51, 66, 71–76, 97, 102, 104, 112, 122, 123, 155, 165, 174

The Eternal, 83, 93–99, 100–101, 105–107, 114, 174, 188

eternal objects: pure, vii, 11–13, 14, 15–16, 16, 17–19, 21, 25, 29, 37, 58, 62, 67, 107, 134; relative, 12–13, 14, 17–18, 19, 20, 26, 30, 35, 42, 46, 49, 52, 61, 64–65, 66, 68, 95, 101, 115–116, 137

Eros. *See* basic notions, metaphysical

evil, ultimate. *See* God: consequent nature

fallacy: of misplaced concreteness, 32, 88, 106, 113–118, 119, 125, 134, 148; of misplaced abstractness, 88; of the perfect dictionary, 149

final causes, 76–81

Ford, Lewis, 64, 68

Frodo, 135

Galileo, 122

God, vii, ix, 1, 25, 27, 105–108, 114, 137, 156, 168, 170, 188; primordial nature of, 1, 2, 8–11, 11, 13, 15–21, 29, 31, 39, 55, 56, 56–59, 61, 64–65, 67, 77, 106, 107, 114, 115–117, 134, 137; consequent nature of, 1, 21–24, 59, 106, 107, 114, 117, 163, 174–179; critique of, 16, 18–20, 23–25, 27, 30, 31–32, 51, 59–60, 77–78, 98, 142, 156, 172, 174–175, 179–180, 184, 186, 188

Great Chain of Being, 140

Griffin, David, 176, 177–178, 178–179, 181

grounding things: background, 21, 47, 50, 64, 84, 86, 122, 141, 144–145, 146, 155, 167, 170; foundation, 3, 4, 8, 9–10, 22, 24, 39, 56, 59, 79, 85, 96, 99, 109, 114, 132, 134, 140, 143, 166, 174; reason, 56, 68, 76, 83, 89, 106, 112, 125, 129, 134, 158, 180; ultimate, 5, 8, 83, 93, 94–96, 97, 99, 104, 105–106, 114, 176, 178. *See also* The Eternal; God: consequent nature; God: primordial nature

Hartshorne, Charles, 176–179, 181

Harvard/Radcliff lectures, 83–108

Hume, David, 57, 58, 164

ideals : normative, 49, 52, 71–76, 76, 78–81, 117, 126–127, 130, 132, 133, 135, 139, 140, 155, 164–173, 183, 185–186, 187, 189; civilizing, 156–162, 163, 164, 168, 171–172, 176, 178, 178–179, 180, 187; failed, 186, 187–188, 189; intrinsic, 180–184. *See also* possibilities: relative

James, William, 154, 158–160, 170, 179

Keats, John, 97, 103

Locke, John, 64, 86

method of inquiry: analogical, 4–8; hypothesizing, viii, x, 39, 46, 49–50, 78, 83, 87, 88–90, 107, 118, 163; intuitive, 8–10, 17, 21–22, 24, 31, 39, 97, 119, 134, 153, 157, 165, 172, 172–173, 179, 180, 187, 189; metaphysical, 84–88, 99, 158–162; the Peacock's way, 88, 89; poetic, 80–81, 84–85, 85–86, 87, 89, 91, 95, 100, 104, 106–108, 135, 156–158, 160–162, 168, 173;

metaphoric, 24, 32, 75, 100, 127, 149–153, 155–101, 156, 157–162, 177; scientific, 83, 84, 85, 88–91, 91, 104; statistical, 2–4; mattering, 137, 138–143, 152, 164, 168, 176, 178, 187, 188, 189
morality, 126–130, 127–128, 140, 141–142, 142, 147, 156, 178
myths. *See* method of inquiry: poetic

nature: its open-endedness, 83, 88–93, 99, 102, 104, 106, 107, 140–141, 162, 168, 169, 170, 172, 173, 189; its relatedness, 13, 25, 61, 84, 92, 151, 181; its order, 1, 9, 15–16, 17, 19, 21, 39, 42, 43, 44, 46–48, 70, 71, 72–73, 75–76, 76–79, 83, 91–93, 95–96, 99, 104–105, 107, 109, 112, 114–115, 121, 132, 133, 135, 140, 149, 152, 161, 165, 170, 172, 175, 181, 187; its solemnity, 170–171, 173
nature of things, in the, 2, 9, 22, 30–31, 40, 52, 134, 164, 185, 189
niches. *See* nature: its open-endedness

ontological principle, 15, 25, 60

Peace : concept of, 109, 119, 163, 163–167, 173, 184–185, 186–187, 189; reality of, 2, 55, 158
perspective, ix, 89, 127, 131, 142, 144–149, 155, 170
Plato, vii–viii, ix, 55, 71, 85, 101, 109, 110–113. *See also* basic notions
possibilities. *See* eternal objects
power, vii–viii, 26, 32, 56, 67; of finite agents, x, 13, 14, 17, 18, 31, 32, 56, 67, 73, 76–77, 102–104, 111, 112, 114, 116, 117, 118, 121–122, 124, 125–126, 128, 130, 131, 133, 134–135, 143, 146, 149, 153, 155, 156, 167, 168, 170, 173, 175, 184, 188–189; of the past, 7, 76–81, 96, 97–99, 101–102, 117; of the present, 29–53; of abstract agents, ix, 18, 25, 26, 32, 55, 77, 96, 113–118, 133, 134, 184, 188
propositions, 46, 119–122, 128. *See also* eternal objects: relative
Psyche. *See* basic notions, metaphysical

rationalizing. *See* method of inquiry: metaphoric
Reality, 119, 120, 121, 123, 128–129, 131, 134, 135, 143, 166, 187
reification. *See* fallacy: of misplaced concreteness
religion, 10, 24, 140, 146, 172, 175, 176, 179
ragged edges. *See* nature: its open-endedness

science, 29, 48, 85–86
shadow of truth, 83, 100–105, 106, 107
simplification, 84–88, 91–92, 122, 142–143, 144–145, 148, 149, 151–153, 174
societies. *See* enduring objects
soul, finite. *See* basic notions: Eros; basic notions: Psyche
standpoint. *See* perspective
stories. *See* method of inquiry: poetic
strains of control. *See* power: of finite agents
suitability bias, 4–5, 16, 21, 39
systems: hierarchical, 1, 15, 25, 72–73, 77, 140, 147–149, 155, 172; functional, 27, 47, 51, 71, 76, 79–80, 91–93, 95, 99, 100, 102, 104, 106–107, 115–116, 141–149, 155, 160, 161–162, 169, 170, 172, 173
schema. *See* method of inquiry: metaphoric

teleonomic. *See* aims
Tennyson, Alfred, 157–158
Totality, 163, 167–173, 189
Tragic Beauty, 184–189
Transcendentals, 33; Aristotelian, 33–38, 41, 44, 51, 56, 65, 111, 126; Leibnizian, 38–43, 44, 51, 56, 66, 111, 126; Hobbesian, 44–51, 51, 75, 112, 114, 132. *See also* categoreal obligations
Truth : concept of, 55, 59, 89, 90–91, 97, 98, 100–101, 102, 104, 106, 107, 109, 119–125, 128, 128–129, 130, 135, 143, 140, 152, 156, 158 160, 163, 166, 174, 179, 184, 185, 186, 187; reality of, x, 2, 10, 39, 49, 50, 71, 83, 87, 98, 102, 124, 140, 142, 156, 159–160, 180

ultimate notions: importance, 138, 142, 144, 145, 147–148, 149, 152, 155, 158, 164, 168–169, 170–171, 176, 177; matter-of-fact, 46, 138–139, 143, 144, 145, 147, 148, 149–150, 151, 151–152, 154, 155, 164, 168–169, 170

values. *See* ideals: normative
Vermeer, Johannes, 182
Voltaire, 50

Wittgenstein, Ludwig, 154

ABOUT THE AUTHOR

George Allan is emeritus professor of philosophy at Dickinson College, where he taught for thirty-three years, the last twenty-one of which he was also the college's senior academic officer. Allan has published three books on the metaphysical foundations of social value, most recently *The Patterns of the Present: Interpreting the Authority of Form*, and three books in philosophy of education, most recently *Modes of Learning: Whitehead's Metaphysics and the Stages of Education*. He is coeditor of two collections of essays, and has published around ninety articles and book chapters in metaphysics, social philosophy, philosophy of history, philosophy of education, and issues in higher education, usually from a process/pragmatic perspective. His current projects include exploring the relevance of Susanne Langer's ontology of the Act for an interpretation of the conditions of civilized existence.

www.ingramcontent.com/pod-product-compliance
Lightning Source LLC
Chambersburg PA
CBHW050905300426
44111CB00010B/1391